Marx, Engels, and Marxisms

The Marx renaissance is underway on a global scale. Wherever the critique of capitalism re-emerges, there is an intellectual and political demand for new, critical engagements with Marxism. The peer-reviewed series Marx, Engels and Marxisms (edited by Marcello Musto & Terrell Carver, with Babak Amini, Francesca Antonini, Paula Rauhala & Kohei Saito as Assistant Editors) publishes monographs, edited volumes, critical editions, reprints of old texts, as well as translations of books already published in other languages. Our volumes come from a wide range of political perspectives, subject matters, academic disciplines and geographical areas, producing an eclectic and informative collection that appeals to a diverse and international audience. Our main areas of focus include: the oeuvre of Marx and Engels, Marxist authors and traditions of the 19th and 20th centuries, labour and social movements, Marxist analyses of contemporary issues, and reception of Marxism in the world.

More information about this series at
https://link.springer.com/bookseries/14812

Kei Ehara
Editor

Japanese Discourses on the Marxian Theory of Finance

palgrave
macmillan

Editor
Kei Ehara
Faculty of Economics
Oita University
Oita, Japan

This publication is funded by Ishii Memorial Securities Research Promotion Foundation.

ISSN 2524-7123 ISSN 2524-7131 (electronic)
Marx, Engels, and Marxisms
ISBN 978-3-030-83323-7 ISBN 978-3-030-83324-4 (eBook)
https://doi.org/10.1007/978-3-030-83324-4

Cover illustration: DAJ/Getty Images

This Palgrave Macmillan imprint is published by the registered company Springer Nature Switzerland AG
The registered company address is: Gewerbestrasse 11, 6330 Cham, Switzerland

Titles Published

1. Terrell Carver & Daniel Blank, *A Political History of the Editions of Marx and Engels's "German Ideology" Manuscripts*, 2014.
2. Terrell Carver & Daniel Blank, *Marx and Engels's "German Ideology" Manuscripts: Presentation and Analysis of the "Feuerbach Chapter"*, 2014.
3. Alfonso Maurizio Iacono, *The History and Theory of Fetishism*, 2015.
4. Paresh Chattopadhyay, *Marx's Associated Mode of Production: A Critique of Marxism*, 2016.
5. Domenico Losurdo, *Class Struggle: A Political and Philosophical History*, 2016.
6. Frederick Harry Pitts, *Critiquing Capitalism Today: New Ways to Read Marx*, 2017.
7. Ranabir Samaddar, *Karl Marx and the Postcolonial Age*, 2017.
8. George Comninel, *Alienation and Emancipation in the Work of Karl Marx*, 2018.
9. Jean-Numa Ducange & Razmig Keucheyan (Eds.), *The End of the Democratic State: Nicos Poulantzas, a Marxism for the 21st Century*, 2018.
10. Robert X. Ware, *Marx on Emancipation and Socialist Goals: Retrieving Marx for the Future*, 2018.
11. Xavier LaFrance & Charles Post (Eds.), *Case Studies in the Origins of Capitalism*, 2018.

12. John Gregson, *Marxism, Ethics, and Politics: The Work of Alasdair MacIntyre*, 2018.
13. Vladimir Puzone & Luis Felipe Miguel (Eds.), *The Brazilian Left in the 21st Century: Conflict and Conciliation in Peripheral Capitalism*, 2019.
14. James Muldoon & Gaard Kets (Eds.), *The German Revolution and Political Theory*, 2019.
15. Michael Brie, *Rediscovering Lenin: Dialectics of Revolution and Metaphysics of Domination*, 2019.
16. August H. Nimtz, *Marxism Versus Liberalism: Comparative Real-Time Political Analysis*, 2019.
17. Gustavo Moura de Cavalcanti Mello and Mauricio de Souza Sabadini (Eds.), *Financial Speculation and Fictitious Profits: A Marxist Analysis*, 2019.
18. Shaibal Gupta, Marcello Musto & Babak Amini (Eds.), *Karl Marx's Life, Ideas, and Influences: A Critical Examination on the Bicentenary*, 2019.
19. Igor Shoikhedbrod, *Revisiting Marx's Critique of Liberalism: Rethinking Justice, Legality, and Rights*, 2019.
20. Juan Pablo Rodríguez, *Resisting Neoliberal Capitalism in Chile: The Possibility of Social Critique*, 2019.
21. Kaan Kangal, *Friedrich Engels and the Dialectics of Nature*, 2020.
22. Victor Wallis, *Socialist Practice: Histories and Theories*, 2020.
23. Alfonso Maurizio Iacono, *The Bourgeois and the Savage: A Marxian Critique of the Image of the Isolated Individual in Defoe, Turgot and Smith*, 2020.
24. Terrell Carver, *Engels Before Marx*, 2020.
25. Jean-Numa Ducange, *Jules Guesde: The Birth of Socialism and Marxism in France*, 2020.
26. Antonio Oliva, Ivan Novara & Angel Oliva (Eds.), *Marx and Contemporary Critical Theory: The Philosophy of Real Abstraction*, 2020.
27. Francesco Biagi, *Henri Lefebvre's Critical Theory of Space*, 2020.
28. Stefano Petrucciani, *The Ideas of Karl Marx: A Critical Introduction*, 2020.
29. Terrell Carver, *The Life and Thought of Friedrich Engels, 30th Anniversary Edition*, 2020.
30. Giuseppe Vacca, *Alternative Modernities: Antonio Gramsci's Twentieth Century*, 2020.

31. Kevin B. Anderson, Kieran Durkin & Heather Brown (Eds.), *Raya Dunayevskaya's Intersectional Marxism: Race, Gender, and the Dialectics of Liberation*, 2020.
32. Marco Di Maggio, *The Rise and Fall of Communist Parties in France and Italy*, 2020.
33. Ryuji Sasaki, *A New Introduction to Karl Marx: New Materialism, Critique of Political Economy, and the Concept of Metabolism*, 2020.
34. Kohei Saito (Ed.), *Reexamining Engels's Legacy in the 21st Century*, 2021.
35. Paresh Chattopadhyay, *Socialism in Marx's Capital: Towards a Dealienated World*, 2021.
36. Marcello Musto, *Karl Marx's Writings on Alienation*, 2021.
37. Michael Brie & Jörn Schütrumpf, *Rosa Luxemburg: A Revolutionary Marxist at the Limits of Marxism*, 2021.
38. Stefano Petrucciani, *Theodor W. Adorno's Philosophy, Society, and Aesthetics*, 2021.
39. Miguel Vedda, *Siegfried Kracauer, or, The Allegories of Improvisation: Critical Studies*, 2021.
40. Ronaldo Munck, *Rethinking Development: Marxist Perspectives*, 2021.
41. Jean-Numa Ducange & Elisa Marcobelli (Eds.), *Selected Writings of Jean Jaurès: On Socialism, Pacifism and Marxism*, 2021.
42. Elisa Marcobelli, *Internationalism Toward Diplomatic Crisis: The Second International and French, German and Italian Socialists*, 2021.
43. James Steinhoff, *Automation and Autonomy: Labour, Capital and Machines in the Artificial Intelligence Industry*, 2021.
44. Juan Dal Maso, *Hegemony and Class Struggle: Trotsky, Gramsci and Marxism*, 2021.
45. Gianfranco Ragona & Monica Quirico, *Frontier Socialism: Self-organisation and Anti-capitalism*, 2021.
46. Tsuyoshi Yuki, *Socialism, Markets and the Critique of Money: The Theory of "Labour Notes"*, 2021.
47. Marcello Musto, *Rethinking Alternatives with Marx*, 2021.
48. Marcello Mustè, *Marxism and Philosophy of Praxis: An Italian Perspective from Labriola to Gramsci*, 2021.
49. Gustavo Moura de Cavalcanti Mello & Henrique Pereira Braga (Eds.), *Wealth and Poverty in Contemporary Brazilian Capitalism*, 2021.

50. Paolo Favilli, *Historiography and Marxism: Innovations in Mid-century Italy*, 2021.

Titles Forthcoming

Vesa Oittinen, *Marx's Russian Moment*

Kolja Lindner, *Marx, Marxism and the Question of Eurocentrism*

Adriana Petra, *Intellectuals and Communist Culture: Itineraries, Problems and Debates in Post-war Argentina*

George C. Comninel, *The Feudal Foundations of Modern Europe*

Spencer A. Leonard, *Marx, the India Question, and the Crisis of Cosmopolitanism*

Joe Collins, *Applying Marx's Capital to the 21st century*

Levy del Aguila Marchena, *Communism, Political Power and Personal Freedom in Marx*

Jeong Seongjin, *Korean Capitalism in the 21st Century: Marxist Analysis and Alternatives*

Satoshi Matsui, *Normative Theories of Liberalism and Socialism: Marxist Analysis of Values*

Shannon Brincat, *Dialectical Dialogues in Contemporary World Politics: A Meeting of Traditions in Global Comparative Philosophy*

Francesca Antonini, *Reassessing Marx's Eighteenth Brumaire: Dictatorship, State, and Revolution*

Thomas Kemple, *Capital After Classical Sociology: The Faustian Lives of Social Theory*

V. Geetha, *Bhimrao Ramji Ambedkar and the Question of Socialism in India*

Xavier Vigna, *A Political History of Factories in France: The Workers' Insubordination of 1968*
Attila Melegh, *Anti-Migrant Populism in Eastern Europe and Hungary: A Marxist Analysis*
Marie-Cecile Bouju, *A Political History of the Publishing Houses of the French Communist Party*
Peter McMylor, Graeme Kirkpatrick & Simin Fadaee (Eds.), *Marxism, Religion, and Emancipatory Politics*
Mauro Buccheri, *Radical Humanism for the Left: The Quest for Meaning in Late Capitalism*
Rémy Herrera, *Confronting Mainstream Economics to Overcome Capitalism*
Tamás Krausz, Eszter Bartha (Eds.), *Socialist Experiences in Eastern Europe: A Hungarian Perspective*
Martin Cortés, *Marxism, Time and Politics: On the Autonomy of the Political*
João Antonio de Paula, Huga da Gama Cerqueira, Eduardo da Motta e Albuquer & Leonardo de Deus, *Marxian Economics for the 21st Century: Revaluating Marx's Critique of Political Economy*
Zhi Li, *The Concept of the Individual in the Thought of Karl Marx*
Lelio Demichelis, *Marx, Alienation and Techno-capitalism*
Dong-Min Rieu, *A Mathematical Approach to Marxian Value Theory: Time, Money, and Labor Productivity*
Salvatore Prinzi, *Representation, Expression, and Institution: The Philosophy of Merleau-Ponty and Castoriadis*
Agon Hamza, *Slavoj Žižek and the Reconstruction of Marxism*
Éric Aunoble, *French Views on the Russian Revolution*
Terrell Carver, Smail Rapic (Eds.), *Friedrich Engels for the 21st Century: Perspectives and Problems*
Patrizia Dogliani, *A Political History of the International Union of Socialist Youth*
Alexandros Chrysis, *The Marx of Communism: Setting Limits in the Realm of Communism*
Stephen Maher, *Corporate Capitalism and the Integral State: General Electric and a Century of American Power*
Paul Raekstad, *Karl Marx's Realist Critique of Capitalism: Freedom, Alienation, and Socialism*
Alexis Cukier, *Democratic Work: Radical Democracy and the Future of Labour*

Christoph Henning, *Theories of Alienation: From Rousseau to the Present*
Daniel Egan, *Capitalism, War, and Revolution: A Marxist Analysis*
Genevieve Ritchie, Sara Carpenter & Shahrzad Mojab (Eds.), *Marxism and Migration*
Emanuela Conversano, *Capital from Afar: Anthropology and Critique of Political Economy in the Late Marx*
Vincenzo Mele, *City and Modernity in George Simmel and Walter Benjamin: Fragments of Metropolis*
David Norman Smith, *Self-Emancipation: Marx's Unfinished Theory of the Working Class*
José Ricardo Villanueva Lira, *Marxism and the Origins of International Relations*
Bertel Nygaard, *Marxism, Labor Movements, and Historiography*
Fabio Perocco (Ed.), *Racism in and for the Welfare State*
Marcos Del Roio, *Gramsci and the Emancipation of the Subaltern Classes*
Marcelo Badaró, *The Working Class from Marx to Our Times*
Tomonaga Tairako, *A New Perspective on Marx's Philosophy and Political Economy*
Matthias Bohlender, Anna-Sophie Schönfelder, Matthias Spekker, *Truth and Revolution in Marx's Critique of Society*

Acknowledgement

I would like to express my gratitude to Iwanami Shoten Publisher, Fumio Miyake, The University of Tokyo Press, and Shigekatsu Yamaguchi for the permissions of translation. I am also grateful to Joel Mark Rasbash for his help in proofreading my English. It is to be greatly regretted that I could not manage to present this volume published to Prof. Yamaguchi.

Contents

Notes on Contributors

Robert Chapeskie (translator of Chapters 2 and 4) is a freelance translator based in Kyoto. His recent English translations include S. Tateiwa's *On Private Property*, Kyoto Books, 2016, *The Philosophy of the Kyoto School*, edited by M. Fujita, Springer, 2018. and Y. Tamanoi, "Economy and Ecology," *The History of Economic Thought (The Japanese Society for the History of Economic Thought)*, Vol. 62, No. 1., 2020.

Kei Ehara (editor, author of Chapters 1 and 7, and translator of Chapter 5) is Associate Professor of Political Economy at Oita University, Japan. His English publications include "From Classical Market View to Marxian Market View: Reinterpreting the Theory of Market Value," *World Review of Political Economy*, Vol. 9, No. 3, 2018 and "The Crisis Theory and the Stages Theory in the Uno School," *Marx Engels Jahrbuch 2017/18*, 2018. His translations include M. Obata, "The Uno Theory and Marx," in N. Yokokawa, K. Yagi, H. Uemura and R. Westra eds., *The Rejuvenation of Political Economy*, London: Routledge, 2016.

Yoshio Miyake (author of Chapter 3) is Late Professor of Rikkyo University, Japan.

Michael Schauerte (translator of Chapter 3) is Research Associate at Miyazaki University, Japan. His recent English translations include S. Kuruma, *Marx's Theory of the Genesis of Money*, Chicago, IL: Haymarket Books, 2019 and S. Kuruma, *In Pursuit of Marx's Theory of Crisis*, forthcoming.

Masashi Shimizu (author of Chapter 6) is Professor at Senshu University, Japan.

Kōzō Uno (author of Chapters 2 and 4) is Late Professor of the University of Tokyo, Japan. Some of his books were translated into English: *Principles of Political Economy*, Sussex: Harvester, 1980; *The Types of Economic Policies under Capitalism*, Leiden: Brill, 2016; *Theory of Crisis*, Leiden: Brill, 2021.

Shigekatsu Yamaguchi (author of Chapter 5) is Late Professor of the University of Tokyo, Japan. His English publications include "On the Varieties of Market Economy," *Problems of Actual Economies*, Tokyo: Ochanomizu Shobo, 2008.

List of Figures

Introduction to Japanese Studies of Marxian Theory of Finance

Kei Ehara

The 2008 world crisis has stimulated a resurgence of interest in the study of finance. Enormous efforts have been devoted to the analysis of what is called "financialization."[1] People have criticized neoliberal micro- and macroeconomics for its failure to attain a proper understanding of financial dynamics. However, it would appear that these efforts have failed to result in any significant breakthroughs. Critiques of neoliberalism aside, we have yet to build a coherent alternative economic theory equipped to deal with the question of finance. As a result, neoliberalism remains the dominant economic paradigm and still shapes global economic policy over a decade from the 2008 crisis.

[1] The general survey of the related literature is available at D. P. Sotiropoulos and A. Hillig, "Financialization in Heterodox Economics," in P. Mader, D. Mertens and N. Zwan eds., *The Routledge International Handbook of Financialization*, Chapter 9, Abingdon: Routledge, 2020; D. Bryan and M. Rafferty, "Financialization," in D. M. Brennan, D. Kristjanson-Gural, C. P. Mulder and E. K. Olsen eds., *Routledge Handbook of Marxian Economics*, Chapter 24, Abingdon: Routledge, 2017.

K. Ehara (✉)
Faculty of Economics, Oita University, Oita City, Japan

K. Ehara (ed.), *Japanese Discourses on the Marxian Theory of Finance*, Marx, Engels, and Marxisms,
https://doi.org/10.1007/978-3-030-83324-4_1

Problems remain even if they are overlooked. We still need to address the issue of constructing an alternative economics of finance that could form the basis for the analysis of financial crises. Over ten years of studies show that we cannot finish this task simply by focusing on empirical analyses. We must connect them with theoretical studies if we are to achieve an overall approach.

A renewal of theory must be based on previous theoretical works. In Japan, there are many studies of the theory of finance from a Marxian economic standpoint. Despite their shortcomings in terms of an investigation of current financial crises, they nonetheless form the starting point for the kind of theoretical work required today.

Despite its achievements, this body of work is hardly known in other languages. For some decades since the end of the Second World War, Japanese Marxian scholars have been developing a number of unique discussions which have remained largely undiscovered within the English language literature. It is therefore difficult to appreciate the latest studies without understanding how Japanese Marxists have dealt with questions of finance theory for the past 70 years.

This book aims to fill the gap in knowledge by providing the non-Japanese-speaking reader an overview of Japanese Marxian finance theory. Here we collect six core essays from Japanese authors, ranging from "classics" to contemporary arguments.[2] The key figure is Kōzō Uno (1897–1977), who had a great impact on Marxian studies in Japan in general. Japanese studies of Marxian finance theory cannot be fully understood without a discussion of Uno's arguments, whether or not one agrees with them, since the fierce debates between Uno's followers and the opponents provide the background to subsequent studies in Japan.

[2] This does not mean that reading six essays is enough to cover Japanese arguments. Limiting the number of essays is mainly due to budget constraint. M. Itoh and C. Lapavitsas, *Political Economy of Money and Finance*, Basingstoke: Macmillan, 1999, has been one of the very few resources accessible to English readers. However, it does not include the historical background to the discussion in Japan, let alone further analyses conducted in the twenty-first century. In particular, it lacks the contributions made by Shigekatsu Yamaguchi, which we consider indispensable for a full introduction of Japanese Marxian studies as shown in the following texts. Meanwhile, C. Lapavitsas, *Profit without Producing*, London: Verso, 2013 provides us with an insightful analysis of "financialization," and in Chapter 5 of the book we find a brief reference to Yamaguchi's achievement.

While Uno's followers were called the "Uno school" or "Unoists," their opponents were labeled the "orthodox school," due to their defense of Marx's arguments in the face of Uno's attempt at critical reorganization. Despite each school having its own internal variants, they still form the basis for classifying the many viewpoints to be found within Japanese Marxian economics today.

1 Uno's Reorganization of Marx's *Capital*

1.1 Reconceptualizing the Historical Transformation into the Stage of Imperialism

It might sound strange to classify Uno as the founder of a Marxian school given his critique of Marx. Nonetheless, Uno criticized Marx's theory in *Capital*, not on the grounds that Marx had been totally wrong. Rather, Uno emphasized the necessity of fixing the structure of the theory in *Capital* in order to underline the importance of Marx's insights for capturing the subsequent development of capitalism in the end of the nineteenth century and thereafter.

From the end of the nineteenth century, capitalism was thought to have transformed into "the highest stage" as Lenin put it. This stage of capitalism was characterized by the emergence of "finance capital," in which monopoly capital coalesced with the banks. The orthodox school in Japan explains this concept from the tendency in capital accumulation depicted in Part 7 of *Capital* Vol. 1, viz. the concentration of capital which results from the process of accumulation. This understanding is generally in accordance with Lenin's description: "The concentration of production; the monopolies arising therefrom; the merging or coalescence of the banks with industry – such is the history of the rise of finance capital and such is the content of that concept."[3]

Uno also used the concept of finance capital and imperialism in his descriptions of the period stretching from the end of the nineteenth century to the outbreak of the First World War, which he labeled "capitalism in its decline." According to Uno, it was the final stage of capitalist history following the stage of liberalism, or "the period of the self-propelled growth of capitalism." However, Uno refused to explain the

[3] V. Lenin, *Imperialism: The Highest Stage of Capitalism*, in *Lenin Collected Works*, Vol. 22, Moscow: Progress Publisher, 1964, p. 226.

stage of imperialism as the simple consequence of capital accumulation during the preceding stage. One of the reasons was the difference in what he saw as the driving force of the accumulation. Uno spelled out the difference in *The Types of Economic Policies Under Capitalism*, a major work which has been recently translated into English. There he states,

> In the era of liberalism, the development of the cotton industry proved most compatible with the operation of individually owned industrial capitals. The latter reproduced pretty much the same pattern of accumulation that one would visualise in studying the behavior of individual capitalists in pure theory. In contrast to this, in the era of imperialism, heavy industries such as iron-and-steel, which required a massive investment in plants and equipment, and which, in consequence, entailed the pooling of capital from a large number of small individual owners, became the norm. This was particularly the case in a country such as Germany, where capitalism started late, and where such conditions as just described gave rise to a new form of capital known as "finance capital."[4]

Here we can observe three points emphasized by Uno which defined the disconnection between the era of liberalism and that of imperialism. First, there was the change in the leading industries, from "the cotton industry" to "heavy industries." Second, while accumulation in the era of liberalism was driven by "the operation of individually owned industrial capitals," that in the era of imperialism was sustained by "the pooling of capital from a large number of small individual owners." This means that the investment in heavy industries took the form of a giant joint-stock company from the beginning, instead of growing organically from the competition between "individually owned industrial capitals." Third, German capitalism started to rise in direct competition with Britain. All these points indicated that the features of imperialism "did not follow straightforwardly from the routine capitalist development which the pure theory of capitalism would lead one to surmise."[5]

Contrary to the orthodox Leninist view, Uno elucidated capitalist history from the nineteenth century to WWI in terms of the tendency for

[4] K. Uno, *The Types of Economic Policies Under Capitalism*, Leiden: Brill, 2016, p. 140.

[5] Ibid., p. 141.

capital to purify itself, and how this process of "purification"[6] had been reversed: "once industrial capital began to be overpowered by finance-capital, ... the erstwhile tendency of capitalism to rid itself of contingent impurities in its development had to be reversed ... Under finance-capital, capitalism no longer tended toward a purely capitalist society."[7]

1.2 Building a Pure Theoretical Image of Capitalism

The starting point for Uno's project lay in the need for a purified theory of capitalism that could serve as a standard to detect the "impurities" in capitalist historical development. Uno thought that such a standard could be achieved by amending key aspects of Marx's *Capital*. For Uno, *Capital* contained defects that had misled people into overlooking emergent forces in the late nineteenth century, which were to reverse capital's previous tendency toward self-purification. By addressing those defects, Uno hoped to construct a more logically compelling theory.

Though Uno's reorganization ranged over the entire system Marx had been developing in *Capital*, there is a consensus that his efforts focused upon two major fields of study: the theory of value and the theory of crisis. Uno's overhaul of *Capital* first appeared as two volumes titled *Principles of Political Economy* in 1950 and 1952. These volumes made a notable contribution to Marxian value theory. Shortly after that, in 1953, he published a small book titled *The Theory of Crisis*. We shall discuss his contribution to value theory and crisis theory, respectively, so long as they are relevant to our main topic.[8]

[6] M. Obata, "The Uno Theory and Marx," in N. Yokokawa, K. Yagi, H. Uemura and R. Westra eds., *The Rejuvenation of Political Economy*, Chapter 2, London: Routledge, 2016, p. 36.

[7] Uno, *Economic Policies*, p. 171. As for Uno's concept of imperialism, see also K. Ehara, "Rethinking Imperialism: A Provisional Reappraisal of Kōzō Uno's Critique of Imperialism," *Oita University Economic Review*, Vol. 71, No. 1, 2019.

[8] The two volumes of *Principles of Political Economy* are combined and republished in 1977 from Iwanami Shoten Publisher. In addition, Uno published an abridged version of his *Principles of Political Economy* in 1964, which was to be translated into English by Thomas T. Sekine (K. Uno, *Principles of Political Economy*, Sussex: Harvester, 1980). The longer version is dubbed *Kyu-genron* (former principles) and the abridged *Shin-genron* (latter principles). In this volume, the former is quoted from the combined edition and referred to as Uno, *Principles 1977* while the latter is quoted from the Sekine's English translation and referred to as Uno, *Principles 1980*.

What is distinctive in Uno's theory of value can be seen in his analysis of value-form. In Sect. 3, Chapter 1 of *Capital* Vol. 1, "The Form of Value or Exchange Value," Marx focused on the concept of the commodity and its relation without considering the will or action of the owners of commodities. The owners, or to be accurate, the possessors of commodities first appear in Chapter 2, "The Process of Exchange." Marx separated the study of commodity relations and that of persons who possess it.

Uno asserted that it is necessary to take into account the desire of the commodity owners in order to fully grasp the nature of value-form. In Uno's view, the simple form of value is the result of the action of the commodity owner who wants a commodity that she/he does not own. With regard to the value-form in Marx's *Capital*, "20 yards of linen = 1 coat, or 20 yards of linen are worth 1 coat,"[9] Uno explains: "A particular commodity, for example linen, expresses its value by a definite quantity of the use value of a certain other commodity desired by the linen-owner. ... He sets aside twenty yards of his own commodity and thereby expresses his willingness to part with them, provided someone comes along with a coat of his liking."[10] Accordingly, the analysis of value-form is reinvestigated to clarify how each form is created by the actions of the commodity owner. Uno's analysis of value-form is, therefore, to explain a logical evolutionary process of value-form in accordance with the economic activities of the commodity owner.

This method had a great influence upon theoretical studies following Uno. The method in Uno's value-form analysis was also applied to reconstruct Uno's theory of interest, which included analyses of the credit system and the market system. When reconstructing the theory of interest, the method is named "differentiation and development method (DDM)." The method was designed to explore the relationship of industrial capital to the two kinds of capital which are seen as operating in the market system, i.e., bank capital and commercial capital. In the Uno school, these are regarded as differentiations that had developed from industrial capital as an embryonic entity. Here, the concept of capital is used to denote an independent and individual market actor, becoming

[9] *Marx Engels Collected Works*, Vol. 35, London: Lawrence & Wishart, 2010, p. 58. *Marx Engels Collected Works* are hereafter abbreviated as MECW in this book.

[10] Uno, *Principles 1980*, p. 5.

almost a synonym for a capitalist. In other words, an individual capital is a fetishized form of an individual capitalist, and the market system evolves in the midst of these competing capitals. These above studies took Uno's value-form analysis as a methodological standard.[11]

While Marx himself managed to finish his value-form analysis in the early chapters of *Capital*, he did not leave us a completed theory of economic crisis under the capitalist mode of production. However, we know from his manuscripts that the economic crisis had been one of the topics that interested Marx. It attracted attention from many Marxian economists and Uno was also engaged in the debate.[12]

Uno's theory of crisis has two key areas of focus, namely the fundamental cause of crisis and the dynamics in the credit system that are expressed at an outbreak of a crisis.

In contrast to a number of orthodox Marxists at the time, Uno did not use reproduction schema to identify the fundamental cause of crisis. He insisted that reproduction schema just illustrated the resultant intersectoral equilibrium within the capitalist economy and that it cannot be adapted to examine factors of disequilibrium. He maintains "it would be completely incorrect to assert that the reproduction of a capitalist society follows the numerical relation of the [reproduction] schemes exactly or

[11] As for Uno's value-form analysis, see also M. Itoh, "A Study of Marx's Theory of Value," in M. Itoh, *Value and Crisis*, 2nd ed., New York, NY: Monthly Review, 2021; T. T. Sekine, "Uno School Seminar on the Theory of Value," in T. T. Sekine, *Towards a Critique of Bourgeois Economics*, Berlin: Owl of Minerva Press, 2013; and K. Nagatani, "Value-Form and the Mystery of Money," *Capital & Class*, Vol. 44, No. 1, 2020. On the other hand, Uno had to face a fierce criticism from other Marxian economists. One of the most important critiques of Uno was given by S. Kuruma, *Marx's Theory of the Genesis of Money*, Chicago, IL: Haymarket Books, 2019, which was translated by Michael Schauerte. Uno made a rebuttal of Kuruma and the debate between the two lasted over 20 years. E. Lange, "Failed Abstraction," *Historical Materialism*, Vol. 22, No. 1, 2014 is available in English as a review on this Kuruma-Uno debate, but this introduction is far from impartial. It is too one-sided for Kuruma and contains few reflections on Uno's method.

[12] There is another Kuruma-Uno debate regarding this issue. While Uno condemned Marx for failing to describe the theory of economic crisis in a satisfactory manner, Kuruma defended Marx, insisting *Capital* was not intended to have a fundamental theory of crisis. Kuruma's essays on this debate will be available soon in English, translated by Michael Schauerte. On the other hand, Uno's essays are in an appendix of K. Uno, *Theory of Crisis*, Leiden: Brill, 2021, which was translated by Ken Kawashima.

that the schemes can possibly represent an unbalanced development of the relation of reproduction in a capitalist society."[13]

Instead, Uno emphasizes the falling rate of profit as the fundamental cause of crisis, which Marx discussed in Part 3 of *Capital* Vol. 3. Nonetheless, Uno criticizes certain aspects of Marx's account. Most especially he notes that, while Marx's law of the tendential falling rate of profit is caused basically by the rise in the labor productivity, it cannot be the cause of abrupt downturn in the business conditions. Uno remarks, "the falling tendency of the profit-rate is a normal consequence of the rising organic composition of capital and that the law itself does not imply any 'internal contradictions' capable of generating an economic crisis. ... this chapter fails to develop a fully satisfactory theory of economic crises."[14]

According to Uno, the fundamental cause of crisis must lie in a sudden fall of the profit rate, such as when there is a profit squeeze caused by the high cost of labor power. To explain this, Uno notes that in the capitalist economy, production of a certain commodity can be increased when the demand is increased. However, the one exception to this is labor power, because it is the only commodity that capital cannot produce by any means. As capitalist accumulation goes on, it is likely that the labor power becomes scarce. This scarcity of labor power as a commodity results in the rise of wages, reducing the rate of profit. As Uno formulates the problem: "The phenomenon of economic crisis, which the capitalist economy cannot avert, arises fundamentally from the super-abundance of capital due to this sudden fall in the rate of profit."[15]

Nevertheless, a more important point for us is that Uno's crisis theory placed great emphasis on the dynamics of credit system. According to Uno, even when capital is faced with the decrease in the profit rate, "individual capitals still endeavor to compensate for the fall of the profit-rate with a desperate attempt at further accumulation."[16] This "attempt" must be abandoned when "the rate of interest rises as the rate of profit falls."[17]

[13] Uno, *Principles 1980*, p. 69. All additions in the square brackets ([ ]) in this volume are made by the editor (Kei Ehara) unless otherwise noted.

[14] Ibid., p. 95.

[15] Ibid., p. 88.

[16] Ibid.

[17] Ibid. This sentence is followed by: "When the two rates are equal, prosperity turns abruptly into a crisis." I cannot find the correspondent sentence in the original Japanese version of Uno's *Principles 1980*. This argument is simply wrong, since the two rates,

Thus, in Uno's theory of crisis, the movements of the two kinds of rates, the profit rate and the interest rate, play a crucial role. In order to clarify this issue, Uno had to study the credit system in relation to the structure of the social production. In chapter "On Money Capitalists in the Theory of Interest in *Capital*" of this volume, we have republished Uno's original analysis of the problem. What follows here is a summary of his theory of credit.

2 Uno's Theory of Interest

Uno's theory of interest, the outline of which is available in English in T. T. Sekine's translation (Uno, *Principles 1980*), is radically different from that of Marx. It begins with commercial credit among industrial capitalists, which is later developed into bank credit.[18] Uno's critique of Marx's theory of interest is summarized in a footnote, yet we assume it is too short to be convincing enough.[19] The article in chapter "On Money Capitalists in the Theory of Interest in *Capital*" of our book should be read together to understand how Uno felt dissatisfied with Marx's argument.

The original Japanese title of this chapter is 『資本論』の利子論における貨幣資本家について. The article was first published in 1958 and provides a brief introduction and overview of the ideas Uno had dealt with at length in the latter half of *Principles of Political Economy* in 1952. The 1952 book was to arouse Yoshio Miyake's criticism, which we have reproduced in chapter "Interest-Bearing Capital: Response to the Explanation of Kōzō Uno" of this volume. In this essay in 1958, Uno relates his arguments with the texts of *Capital* Vol. 3 and elucidates in detail why he felt necessary to challenge Marx's view. Comparing Marx and Uno, readers will be able to grasp the points at issue.

Uno's 1958 essay consists of an introduction, four untitled sections, and a conclusion. In Sect. 1, Uno introduces Marx's concepts of the

the interest rate and the profit rate, are not directly compared by any capitalists. We shall discuss the difference between the two concepts in our chapter "Theorizing Bank Capital: Neo-Unoist Approach". For more discussions on Uno and Unoist crisis theory, see K. Ehara, "The Crisis Theory and the Stages Theory in the Uno School," *Marx Engels Jahrbuch 2017/18*, Berlin: De Gruyter, 2018.

[18] Uno, *Principles 1980*, pp. 109–113.

[19] Ibid., pp. 120,1.

"money capitalist" and the "functioning capitalist," which appear in Chapter 21 of Part 5, *Capital* Vol. 3, titled "Interest-bearing Capital." In Marx's text, a "money capitalist" lends £100 of money to the other capitalist, viz. the "functioning capitalist," who puts the money into a process of valorization. Here, the borrowed money turns itself into "interest-bearing capital." This relation is plain to see at first glance. However, Uno raises a question: where does this "money capitalist" come from in theory?

In Sect. 2, Uno illustrates his interpretation as follows: the "functioning capitalist," who runs the business with £10,000 of capital, borrows £100 of money, and pays the interest from the profit yielded by the business. According to Uno, Marx's example of borrowing and lending of £100 should be regarded as a partial scene abstracted from the whole movement of industrial capital. The "functioning capitalist" becomes a capitalist not by borrowing money from the "money capitalist": it is not reasonable to lend money to those who possess no ability to pay back. The "functioning capitalist" can borrow money because she/he has already launched some profitable activity as a capitalist before borrowing money.

In the same vein, Uno asserts that the "money capitalist" must also be a capitalist even if she/he does not lend the money to someone else. It is true that, in reality, there is a rentier who does not engage in any business and just lends money to get interest. In the pure theory of capitalism, however, this particular "class" should not be taken into consideration, since the rentiers are undistinguishable from capitalists in pre-modern societies, viz. usurers' capital which takes "so to speak antediluvian forms."[20] We cannot treat them equally as three basic classes in the modern capitalist society, i.e., capitalists, landowners, and workers.

This is why in Sect. 3 Uno refutes Marx's argument by arguing that Marx's theory of credit relations is not organically related to his analysis of social reproduction. If we are to build the theory of credit under the capitalist mode of production, the source of lending money capital must be found within the process of social reproduction and the way this has been managed by industrial capitalists. In this scenario, the "money capitalist" is replaced with the industrial capitalist who possesses surplus money capital that is enough to make him/her into a creditor. According

[20] MECW, Vol. 35, p. 174.

to Uno, it is only by locating the source of finance within the social reproduction process that we are able to reveal the logic of finance within capitalism, including the modern banking system. As we have noted above, his theory of crisis rested upon the same premise, in which he had hoped to construct a theory of crisis based upon the dynamic interplay between the credit system and the process of industrial accumulation. Yet, because the "money capitalist" provides monetary funds from outside the process of social reproduction, Uno argues that it is not possible to analyze his/her activity without adding further levels of analysis.[21]

In the last section, Uno focuses on Marx's theory of interest and ground rent, setting out the differences between his and Marx's approach to different levels of abstraction. For Uno, Marx clearly distinguishes the modern form of landed property from pre-modern forms like feudalism, but by abstracting from their continued empirical existence, he was able to demonstrate how ground rent had enabled the formation of a landowning class within capitalist society and the mechanism which had prevented the capitalists from gaining a monopoly of land ownership.

On the other hand, Uno felt that Marx's theory of interest failed to make a clear distinction between theoretical matters and actual states, as we have discussed: the "money capitalist" seems to be associated with rentiers, who are not grounded upon the basic theory. As a result, it is difficult to find out why the "money capitalist" does not form a specific class while the landowners do. In Uno's reformulation, the credit relationship in capitalist society does not require a certain class of creditors: the surplus funds of industrial capital are financed to those who are temporarily short of money. There is no room for the "money capitalist," let alone for the fourth type of class.

It is noteworthy that Uno here refers to a passage in Marx's account that is most discussed in the field: "An exhaustive analysis of the credit system and of the instruments which it creates for its own use (credit money, etc.) lies beyond our plan. We merely wish to dwell here upon a few particular points, which are required to characterize the capitalist mode of production in general. We shall deal only with commercial and bank credit. The connection between the development of this form of

[21] See also M. Itoh, *Basic Theory of Capitalism*, London: Macmillan, 1988, pp. 257–60; C. Lapavitsas, "Two Approaches to the Concept of Interest-Bearing Capital," in C. Lapavitsas, *Marxist Monetary Theory*, Chicago, IL: Haymarket Books, 2017.

credit and that of public credit will not be considered here."[22] Uno argues this is an appropriate approach to credit theory, although he states that it is not one that Marx follows himself. Most Japanese Marxian economists have followed Uno's interpretation in their "analysis of the credit system" insofar as it focuses on "commercial and bank credit." However, this paragraph from *Capital* Vol. 3 differs in significant respects from what Marx wrote in the original manuscript. We shall later discuss Teinosuke Otani (1934–2019), who has based his analysis on the manuscripts made available in the *Marx Engels Gesamtausgabe* (MEGA) and consider its impact upon previous Japanese studies.

Referring back to the concluding section in Uno's article, he developed his own approach to capital fetishism, or "capital as an automatically interest-bearing force." According to Uno, the borrowing and lending relation does not contain mysterious or fetish character: it is grounded upon the social reproduction and the demand of and supply for funds, which then determine the rate of interest. This credit system stimulates competition among capitalists which results in the equalization of the rate of profit. On the other hand, Uno redefines the concept of fetishism in relation to his original form of capital, in the sense of "capital as an automatically interest-bearing force." Unfortunately, there is insufficient space here to elaborate on this unique concept.[23]

3 Uno-Miyake Debate

Uno's critique of Marx's theory of interest was just one of a number of criticisms of *Capital* set out in *Principles of Political Economy* (1950 and 1952). The scale and scope of his critique provoked a storm of reaction from Marxian economists at the time, which resulted in a protracted debate in which Uno gradually gained ground. These discussions are indispensable for anyone seeking fully to appreciate the significance of the Japanese studies of Marxian economics.

Yoshio Miyake (1916–1996) was one of the main critics of Uno's theory of interest. He had already been one of the earliest scholars to have emphasized the significance of Marx's concept of interest-bearing

[22] MECW, Vol. 37, p. 397.

[23] See S. Shibasaki and K. Ehara, "What Is Commercial Capital? Japanese contributions to Marxian market theory," *Capital & Class*, OnlineFirst, July 9, 2021, Section 1.

capital and fetishism. His studies also influenced the works of T. Otani. Miyake and Uno engaged in a highly polemical and protracted debate, which included mutual rebuttals and counter-rebuttals Chapters 3 and 4 aim to give the reader a sense of the debate. Chapter 3 consists of an excerpt from Miyake's essay from 1953 and sets out some of the classical questions that one can expect regarding Uno's theory of interest, while Chapter 4 consists of Uno's rebuttal. Here readers are provided with materials for a better understanding of Uno's notion of interest and those who opposed him.

The original Japanese title of chapter "Interest-Bearing Capital: Response to the Explanation of Kōzō Uno" is 続利子生み資本小論: 宇野弘蔵氏の所説によせて. This article is first published in 1953. It is a part of Miyake's essay that criticizes his contemporaries. The original article is longer and includes the critique of Ichirō Kawai (1918–1979) and Tomoyoshi Fujitsuka (1916–1993) as well as that of Uno. Note that Miyake's criticism is made on Uno's *Principles of Political Economy* published in 1950 and 1952, not on Uno's 1958 article or on his abridged version of *Principles* that has an English translation. Chapter "How a Theory of Interest Should Be Developed: Answering Yoshio Miyake's Critique of the Theory of Interest in My *Principles of Political Economy*" is Uno's answer, which is originally titled 利子論はいかに展開されるべきか: 三宅義夫氏の拙著『経済原論』における利子論の批評に答う. This article is also first published in 1953.

In Sect. 1 of Miyake's essay, he questions Uno's explanation of "loan capital." According to Uno, "loan capital" cannot be simply be described as capital just because it is lendable. It can be lent because it is in a money form. Miyake guesses, therefore, "loan capital" is considered by Uno a capital since it begets interest. This is not a reasonable definition since "loan capital" in Uno's sense fails to be a capital when the borrower cannot pay back the interest. Here we can see that for Miyake, the concept of "interest-bearing capital" cannot be replaced with that of "loan capital." Rather, "interest-bearing capital" still functions as capital within the hands of the lenders even before it is offered for lending, regardless of the credibility of the borrowers.

We can find the term "loan capital" also in the text of English translation of Uno's *Principles*. There we observe that the concept of "loan capital" is related to the activity of banks: "Banks pay an interest in collecting deposits and charge interest in making loans; they earn the interest-differential as profit on their own capital invested in the operation of finance, that is to say, in the function of intermediating the capitalist-social utilization of idle funds. This function … is carried out by the banks according to the formula M … M' of *loan-capital*."[24] Here the "loan capital" does not function as an equity capital invested by a certain capitalist. It is just a description of the movement of "funds" through the banking system.

This is the basic reason why Uno rejected Miyake's critique as irrelevant. The formula of "loan capital" exists when "interest conclusively becomes the price for the use of 'funds' during a specified period of time."[25] Even when the borrowers fail to pay interest, they must do so somehow just as the buyers must pay money for commodity they took away from the store. This principle has nothing to do with the concept of capital.

Admittedly, the concept of "loan capital" has largely faded from view. It is an ambiguous concept in that it seeks to separate the formula of capital from equity. To reflect this shift, we have decided to focus the last two chapters of the book on more recent attempts to deepen the concept of bank capital in order to develop a clearer picture of the significance of banking.

The second point of contention between Uno and Miyake rests on the concept of the "value of capital." For Uno, capital cannot be commodified in the relation between the "money capitalist" and the "functioning capitalist," since it is only money that is commodified insofar as money is borrowed and lent. The interest is the price of the right to use the money during certain period. Uno argues, therefore, that interest represents not the "value of capital" but the value of monetary "funds." On the other hand, Miyake points out Marx does not refer to the concept of the "value of capital" in this context, since capital is, in Marxian terms,

[24] Uno, *Principles 1980*, p. 110.

[25] Ibid., p. 111.

value in motion. It can be assumed that Miyake believes that "interest-bearing capital" is value in motion just as is the case for all other forms of capital and that it is not interest that should be counted as the value of "interest-bearing capital" but the value of "fictitious capital." Thus, while Uno focuses on banking, Miyake seems to consider a broader foundation of finance.

This raises a third point on the use of terminology. Uno often uses the word "funds" when referring to the idle money in the course of the circulation of industrial capital. This terminology was not common at that time among Marxian economists. Miyake asserts it can be just called hoarded money, the concept of which is much more familiar to Marxists. According to Miyake, people in pre-capitalist society hoard money for different objectives than those in capitalist society: in pre-capitalist society, money hoarding is in itself a goal, while money is just a means of valorization in capitalist society. Miyake thus recognizes the difference in the concept of hoarded money and insists that what Uno calls "funds" is identical with hoarded money in a capitalist society.

Uno's conceptualization of the term is certainly unclear. In Uno's *Principles* in 1950 (the first half of Uno, *Principles 1977*), we observe that he adheres to Marx's threefold classification of the functions of money: viz. money as the measure of values, as a means of circulation, and simply as "money." The final one, which is also called "money as such," is divided into three: hoarding, the means of payment, and world (universal) money. Meanwhile, in the body text, we find the concept of "funds" as a new function of money. According to Uno, gold, as the form of world money, "moves back and forth between the circulation market and the pool of monetary saving, where it often takes the form of bullion. But gold in its bullion state can no longer be considered as money in the ordinary sense; it is rather money at rest or *idle funds* (shikin) laid aside from the circulation market characterised by the ceaseless motion of prices."[26] Nevertheless, it is obvious that the term "funds" cannot be reduced to world money in Uno's context. The "funds" are neither hoarded money,

[26] Ibid., p. 12. This quotation is followed by the following sentence: "Whereas money as the means of payment is required to meet pre-arranged obligations, idle funds are accumulated for no specific purpose." We cannot know from this distinction how idle funds "accumulated for no specific purpose" are different from hoarded money. Actually, this English translation of the sentence is not quite accurate: in the original Japanese text, Uno just emphasizes the necessity in distinguishing this new function from the means of payment.

means of payment, nor world money, but are included in the category of "money as such."

Indeed, it was not only Miyake but also Uno's followers who were confused by this shifting terminology. As we shall see in the next section, his supporters subsequently sought to remove the ambiguity that persisted with Uno's use of the word "funds."

The fourth and the last point is on the fetishism of capital. Miyake indicates that Uno overlooks this significant concept and that this is the root of Uno's misunderstanding of Marx. According to Miyake, Uno fails to appreciate the concept of "interest-bearing capital" since he does not consider the "interest-bearing capital" as a reified form of capital, in which the interest is regarded as its inherent nature. As we have noted above, Uno discusses the fetishism of capital originally with regard to the concept of "capital as an automatically interest-bearing force." Miyake poses a question on this reorganization: why does Uno disregard the concept of reification at the beginning of the theory of interest and revisit it at the end? In other words, how does Uno justify the assumption that the borrowing and lending of money do not reify the nature of "interest-bearing" while the joint-stock company does?

Uno's answer is that the fetishism of capital first appears in the form of a joint-stock company because the rate of interest is theoretically given for the stock market or the capital market. It is the money market, not the capital market, that determines the rate of interest, which is used in calculating the stock price. Uno asserts that the nature of "interest-bearing" must not be presumed, but must be deduced through the theoretical development of the financial system within the capitalist economy.

Nevertheless, this does not fully address Miyake's question. Miyake understands the concept of "interest-bearing capital" and capital fetish as belonging fundamentally to the capitalist system of credit and finance. It is not only the capital in the stock market but the whole capital, whether it is traded in the stock market or not, that is fetishized. Due to Uno's inability to grasp the contagious effect of his concept of "capital as an automatically interest-bearing force" upon the whole of capitalist society, Miyake is left wondering why Uno rejected the capital fetish at the outset, while accepting it at the other end of the process.

Due to these inconsistencies, those influenced by Uno have increasingly abandoned the concept of capital fetishism from their theories of interest, preferring to concentrate on the theoretical development of commercial and bank credit.[27]

4 Yamaguchi's Methodological Change

Uno greatly influenced Japanese Marxism and had many followers. Makoto Itoh (1936–) and Thomas T. Sekine (1933–2022) are the best-known scholars among Unoists in the English-speaking world. It goes without saying that their achievements are important, yet it was Shigekatsu Yamaguchi (1932–2021) who made the greatest innovations in this field of study after Uno. While largely unknown in the English-speaking world, Yamaguchi's work has had a far from negligible impact on Marxian economics in Japan.

Let us begin briefly by introducing Yamaguchi's study of Marxian economics as a whole. His first monograph is on the theory of commercial capital, titled *Competition and Commercial Capital* in 1983.[28] There he criticized Uno's theory of commercial capital, for failing to provide a sufficient analysis of the competitive relations between commercial capital to industrial capital, and rectified the role of commercial capital in the formation of capitalist market system in the fundamental theory. The method of emphasizing competition taken in this book is also applied to the theory of finance. In 1984, Yamaguchi published another monograph titled *The Theory of Financial Systems*, in which chapter "A Systematic Approach to Marxian Credit Theory Based on the Uno Theory" of our book is included, and in 1987 he published *The Scope of Value Theory* which makes a contribution to the development of the theory of value, not least in terms of the Unoist interpretation of the "transformation problem." All of these achievements are systematically brought together

[27] E. Lange, *Value without Fetish: Uno Kōzō's Theory of 'Pure Capitalism' in Light of Marx's Critique of Political Economy*, Leiden: Brill, 2021, pp. 282-91, includes the latest critique of Uno's theory of credit available in English. Although Lange argues that "banking activities are *presupposed*" (p. 290) in Uno's discussion, essays included in the present volume will show that the existence of bankers is regarded as an *explanandum*, rather than *explanans*, in the Uno school. Lange's monograph is wholly dedicated to the criticism against Uno and the Uno school who do not follow Marx's method on the critique of fetishism. As seen in Miyake's essay, this type of criticism is not new in Japanese studies of Marxism.

[28] Shibasaki and Ehara, "What Is Commercial Capital?" discusses Yamaguchi's achievements on the theory of commercial capital in detail.

in his textbook of Marxian economics, *Lectures on the Principles of Political Economy*, published in 1985. He worked long at the University of Tokyo together with M. Itoh and educated many Marxian economists.

Yamaguchi's innovations in the field of the theory of finance center on three main topics: credit creation, central banking, and the capital market. Chapter 5 of our book mainly concentrates on the first of these by republishing an article he wrote originally in 1980 (the original Japanese title of the chapter is マルクス信用理論の体系化: 宇野理論の展開). In this essay, Yamaguchi summarizes the gist of Uno's theory of interest and develops it on his own terms. While Yamaguchi's summary of Uno's theory is clear and valuable in itself, the third section is the most important because it includes Yamaguchi's own departure from Uno's view, which turns the theory of interest into what should be renamed the theory of credit, so to speak.

4.1 Credit Creation

The third section has four subsections, titled "commercial credit," "bank credit," "central banking," and "credit creation," respectively. Yamaguchi's description of the development of the relationship between commercial credit and central banking is almost the same as that which Uno described, but Yamaguchi points out that we can observe credit creation in the sense that the purchasing power is newly created in each stage. Most fundamentally he believes it is possible to observe credit creation in the sense of commercial credit.

Let us examine Yamaguchi's example. B, a weaver, purchases yarn by a promissory note of £100 from A, who is a spinner. Since A has £40 of money to continue his/her process of production, she/he does not need to sell his/her commodity in cash. Though the commodity yarn would sell at a price of £80 in cash, A chooses to sell it on credit. Meanwhile, B is running out of cash. B can buy the yarn on credit since B would sell his/her commodity, cotton fabrics, at a price of £100 in future. Here, £100 of additional purchasing power is created on the basis of B's creditworthiness.

This relation can be illustrated in a balance sheet-like figure. The signs C, M, N denote commodity, money, credit or obligation, respectively. When N is put on the left side of the balance sheet, it means a claim; if N is on the right side, it is a debt. The superscript shows the price and the

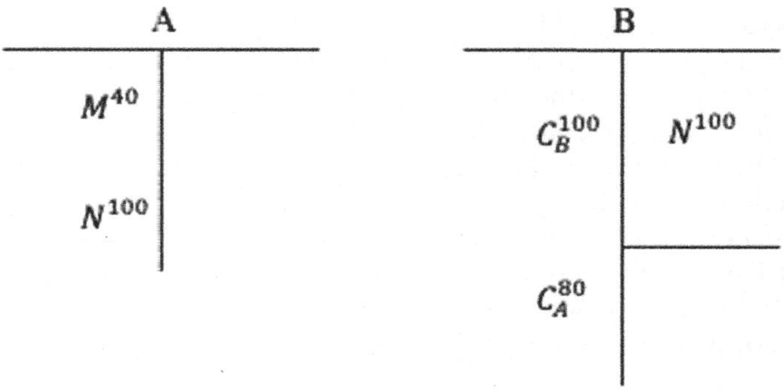

Fig. 1 Commercial credit

subscript of C refers to the person who has produced it. After B buys A's commodity by a promissory note, their assets and debts can be illustrated in Fig. 1.

It is important to note that A's money capital, £40 in this example, is not directly financed to B. This idle money capital, or "funds," is necessary for A to give a credit, but this is not a direct source of finance. If A lent £40 of money to B, there would be no additional purchasing power in this relation. Moreover, A would get less benefit. In this case of commercial credit, the substantial rate of interest is 25%: since A sells a commodity that would sell at £80 in cash at the price of £100 on credit, 100 – 80 = £20 could be conceived as interest. The substantial principal is 80. Thus, if A lent £40 directly to B, A's gain would be as low as £10 in an equilibrial state (40 * 0.25 = 10). We can assume A has an incentive to sell his/her commodity on credit, rather than lending his/her idle money capital, if she/he has more commodity capital to sell than the amount of money capital.

Hence, the role of "funds" is finally clarified by Yamaguchi, and the misleading aspects of Uno's terminology are exposed.[29] For Uno, "funds" are defined as "independent money, separate from the direct

[29] Ichirō Kawai, who was criticized by Miyake, substantially discussed the credit creation before Yamaguchi. Kawai worked at Osaka City University and his monograph titled *Capital and Credit*, published in 1954, was influential in Marxian finance theory at the time. We can assume Yamaguchi incorporated Kawai's idea on the credit creation in Uno's theory of finance.

process of circulation and different from money as a means of circulation, *that can be put into circulation at any time as something that purchases commodities*," and as "the object of demand and supply, and … the object of sale and purchase from being commodified."[30] However, as shown in £40 in the hand of A in the above example, it is never supplied or "commodified" itself in the relations of credit. The "funds" generated in the reproduction process are certainly the basis of credit relations, yet they are not lent to the debtor themselves but are spent in order to maintain the creditor's production process during the term of credit. In this sense, we do not need a special term for this sort of money capital.

4.2 Central Banking

As Yamaguchi argues, it was Uno who first theoretically discussed the relations between banks and the formation of central banking. However, Yamaguchi casts doubt on the logic of taking a deductive approach to central banking. There can be some sort of division of labor between banks in theory: some banks engage in receiving deposits and others issue banknotes. Nevertheless, it is difficult to prove that these roles are fixed or monopolized. Yamaguchi thus maintains that central banking should be analyzed in its actual historical process and cannot be deduced in theory.

As a result, there exists no central bank in Yamaguchi's fundamental theory. Instead, we have an organizational banking system that is formed by banks amid their competition. A central banking system emerges as one of the many historical possibilities contained within Yamaguchi's theory of an organizational banking system. It is not only theoretical development but also historical factors that should be considered in order to analyze how a central banking system is established. Yamaguchi thus draws a clear line of demarcation between theory and historical studies.

4.3 Capital Market

While Uno discussed the capital market with regard to his own concept of "capital as an automatically interest-bearing force," he scarcely related it to the movement of industrial capital. In Uno's theory, the credit system and commercial capital both play a role in assisting the process of profit

[30] Uno, *Principles 1977*, p. 457. Quoted by Miyake on p. 68 in our book.

rate equalization among industries, yet the capital market does not. By defining "capital as an automatically interest-bearing force" he is stating that it is just an ideal concept: it does not realize itself without a concrete institutional structure, such as a stock market system.

For Yamaguchi, the capital market forms part of his deductive theoretical system in that it is developed as part of the capitalist market system together with commercial capital and banking system in the fundamental theory. The capital market is necessary if fixed capital is removed from one industry to be employed in another industry. This movement of fixed capital does lead to the formation of general rate of profit. It is true that the stock market must be institutionalized somehow, yet there must be an abstract form of the capital market even in a pure theory. In Yamaguchi's theory, therefore, the capitalist market system has a three-layered structure: the commodity market with commercial capital, the money market with bank capital, and the capital market with securities capital.[31]

According to Yamaguchi, Uno failed to develop the theory of market system because Uno stuck to the theory of fetishism in Marx's theory of interest. As we have discussed, Uno tried to refurbish Marx's concept of fetishism of capital in his own way which led to Miyake's objection. Yamaguchi argues that the theory of fetishism is incompatible with Uno's reformulation of constructing the theory of credit on the basis of idle money generated in the circuit of industrial capital. If the method of the latter is thoroughly employed, the theory of finance will be reconstructed as a developmental process of the abovementioned three-layered market system, which can be associated with Uno's value-form analysis. As Uno based his developmental sequence of value-forms on the basis of relations among commodity owners, so Yamaguchi theorizes a sequential development of the market system by focusing on the relations of individual industrial capitals. Instead of pursuing the issue of fetishism, Yamaguchi chooses to establish a new method for developing the theory of finance, which is called the "differentiation and development method (DDM)."

DDM considers the economic incentives of market actors as they engage in certain transactions as we have seen regarding the credit creation. For example, if both parties deem the circulation cost would be lowered, the trade between industrial capitalists generates the actor

[31] See Shibasaki and Ehara, "What Is Commercial Capital?," Table 1.

who exclusively engages in the trade activity, viz. a commercial capitalist. This style of reasoning is used to analyze the structure of financial system.

5 Post-Yamaguchi: Bank Capital and "Interest-Bearing Capital" Revisited

5.1 Equity Capital in Banking

I assume that many Marxists feel that Yamaguchi waters down Marxian theory by rejecting the theory of fetishism. Nevertheless, Yamaguchi's method attracted many researchers and stimulated rigorous studies of financial theory. DDM is based on, as it were, micro viewpoints, but today's standard mainstream microeconomics usually lacks the full-fledged theory of finance. Meanwhile, the mainstream macroeconomics premises that all financial structures are given, consequently failing to reveal the role of credit creation in the relations of two individuals. Yamaguchi's theory fills the gap left by mainstream economics, thus establishing itself as an alternative economic theory that gives a penetrating insight into the capitalist system of finance.

Within DDM, Yamaguchi first focuses on the activities of individual industrial capitalists by sequentially following their activities through the three-layered market system, i.e., the commodity market, the money market, and the capital market. With the establishment of this tripartite market system, Yamaguchi's followers have refined and reinforced the scheme. However, once this multistory system is established, scholars have started paying attention to its applicability to the activities of other types of capitalists. Shimizu's article in chapter "Bank Capital and Credit System" is one of the first attempts to shed light on the relationship between banking and the capital market, rather than that between industrial capital and credit system.

Masashi Shimizu (1970–) is one of the current leading Japanese Marxian economists. Shimizu wrote his dissertation on the concept of commercial capital, which was published in 2006 as *The Scope of Commercial Capital Theory*. In this monograph, he investigates multilateral relations centered on commercial capital within the three market systems. It has four chapters, which, respectively, study the fields of the commodity market, commercial credit, bank credit, and the capital market. The article in our book provides the materials for his understanding on bank credit (which was originally published as 銀行資本と信用機構 in 2004).

The most important point in this article is that bank capital needs a form of equity capital that cannot be financed by deposits. As we have seen above, financial theorists have been mostly analyzing credit relationships which are formulated as movements of "loan capital," or M ... M'. This "M" is not owned by banks themselves but is a deposit from others. As a result of focusing on credit relationships, they tend to neglect the role of equity capital in a bank and consequently ignore how a bank valorizes itself as one type of capital.

Shimizu discusses what he calls the "reserves" necessary for the banking industry and classifies it into two types, i.e., reserves as ready cash and reserves for non-performing loans. Shimizu labels them the "monetary reserves" and the "asset reserves," respectively. While the "monetary reserves" must be ready in cash, or at least held in the form that can be immediately changed into the cash form, the "asset reserves" do not necessarily take the form or semi-form of cash, but are forms of asset that retain reliable values. Though the demand for the "monetary reserves" could be satisfied by collecting deposits, the "asset reserves" must be invested as equity capital. Bank capitals can augment the value of the "asset reserves" from their own profit-seeking activities, but they can also reinforce their "asset reserves" by collecting investment from other capitalists. According to Shimizu, bank capitals thus have a notable incentive for creating and participating in a capital market.

Based on Shimizu's emphasis on the equity of bank capital, we can finally give a full description of a bank credit relationship. Let us use Yamaguchi's example of commercial credit shown in Fig. 1. Assuming that A is the creditor and B is the debtor, when B applies to A for credit, but A does not believe that B will repay the loan, A will refuse B's credit application and there is, thus, no commercial credit relationship between the two (Phase 1 in Fig. 2).

Bank capital plays a role here as an intermediary. A will accept now a note if the bank capital guarantees B's deferred payment. Then, B tries to get credit from the bank capital. If B succeeds, the bank gives credit to B and at the same time B becomes a creditor to the bank. The bank does not give his/her own cash to B: the bank is an agent retaining credibility that is strong enough to make his/her own debt circulate through the credit nexus. Thus, when the bank provides a credit, she/he simultaneously owes a debt. The bank can earn from the difference between the credit and the debt, usually collected as an interest. In this example, the bank provides a £90 credit (*N'*) to B instead of getting a £100 credit

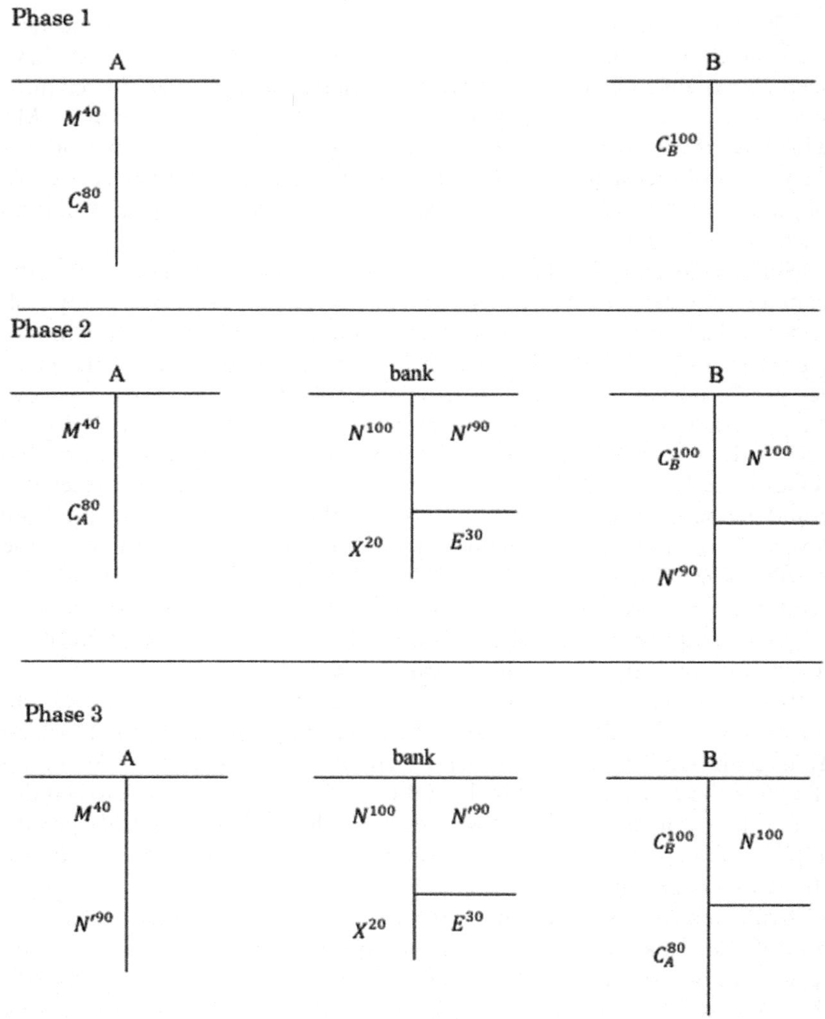

Fig. 2 Bank credit

(N): for instance, the bank discounts B's bill of £100 to £90. The interest or discount rate is ten percent.

The bank capital can be distinguished from other types of capital because his/her own equity capital is invested exclusively for the purpose of credit mediation, as we utilize what Shimizu refers to as the equity capital of the bank as "asset reserves." This forms the foundation of the bank's high creditworthiness. Some portion of the bank's assets must be his/her own property, say X, and it corresponds to his/her equity, E. In this case, E becomes larger than the value of X, since it is augmented by gaining the interest (Phase 2 in Fig. 2).

Thanks to the mediation of the bank, B is now able to buy A's commodity. N' and C_A are exchanged with each other. The debt of the bank is here counted as the means of payment, regardless of whether it takes a form of deposit or banknote. As a result of all these transactions, the bank owes a debt to A, an original creditor, and gives a credit to B, an original debtor. However, this does not mean that the bank lends to B the money that is collected from A. As we have seen in the relation of commercial credit, A's money capital is not directly financed to B. In the same vein, A's money capital remains in A's hands in the bank credit relation. It is B's creditworthiness based on his/her commodity capital that is an ultimate source of the bank credit (Phase 3 in Fig. 2).

5.2 Revisiting "Interest-Bearing Capital"

With Shimizu, we start to see the kernel of banking system, and how this relates to the reconstruction of Marxian finance theory as developed by Uno and Yamaguchi. Nevertheless, we cannot stop here as we are confronted with the recent development of "financialization." The foundation of Uno-Yamaguchi's finance theory lies in the idle money generated during the circuit of industrial capital. It is true that Yamaguchi took credit creation into account, yet the amount of finance is fundamentally determined by the amount of idle money generated in social reproduction. On the other hand, the phenomena of "financialization" points to the radical expansion of finance and its increased isolation from the real economy. While this suffices as a phenomenal description, it has remained under-theorized.

T. Otani insists on the importance of a more careful reading of Marx in the analysis of contemporary financial phenomena. According to Otani, it was a fatal mistake to focus on the formation of commercial and bank credit by disregarding the concept of "interest-bearing capital." Otani reemphasizes the significance of the concept of "interest-bearing capital" by his intensive and comprehensive study of Marx's manuscripts of *Capital* Vol. 3, generally in accordance with the Kuruma and Miyake tradition.

Let us take a typical example. As we have mentioned, most Japanese Marxian economists analyzed the relations of commercial and bank credit, following Uno's approach. Uno grounded his arguments upon Marx's statement, which I here quote again:

> An exhaustive analysis of the credit system and of the instruments which it creates for its own use (credit money, etc.) lies beyond our plan. We merely wish to dwell here upon a few particular points, which are required to characterize the capitalist mode of production in general. We shall deal only with commercial and bank credit. The connection between the development of this form of credit and that of public credit will not be considered here.

This statement can easily be interpreted to suggest that the study of commercial and bank credit does not constitute an "exhaustive analysis" of the credit system, whereas "the development of state credit" would feature in an "exhaustive analysis" and thus "lies beyond our plan." This interpretation has led most Marxian economists to focus on the study of commercial and bank credit, which was considered as included in Marx's "plan" as a *non-exhaustive* analysis of the credit system.

Otani reveals that this passage was actually modified by Engels. The original sentences are as follows:

> It lies outside the scope of our plan to give an analysis of the credit system and the instruments this creates for itself, such as credit money, etc. Only a few points will be emphasised here, points which are necessary for the characterisation of the capitalist mode of production in general. In this connection we shall simply be dealing with commercial credit. The connection between commercial credit's development and the development of state credit remains outside our consideration.[32]

[32] *Marx's Economic Manuscript of 1864–1865*, Chicago, IL: Haymarket Books, 2017, p. 500. See also, *Marx Engels Gesamtasugabe*, II-4.2, S. 469. *Marx Engels Gesamtasugabe* is hereafter abbreviated as MEGA in this book.

At first glance, there is no important change. However, Otani points out two small but significant modifications here. First, Engels inserted the adjective "exhaustive" in the first sentence. As a result of this modification, people believe that Marx here launches a brief study of the credit system so long as it is necessary for characterizing the capitalist mode of production in general. Consequently, Part 5 of *Capital* Vol. 3 is largely divided into two pieces: the first four chapters, Chapters 21–24, are about the concept of "interest-bearing capital," and the remaining chapters are on the credit system. This division led Japanese Marxists to concentrate on the latter and the Uno school was the most extreme example, who dismissed altogether the concept of "interest-bearing capital." Otani asserts that this is a wrong interpretation, because Marx simply places "an analysis of the credit system" outside the scope of his plan. According to Otani, Marx conducts the analysis of "interest-bearing capital" throughout the texts of Part 5 and the credit system is referred to insofar as it is related to the concept of "interest-bearing capital," not as an independent set of institutions.

Second, Marx originally says he will deal with only "commercial credit," not "commercial and bank credit." Otani insists that the term "commercial credit" is here used as an antonym for "state credit" or "public credit," not as that of bank credit as seen in other parts.[33] Marx here just puts to one side the role of the state and does not intend to proceed to the issue of developing the relations of commercial credit into those of banking, which Japanese Marxian economists have tried to address. This modification also resulted in diverting their attentions away from the concept of "interest-bearing capital," according to Otani.

Otani indicates numerous other points of difference between Engel's edition and Marx's manuscript, thereby emphasizing the consistency in Marx's original theoretical study of "interest-bearing capital." As we have seen above, it was Miyake who stressed the importance of the concept in the debate with Uno, while Miyake also interpreted Part 5 as dealing with two different issues, "interest-bearing capital" and the credit system. Otani's critique is directed to this interpretation of Miyake's, provoking a heated debate between the two. However, it should be noted that Otani's

[33] See, for example, MECW, Vol. 37, p. 478.

reinterpretation has a potential impact on the whole trajectory of Marxian studies of credit theory in Japan.[34]

On the basis of the study of the manuscript, Otani builds his own theory of "interest-bearing capital," which is available in English translation in his textbook of Marxian economics *A Guide to Marxian Political Economy*.[35] Chapter 19 is named "Interest-bearing Capital and Interest" and it has two sections, the latter of which, "Bank Capital and Banking System," shows Otani's theorization of the connection between the "interest-bearing capital" and the banking system.

Otani argues that "The banking system has two aspects: the credit-dealing system and the institution for the management of interest-bearing capital."[36] As for the first aspect, he states: "Whereas *commercial credit is the foundation of the credit system*, the *banking system is its superstructure*, and together are the two constituents of the credit system under capitalist production."[37] This is equivalent to what most Japanese Marxist economists have intensively studied, the Uno school in particular. However, they have overlooked the other aspect, viz. what Otani calls "the management of interest-bearing capital." In Marx's manuscript, "interest-bearing capital" is labeled under the banking system as "monied capital" or "moneyed capital." Accordingly, Otani states that banks "*make the borrowing and lending of money their own proper function and mediate and manage moneyed capital as interest-bearing capital*."[38]

Otani goes on to discuss the concept of "fictitious capital" as a main consequence of the development of the "interest-bearing capital." "Because money lent as interest-bearing capital brings about interest at the given rate of interest settled on in the market, a *regularly obtainable money revenue* is conceived of as *interest* on some sort of «capital», and in turn, the *revenue source* generating this «interest» is conceived of as

[34] Otani's extensive study of this theme is published in four volumes together with the first complete Japanese translation of Marx's manuscript of Part 5 in *Capital* Vol. 3 in MEGA, II-4.2. T. Otani, *Marx's Theory of Interest-Bearing Capital*, Tokyo: Sakurai-Shoten, 2016. My brief review of these volumes is available in English in *Marx Engels Jahrbuch 2017/18*, Berlin: De Gruyter, 2018.

[35] T. Otani, *A Guide to Marxian Political Economy: What Kind of a Social System Is Capitalism?* Berlin: Springer International, 2018. The translator is Michael Schauerte.

[36] Ibid., p. 418.

[37] Ibid., p. 420.

[38] Ibid., p. 424.

capital. ... The «capital» conceived of through this capitalisation is ... called **fictitious capital**."[39] Banks, as managers of the "interest-bearing capital," invest in the "fictitious capital" in the forms of various types of securities such as bonds and stocks to obtain so-called income gains and capital gains, making themselves exposed to speculative activities. Consequently, "When, *for whatever reason*, one part of the fictitious capital seeks to be transformed into real value, the fictitious character of this enormous totality of capital is immediately brought to light, and the banking system itself undergoes a disturbance to a greater or lesser extent."[40]

In Otani's theory of the banking system, we observe securities investment, which is an indispensable topic for analyzing today's financial phenomena, as one of the forms of the finance provided by banks. This aspect of banks is largely neglected in the conventional Unoist approach. For example, in Yamaguchi's theory, the money market and the capital market are managed by two different forms of capital, viz. bank capital and securities capital, while the concept of "fictitious capital" does not appear in Uno-Yamaguchi's theory. Through scrutinizing Marx's manuscript, Otani sheds light on Marx's original concept of "interest-bearing capital" and practically expands the scope of Marxian finance theory developed in Japan, thereby laying the basis for today's questions.[41]

5.3 *Bank Capital and Financial System*

While Otani recaptures the richness of Marx's study of "interest-bearing capital," it is necessary to assess whether those ideas are logically compelling. We admit the concept of "interest-bearing capital" enables us to examine the issues of finance to a greater extent than the conventional configuration of Japanese theories of credit. However, we must carefully check its compatibility with other concepts and also consider whether it is the only way to a breakthrough.

The essay in chapter "Theorizing Bank Capital: Neo-Unoist Approach" of our book aims to reconstruct the theory of credit and

[39] Ibid., pp. 432,3.

[40] Ibid., p. 435.

[41] As for the development of Otani's finance theory, see also K. Miyata, "Karl Marx's Credit Theory," *Marx Engels Jahrbuch 2015/16*, Berlin: De Gruyter. 2016.

finance by both accepting and criticizing the previous studies including Uno-Yamaguchi's theoretical achievements and Otani's detailed study of Marx's manuscript. In line with Uno-Yamaguchi's theory, it does not make use of the concept of "interest-bearing capital," yet it takes a critical attitude to the main methodology established by Yamaguchi. Meanwhile, the author of the chapter fully appreciates the significance of Otani's study and its extended scope of analysis, though he casts doubt on the consistency of the essential term "capital." The article was originally published in 2019 in Japanese (with the original title of 銀行業と資本: 分化・発生論批判), yet it is entirely rewritten for this volume with new developments added.

In Japanese studies of Marxian theory of finance, "the differentiation and development method (DDM)" has been a dominant theoretical method, which was established by Yamaguchi. According to DDM, commercial and bank credit is formed within the movement of industrial capital faced with the "indeterminate nature of the circulation process." However, current financial phenomena are undermining these conclusions as financial transactions have expanded irrespective of industrial growth. It was thanks to DDM that Japanese Marxian economists successfully captured the structure of the banking system, yet it falls short when analyzing recent developments.

This is why the concept of "interest-bearing capital" is again gaining more attention these days. It has led us to pay attention to the significance of "fictitious capital." Meanwhile, the concept of "fictitious capital" is inconsistent with other types of capital in two senses. First, it is just named as "capital" by capitalizing the revenue by the rate of interest and must be distinguished from other forms of capital that do not require such a special process of calculation. As we have quoted above, Otani himself explains the concept first by placing the term capital within guillemets ("«capital»"), suggesting that it is not the same with industrial capital or commercial capital, but he removes the guillemets when referring to "fictitious capital" without giving an explanation. This makes it difficult to know whether or not the "fictitious capital" is one of the types of capital in a theoretical sense.

Second, if the "fictitious capital" is termed as capital in its original sense, it must compete with other types of capital in terms of the profit rate. In other words, the return on "fictitious capital" must be compared with the rate of profit for other investment spheres. The competition among capitals theoretically results in profit equalization. Since the return on "fictitious capital" corresponds to the rate of interest by definition, it would lead us to assume the rate of interest must have a tendency toward being equalized with the rate of profit. This is not a desirable consequence. As Otani also admits, even for banks, their profits are not "*definitely limited to interest*."[42] We must strictly distinguish the category of profit and that of interest. Capital generates profit, not interest. The concept of "fictitious capital" blurs this fundamental conceptual distinction.

In my view, as a result of trying to adopt the idea that capital begets interest, Otani ended up creating a lot of terminological confusion as regards banking and capital. While Otani successfully describes the financial structure of banks using a balance sheet-like figure, he uses two kinds of "capital" on the side of "Capital & Liabilities," viz. "owned capital" and "borrowed capital." According to Otani, the proportion of profit vis-à-vis the "owned capital" is the rate of profit and it "does not generate any interest." It has another name called "bank capital." On the other hand, the "borrowed capital" is regarded as generating interest and named as "banking capital."[43] I understand this terminology is derived from Otani's detailed analysis of Marx's manuscript, especially that of Chapter 29, "Banking Capital's Component Parts." However, if we are to theorize the banking system, we do not have to follow all of Marx's practices. I assume it is better to use the term "capital" only for the "owned capital," and what Otani mentions as the "borrowed capital" should be considered as liabilities, not a perverted concept of "capital" earning interests. Accordingly, the "owned capital," or bank capital, is the only part that deserves to be called capital. This is equivalent to what Shimizu mentions as an equity capital of banks.

By clarifying the meaning of the term "capital," we can now formulate the rate of profit for banking. Based on this formulation of the profit rate within banking, we can conduct a more detailed analysis of the financial system without relying upon the concept of "interest-bearing capital" or "fictitious capital." In order to raise the profit rate, banks need to increase not only the interest rate but also the size of their assets. Whereas the increase in the rate of interest dampens the demand for finance, banks do not necessarily increase their reserves in proportion to the rise in their

42 Otani, *Marxian Political Economy*, p. 425.

43 Ibid., pp. 425–7.

assets, the effect of which is down to achieving economies of scale. Banks have an incentive to maintain and reinforce their creditworthiness on the basis of their equity capital so as to be more attractive as a financial mediator, thereby enlarging the size of their assets. The growth of such assets leads to an increase in profits even where the interest rate is constant.

Therefore, financial expansion does not always result in financial instability. Banks purchase securities especially when the demand for loans is stagnant, but as long as the creditworthiness of banks is not undermined, the increase in the banking assets is not problematic. However, banks try to maintain their creditworthiness insofar as it is necessary to expand their assets. When the securities market booms for some reason, the assets in the banking industry grow regardless of banks' credibility and yield profit for banks. Financial boom occurs in this case along with the credit expansion, which is highly likely to result in an economic crisis. We should assume banks have two contradictory aspects: the one which maintains financial stability and the other which leads to financial instability. Both of these aspects are the logical consequence of the profit-seeking activities of banks.[44]

6 Conclusion

Japanese Marxian economists have devoted over half a century to the study of financial systems and developed a highly sophisticated conception of the field. Much of this work was stimulated by Uno's reformulation of Marx's theory of interest and can be seen as various attempts to refine and develop certain key concepts that remain unclear such as "loan capital" and "funds," which have been re-criticized and mostly abandoned. Miyake's critique of Uno's terminology was relevant in some respects, though it was Uno's followers, including Yamaguchi and Shimizu, who did the most to reveal the structure of financial systems and refined the terminology.

[44] We assume that this viewpoint is basically in line with Lapavitsas, *Profit without Producing*, in which he asserts "at the root of financialization lie the vast banks of mature and other economies." (ebook, Kindle) We also share his warning of the danger of using the concept of "fictitious capital." However, if we are to focus on banks in contemporary capitalist economies, we think we must update the Japanese theoretical studies so far, which Lapavitsas appreciates in his work, as we will see in chapters "Bank Capital and Credit System" and "Theorizing Bank Capital: Neo-Unoist Approach".

It remains to be discussed whether the very concept of "interest-bearing capital" is useful or not. I myself think that this concept refers to what should be considered as financial assets or commodities rather than capital and that the terminology is therefore confusing. Also, the inner relation between banking and the securities market, which is essential in analyzing "financialization" today, can logically be developed without using the concept of "interest-bearing capital." As shown in chapters "Bank Capital and Credit System" and "Theorizing Bank Capital: Neo-Unoist Approach," bank capital has an incentive to reach out the securities market itself.

Meanwhile, as Miyake and Otani suggested, the theory of "interest-bearing capital" is connected to revealing the fetishism of capital, which is widely regarded as crucial for the critique of capitalism. While Unoist studies of the financial system have become more accurate and refined, the same cannot be said for the fetish character of capital. Consequently, the Unoist theory of finance does not tell us much about how the wealth in capitalist society is fetishized in the form of capital and how this notion permeates through our society.

It should be noted here that the capital fetish should not be regarded as an accomplished ideology but as an incessantly regenerating and expanding one. What should be grasped is not fetishism itself but fetishization, as it were. In this sense, the source of fetishism must be critically located; we cannot take for granted the fetish power of "interest-bearing capital." For this reason, we should reexamine not only the theory of finance but also the theory of capital itself. As we mention in Chapter 7, Uno and Unoists have studied the theory of capital within the original theoretical field of the market and circulation, called the theory of circulation. Since the fundamental form of the motion of capital is analyzed there, it could be regarded as the best place to expand upon the study of capital fetishism.

As mentioned in the final part of Chapter 7, some of the contemporary Japanese Marxian economists reorganize conventional Unoists frameworks and are redeveloping a new theory of political economy that could serve as a foundation of understanding today's capitalism. This trend can be identified as a "neo-Unoist" approach. The theory of capital is one of the topics that are discussed by recent neo-Unoists. Whereas the long discourses of Japanese Marxian studies are worth investigating, we hope further researches on fundamental theory in Japan will also gain wide attention.

Uno-Miyake Debate: Formation of Marxian Theory of Finance

On Money Capitalists in the Theory of Interest in *Capital*

Kōzō Uno

I have already had the opportunity to discuss this elsewhere,[1] but when *Capital* develops its theory of profit, or theory of rent, and when it develops its theory of interest, the capitalist society that serves as a foundation for this theoretical development, while a markedly abstract, pure

[1] Kōzō Uno, "How a Theory of Interest Should Be Developed: Answering Miyake Yoshio's Critique of the Theory of Interest in my *Principles of Political Economy*" [included as Chapter 4 of this book].

Translated by Robert Chapeskie.
[This essay was first published in Japanese in Tatsuo Morito and Hyoue Ouchi eds., *Issues on Economics: Collection Commemorating the 60th Birthday of Prof. Samezo Kuruma*, Tokyo: Hosei University Press, 1958. The translation is based on *Kōzō Uno Collected Works*, Vol. 4, Tokyo: Iwanami-Shoten, 1974, pp. 163–85—editor. All additions in the square brackets ([ ]) in this volume are made by the editor (Kei Ehara) unless otherwise noted.]

K. Ehara (ed.), *Japanese Discourses on the Marxian Theory of Finance*, Marx, Engels, and Marxisms,
https://doi.org/10.1007/978-3-030-83324-4_2

capitalist society in the case of the former, is in contrast quite concrete in the case of the latter; at least, it cannot be described as a pure capitalist society—one cannot help but see it like this. It seems to me that this approach, presumably in connection with the reason it was chosen to begin with, has had an extraordinarily large influence on the theory of interest in *Capital*. The "money capitalists" that emerge from the explication of "interest-bearing capital" can be described as a straightforward manifestation of this. These "money capitalists" can be seen as having already been presented within the "money-dealing capital" laid out in Part 4 [of Vol. 3—trans.] of *Capital*, "Conversion of Commodity Capital and Money Capital into Commercial Capital and Money-Dealing Capital (Merchant's Capital)" prior to the development of Part 5, "Division of Profit into Interest and Profit of Enterprise. Interest-bearing Capital." Describing what sort of position these money capitalists hold in a pure capitalist society, however, is not so easy. At least, I think the idea that some capitalists could actually exist as simply money capitalists still needs to be examined. My doubts about Marx's assertion that with loan capital "capital as capital becomes a commodity," too, arise fundamentally in relation to this point.

1 ["Money Capitalist" and "Functioning Capitalist"]

Marx's explanation of loan capital is as follows:

> Suppose the annual average rate of profit is 20%. In that case a machine valued at £100, employed as capital under average conditions and an average amount of intelligence and purposive effort, would yield a profit of £20. A man in possession of £100, therefore, possesses the power to make £120 out of £100, or to produce a profit of £20. He possesses a potential capital of £100. If he gives these £100 to another for one year, so the latter may use them as real capital, he gives him the power to produce a profit of £20 — a surplus value which costs this other nothing, and for which he pays no equivalent. If this other should pay, say, £5 at the close of the year to the owner of the £100 out of the profit produced, he would thereby

K. Uno (Deceased) (✉)
University of Tokyo, Tokyo, Japan

> pay the use value of the £100 — the use value of its function as capital, the function of producing a profit of £20. The part of the profit paid to the owner is called interest, which is just another name, or special term, for a part of the profit given up by capital in the process of functioning to the owner of the capital, instead of putting it into its own pocket.
>
> It is plain that the possession of £100 gives their owner the power to pocket the interest — that certain portion of profit produced by means of his capital. If he had not given the £100 to the other person, the latter could not have produced any profit, and could not at all have acted as a capitalist with reference to these £100.[2]

It goes without saying that the owner of these £100, as someone who gives this money "to another for one year, so the latter may use them as real capital," is a "money capitalist," and the other person who receives this loan to "use as real capital" is what Marx calls a "functioning capitalist." But what happens when this kind of supposition is made in a pure capitalist society? In a society of capitalists, laborers, and land-owners, since any kind of capitalist first becomes a capitalist as an owner of money—not merely an owner of money as a means of circulation, but an owner of money derived in some way from the circulation of commodities, money as money, or as so-called "monetary property"—it may indeed be acceptable to think that such a capitalist can also loan out this money rather than "use it as real capital" directly, but where exactly does the capitalist who "could not have acted as a capitalist" if the original owner of the money "had not given the £100 to the other person" come from? Of course, I do not mean to deny that capitalists who become "functioning capitalists" through this kind of lending-borrowing relationship exist in practice. The problem is that through this kind of functioning capitalist being assumed from the start in the development of the theory, the capital of the money capitalists itself seems to acquire the same character as the old money-lending capital as simply the owner of monetary property. At the very least, can it not be said that here there is already the assumption of the differentiation between money capitalists and industrial or functioning capitalists that can be thought of as arising on the foundation of the transition from the quantitative division to the qualitative division of profit developed later? It is assumed of a money capitalist that "if he gets

[2] [*Marx Engels Collected Works* (hereafter MECW), Vol. 37, London: Lawrence & Wishart, 2010, p. 337.]

it back, he must always loan it out again, so long as it is to function for him as capital—here as money capital,"[3] and "the functioning capitalist is here assumed as a non-owner of capital"[4] so the former can perhaps be described as simply an investor. For Marx this can be thought of as not necessarily being the case. In the passage already quoted, after saying "if he had not given the £100 to the other person, the latter could not have produced any profit" he adds that the owner of the money "could not at all have acted as a capitalist with reference to these £100," and seems to be considering the process of the establishment of this relationship as one that transitions from a quantitative to a qualitative division. Even so, however, the problem in that case is the conditions of this quantitative division themselves. Here there is a major issue in regard to the method of economic analysis.

2 [The Problem with Marx's Illustration]

It seems that Marx's framing should be understood as follows. He considers an example in which a capitalist who is already operating a business with £10,000 of capital is somehow loaned £100 from elsewhere. This £100 is then added to the £10,000 to expand the business. Provided the rate of profit does not change, a profit of £2020 is obtained and some small amount of interest is paid on the borrowed money from this profit. From this relationship, Marx cuts away and abstracts what relates to the £10,000, thereby extracting and addressing only what relates to these £100. Of course, even in a framing that should be understood in this way, it is not impossible to say that the capitalist who does the borrowing "could not at all have acted as a capitalist with reference to these £100" if he had not received the loan from someone else. But this capitalist was already a capitalist operating a £10,000 business and could not be said to not be a capitalist even if he were unable to borrow these £100 and failed to be a simple functioning capitalist. It is indeed precisely because he was already a capitalist that he was able to borrow £100, and he is not a "functioning capitalist" who is "assumed as a non-owner of capital." The method of assuming such a capitalist "with reference to these £100" must be described as an extremely formal abstraction. But this method is

[3] [Ibid., p. 368.]

[4] [Ibid., p. 371.]

not only problematic insofar as it is no more than merely formal purity. The consequences of this method inevitably appear in the side lending the £100 as well. While the borrowing capitalist becomes simply a functioning capitalist "as a non-owner of capital," at the same time the capitalist who lends the money becomes a money capitalist who "must always loan it out again." To posit Marx's "money capitalists" in this way completely obscures the character of the funds (*shikin*) used for these loans.

After having provided a general description of "interest-bearing capital" in Chapter 21, the first chapter of Part 5, in Chapter 22, "Division of Profit. Rate of Interest. 'Natural' Rate of Interest," Marx points out that in the end the rate of interest is inevitably regulated by the rate of profit, and moreover asserts that "the rate of interest also has a tendency to fall quite independently of the fluctuations in the rate of profit." He presents "two main causes" of this tendency. The first, given in a quote from [George—trans.] Ramsay's *An Essay on the Distribution of Wealth*, is the existence and increase of "rentiers." The second is "the development of the credit system and the attendant ever-growing control of industrialists and merchants over the money savings of all classes of society that is effected through the bankers, and the progressive concentration of these savings in amounts which can serve as money capital."[5] Of course, it must be acknowledged that the existence and increase of loan capital affect the tendency of fluctuations in the rate of interest in actuality, but doesn't incorporating this kind of loan capital into the theoretical development of loan capital in general then become an issue? When we posit a pure capitalist society as a society of capitalists, workers, and landowners and the movement of profit, rent, and interest within it, is it appropriate to consider the kind of "class" described in the passage by Ramsay quoted by Marx?

> For, as a nation advances in the career of wealth, a class of men springs up and increases more and more, who by the labours of their ancestors find themselves in the possession of funds sufficiently ample to afford a handsome maintenance from the interest alone. Very many also who during youth and middle age were actively engaged in business, retire in their latter days to live quietly on the interest of the sums they have themselves

[5] [Ibid., p. 359.]

> accumulated. This class, as well as the former, has a tendency to increase with the increasing riches of the country....[6]

Moreover, when it comes to the "money savings of all classes of society," it goes without saying that "all classes" are not limited to the three major classes of capitalists, workers, and landowners. Of course, when we analyze financial relationships in mid-nineteenth century Britain or describe typical financial relationships at a certain stage of capitalism, we cannot do so without examining and analyzing the existence and increase or decrease of these kinds of "classes." But this is a problem when it comes to the theoretical consideration that yields a fundamental description of interest.

Regarding the role of capitalists in the theory of profit, have we not posited them as distributing the surplus value produced through the production process as profit, and allotting whatever of this is not used for personal consumption to the accumulation of capital? And when it comes to the role of landowners in the theory of rent, have we not posited all of their rental income as going toward their personal consumption? Of course, this is not to deny that in practice there are capitalists who "retire" and become "rentiers." Nor is it to reject the possibility of landowners not personally consuming all of their income from rent and using it instead to start capitalist enterprises or as loan capital. On the contrary, it is when the fundamental description of interest is developed on the foundation of the process of reproduction in a pure capitalist society that such relationships can be examined and analyzed as concrete issues. Bringing such matters into theoretical development needlessly complicates and obscures the principles of the relationship between the formation/supply of the funds loaned as loan capital and the demand for/use of these funds by introducing elements that are at least not directly connected to the movement of the reproduction process. Even if this cannot be said to be straightforwardly identical to the money-lending capital of the past, must it not be examined as something abstract like the money-lending capital given from outside the capital reproduction process by adding factors not directly related to the expansion or contraction of this process? When it comes to loan capital, as something that exists independently in the hands of money capitalists, the interest obtained through making loans increases the accumulation of money capital; this becomes something completely

[6] [Ibid.]

distinct from industrial capital, and the quantity of funds that can be loaned increases without any direct connection to the actual reproduction process of capital. This is not to deny that the formation of such funds occurs in practice. But this inevitably reduces the clarity of the law of the development of purely industrial capitalist productive power, which holds that funds formed within the capital reproduction process are used in a capitalist society manner and the capitalist reproduction process is expanded to its extreme of productive power at various points in time.

Of course, *Capital* does not say that funds formed within the industrial capital movement process—including the formation not only of accumulation and depreciation funds supplied by new surplus value but reserve funds and temporarily idle money capital that become loanable funds with the development of the banking system—are not to be investigated as something fundamental. Nor does it fail to discuss such funds being loaned to industrial capital and being useful in the expansion of its movement. However, the process through which loan capital is theoretically formed from the capital reproduction process, at least, cannot be said to have been considered in a pure form concerning these fundamental elements. Marx genuinely considered commercial credit to be "the basis of the credit system,"[7] but this was nothing more than a supplementary addition to his consideration of the accumulation of money capital. In relation to this point, Marx himself specifies that "we are not concerned here with loans of houses, machines, or other fixed capital. Nor are we concerned with the advances industrialists and merchants make to one another in commodities and within the compass of the reproduction process; although we must also investigate this point beforehand in more detail. We are concerned exclusively with money loans, which are made by bankers, as middlemen, to industrialists and merchants."[8] Of course, the money loaned by "bankers, as middlemen" in this case includes funds that cannot be said to be directly formed "within the compass of the reproduction process." At the same time, as has already been pointed out, this

[7] [Ibid., p. 478.]

[8] [Ibid., p. 477. It is not as evident as Uno suggests that this passage is related to commercial credit in Marx's original conception. Engels edited the paragraphs here and some of them are moved to the beginning of Chapter 33, "The Medium of Circulation in the Credit System." See *Marx Engels Gesamtausgabe* (hereafter MEGA), II-4.2, S. 531–6. See also, *Marx's Economic Manuscript of 1864–1865*, Chicago, IL: Haymarket Books, 2017, pp. 567–72.]

supply itself must inevitably appear as something added from outside the "compass of the reproduction process."

3 [The Concept of Loan Capital]

In thinking about the relationship between the movements of loan capital and industrial capital, while one might suppose Marx's stance would flow naturally out of the approach described above, on the contrary, he adopts an approach of directly connecting them. The movement of money as capital that is loaned from loan capitalist A to functioning capitalist B is illustrated as follows.

> In B's possession the money is actually converted into capital, passes through M—C—M' and returns to A as M', as M + ΔM, where ΔM represents the interest. For the sake of simplicity we shall not consider here the case, in which capital remains in B's possession for a longer term and interest is paid at regular intervals.
>
> The movement, therefore, is
>
> M—M—C—M'— M'.
>
> What appears duplicated here, is 1) the outlay of money as capital, and 2) its reflux as realised capital, as M' or M + ΔM.[9]

But this direct connection is also a problem.

In Marx the connection between the two in this case is examined as one in which "this double outlay of money as capital, of which the first is merely a transfer from A to B, is matched by its double reflux."[10]

> It [the money—trans.] flows back to B only as what he had expended, as functioning capital, but as the property of A. To make its reflux complete, B must consequently return it to A. But in addition to the capital, B must also turn over to A a portion of the profit, a part which goes under the name of interest, which he had made with this capital since A had given him the money only as a capital, i.e., as value which is not only preserved

[9] [MECW, Vol. 37, pp. 338,9.]

[10] [Ibid., p. 339.]

> in its movement, but also creates surplus value for its owner. It remains in B's hands only so long as it is functioning capital. And with its reflux ... it ceases to function as capital. When no longer acting as capital, however, it must again be returned to A, who had never ceased being its legal owner.[11]

The relationship between A and B, in which money is handed over from A to B and then returned to A after a certain period of time is directly combined with "functioning capital" in the hands of B. It becomes a movement of capital that begins with M—M and ends with M'—M'. As I have already pointed out, this separates the funds borrowed by B from B's own capital and makes it independent capital that has been invested. In Marx the reflux of loan capital does not externally appear as a result of the actual movement of capital, but it is emphasized that "these transactions are really determined by the actual reproductive returns."[12] Of course, the movement of loan capital that has its foundation in the capitalist reproduction process is not something that is conducted without any connection to this reproduction process. But can directly connecting individual borrowing and loaning relationships to the production process like this ultimately be said to properly describe loan capital that has its foundation in the movement of capital? Using this method, at very least the formation of funds allocated to loans themselves, as was mentioned earlier, must be separated from the capital reproduction process. This is the case because when it comes to A themselves, the loan that is directly combined with the movement of capital in the hands of B must be seen as funds completely separated from the capital production process. A, owner of the loan capital, is posited as a capitalist owner of money they do not use outside of loans. To put it another way, even if A's funds have come out of the capital reproduction process, they become something with no direct connection to this process, and in this respect are no different from the money-lending capital of the past. This is merely to say that loaned funds do not simply demand interest on the loan, but are put into the capital production process, and since a portion of the surplus value thus produced is distributed, their interest is limited by this surplus value. This is one aspect that can be described as an external limitation. Of course, it can be said that by adding this kind of limitation to the old money-lending capital, the development of the capitalist method of production

[11] [Ibid.]

[12] [Ibid., p. 347.]

transformed it into modern loan capital. This, however, means ignoring the other aspect in which loan capital itself must necessarily emerge within the capitalist reproduction process. Not only can it be said that the target of loans is the capitalist reproduction process but also that it is only as something that emerges out of this process that the loan funds themselves can then be explained on the basis of the capitalist reproduction process.

In fact, in this kind of single-aspect determination, the connection between both movements can only be grasped in an extremely abstract manner. Even in Marx's case, the M—C—M' that M—M' subsumes within its movement (even in this case I think M … M' would be better, as M—M' cannot be said to be simply something occurring within the circulation process, but putting that aside) takes the form of merchant capital as a fundamental form of the movement of capital, and it is not at all the case that commercial capital or merchant capital are being concretely considered. If B is assumed to be someone without other capital, then the investment of these borrowed funds in the production process naturally includes the means of labor and other components of fixed capital, and the reflux of M … M' cannot be simply resolved with the reflux of M—C … P … C'—M'. Marx says, "Later, we shall also have to turn our attention to the form in which interest is paid in the meantime at fixed intervals, but without the capital, whose return follows at the end of a lengthy period"[13] and puts this point aside for the time being, but the problem lies in having taken the loaning of funds through loan capital as a loaning of funds that exists independently of the capital reproduction process—or at least something along these lines—and directly tying the repayment of funds to a reflux that occurs in the actual movement of capital.

Even when loan capital is developed with a capitalist society reproduction process as its foundation, if it is only as a form of movement of capital it can be separated from this kind of foundation and developed as what I have called the form of money-lending capital, and while I think this is something that must be done, substantially its foundation must necessarily be sought in the capitalist society reproduction process. If this is not done, it will be impossible to elucidate the principles underlying this movement, and in that case, while it goes without saying that in

[13] [Ibid., p. 349.]

general the making and collecting of loans is something based on a reflux in the movement of capital, and moreover that the interest paid on loans is limited by the surplus value produced in the production process, this does not mean that we must consider the reflux movement of loan capital directly in connection with actual individual reflux movements of capital. While on the one hand being something that is to a certain extent separate and independent of these movements, on the other hand, loan capital must be described as something that is loaned and collected with them as its foundation. In accordance with loaned funds that can be seen as something temporarily separated from the capital reproduction process, collecting the loans must not be viewed as something comprehensively regulated by actual individual refluxes of capital, but rather as something partially regulated by refluxes defined by particular circulation periods. To put it in terms of a conclusion that can be drawn, loan capital is given a modern capitalist meaning insofar as in a capitalist society idle funds are financed and reduce the portion of circulating capital, which is invested in the capitalist reproduction process to maintain the capital circulation process. In actuality these funds, like those that are not directly connected to the capital reproduction process, such as, for example, those of the "rentiers" I have mentioned above, are not one-sidedly controlled by the capital reproduction process. Capitalists who receive loans, too, are in a relationship in which they receive the funds thinking that they may have to return them according to the needs of the capitalist who has lent them, and the meaning of the banking system is to be found in its ability to provide an antidote to these individual circumstances. But the banking system never transforms these individual loans into simple loan funds. Of course, this is not to deny the fact that here too, in concrete terms, various different banks are created in accordance with the kinds of funds they handle, and they do not necessarily only deal with funds created within the capital reproduction system. It is only to say that we must not use these sorts of concrete facts to immediately obfuscate the essential description of the modern banking system.

In short, what I want to say is that when it comes to the description of loan capital as a fundamental theory, as in other cases, the funds formed in the capital reproduction process within a pure capitalist society must be developed as something used in the manner of a capitalist society. For now, the transformation into loan capital of the income assigned to personal consumption by capitalists, and of course workers, should be abstracted. Moreover, we should abstract the "class of men ... who by the labours of their ancestors find themselves in the possession of funds sufficiently ample to afford a handsome maintenance from the interest alone," those "who during youth and middle age were actively engaged in business, retire in their latter days to live quietly on the interest of the sums they have themselves accumulated," and "the money savings of all classes of society" that become available along with the development of the credit system.[14] As I have already pointed out, Marx cited these sorts of phenomena as the "main causes" of the fact that "the rate of interest also has a tendency to fall quite independently of the fluctuations in the rate of profit," but when *Capital* explicates "the law of the tendency of the rate of profit to fall," the changes in the composition of capital are discussed at first in a pure form, and other effects such as foreign trade are considered as "counteracting influences" on this tendency. Like this loan capital, did the funds handed over from A to B not from the start correspond more closely to funds of "rentiers" than funds necessarily arising within the capital reproduction process?

There is a problem with the development of loan capital occurring from the start through a conflict between industrial capitalists—who moreover do not own capital at all but are abstracted as functioning capitalists—and money capitalists—who become loan capitalists as owners of the money "capital" corresponding to this abstraction. When it comes to explicating borrowing and loaning relationships in a pure capitalist society composed of capitalists, workers, and landowners—in my understanding, in order to clarify the economic laws (*keizai-hosoku*) of a capitalist society we must presuppose this kind of society, and this presupposition does not exist only in our heads; as capitalism itself had been working toward the comprehensive realization of this kind of pure capitalist society at least before entering its late-stage manifestation, we may engage in this presupposition and by doing so develop the general laws of capitalism—can the abstraction that treats industrial capital as functioning capital and loan capital as simply the capital of money capitalists ultimately be said to be the correct approach? To me it is unavoidably dubious. From this method, is it not impossible to explicate the movement of the rate of interest to a certain extent independently from the movement of the rate of profit, even though in the end the former cannot move separately from the latter? Regarding the demand and supply of funds as loan capital, I

[14] [Ibid., p. 359.]

think it is not through a direct combining of loans and the production of surplus value, but rather when they are developed with an indirect combination based on the capital reproduction process that their independence and dependence can be clarified.

In the case of Marx, it is imagined that he fundamentally believed that in the theory of profit it was possible to assume a pure capitalist society and then elucidate its principles, but in the case of the theory of interest this could not be done. We can find many pieces of evidence that give rise to this view. But this is not the case when it comes to the theory of rent that follows the theory of interest; here once again the theory is developed with a pure capitalist society, and this extends as far as the "Classes" in the final part. Of course, this part of *Capital* is based on Marx's manuscripts for Volume 2 onward, and the question of what it would have been like if he himself had seen it through to publication remains, but we have no alternative to engaging in discussion based on the existing version of the text.

4 [The Theory of Interest and the Theory of Ground Rent]

Part 4, "Transformation of Surplus Profit into Ground Rent," of Volume 3 of *Capital* develops a theory of rent, and in Chapter 37, "Introduction," it provides the methodological consideration that is required for the development of a fundamental theory of this phenomenon. Here Marx clearly distinguishes the landed property that appears when agriculture is conducted in a capitalist manner from that which had existed in the past:

> The form of landed property which we shall consider here is a specifically historical one, a form *transformed* through the influence of capital and of the capitalist mode of production, either of feudal landownership, or of small-peasant agriculture as a means of livelihood, in which the *possession* of the land constitutes one of the prerequisites of production for the direct producer, and in which his *ownership* of land appears as the most advantageous condition for the prosperity *of his* mode of production. Just as the capitalist mode of production in general is based on the expropriation of the conditions of labour from the labourers, so does it in agriculture presuppose the expropriation of the rural labourers from the land and their subordination to a capitalist, who carries on agriculture for the sake

> of profit. Thus, for the purpose of our analysis, the objection that other forms of landed property and of agriculture have existed, or still exist, is quite irrelevant. Such an objection can only apply to those economists who treat the capitalist mode of production in agriculture, and the form of landed property corresponding to it, not as historical but rather as eternal categories.[15]

He also writes:

> But the form of landed property with which the incipient capitalist mode of production is confronted does not suit it. It first creates for itself the form required by subordinating agriculture to capital. It thus transforms feudal landed property, clan property, small-peasant property in mark communes—no matter how divergent their juristic forms may be—into the economic form corresponding to the requirements of this mode of production.[16]

And continues as follows:

> As important as it may be for a scientific analysis of ground rent—that is, the independent and specific economic form of landed property on the basis of the capitalist mode of production—to study it in its pure form free of all distorting and obfuscating irrelevancies, it is just as important for an understanding of the practical effects of landed property—even for a theoretical comprehension of a multitude of facts which contradict the concept and nature of ground rent and yet appear as modes of existence of ground rent—to learn the sources which give rise to such muddling in theory.[17]

Marx then presents practical impurities that impede theoretical development concerning rent, identifies issues that must be considered when it comes to methodology, and from Chapter 38 onward develops a theory of rent as a relationship between capitalists—and, indirectly, workers—and landed property or landowners in a pure capitalist society. Of course, for the capitalist method of production, land rented out by landowners, unlike funds in the case of loan capital, is an external entity while also

[15] [Ibid., pp. 608,9.]

[16] [Ibid., p. 611.]

[17] [Ibid., p. 618.]

being an indispensable means of production. It cannot be produced by capital itself. The forms of property before capitalism, therefore, had only negative relationships with the commodity-economy and the forms faced by capitalism in its early period were in markedly different circumstances to those in the case of loan capital. At the same time, even in a capitalist society, land can be owned by those who are not capitalists, and these owners also form a class in contrast to capitalists. The funds of loan capital must not be seen as the same. In other words, the methodological concern Marx raises regarding landed property and rent should not be directly applied to loan capital and interest. That is not to say, however, that for the development of the theory of interest it is not necessary to suppose a pure capitalist society as in the case of the theories of profit and rent.

Marx begins Chapter 25, "Credit and Fictitious Capital," of Part 5, Volume 3 of *Capital*, in which he develops his theory of interest, as follows:

> An exhaustive analysis of the credit system and of the instruments which it creates for its own use (credit money, etc.) lies beyond our plan. We merely wish to dwell here upon a few particular points, which are required to characterise the capitalist mode of production in general. We shall deal only with commercial and bank credit. The connection between the development of this form of credit and that of public credit will not be considered here.[18]

Marx begins by addressing how the "natural basis of the credit system" that is formed along with the function of money as a means of payment is "extended, generalised, and worked out"[19] with the development of capitalism. He then goes on to state that "the other side of the credit system is connected with the development of money-dealing, which, of course, keeps step under capitalist production with the development of dealing in commodity"[20] and recapitulates the points concerning "money-dealing" developed in Chapter 19 of Part 4. In actuality, as has already been stated,

[18] [Ibid., p. 397. This passage contains important corrections by Engels. We discuss the meaning of the changes he makes in Chapter 1 of this volume. See pp. 25 ff.]

[19] [MECW, Vol. 37, p. 397.]

[20] [Ibid., p. 399.]

loan capital is not developed from commercial credit, but is discussed as interest-bearing capital in Part 5, which directly follows Part 4, "Conversion of Commodity Capital and Money Capital into Commercial Capital and Money-Dealing Capital," which includes the issue of "money-dealing capital." This can be thought of as a factor that markedly "distorts" the money capital that is addressed in Part 5. When he later examines commercial credit "purely," Marx says, "When we examine this credit detached from banker's credit, it is evident that it grows with an increasing volume of industrial capital itself. Loan capital and industrial capital are identical here"[21] and "The maximum of credit is here identical with the fullest employment of industrial capital, that is, the utmost exertion of its reproductive power without regard to the limits of consumption."[22] I myself cannot believe this "utmost exertion of its reproductive power" can be realized with commercial credit alone, and I think the role of bank credit comes into play here, but in any case I would suggest that the development of loan capital must not be carried out from the side where it "develops ... as a special function of the money dealers."[23] To put it bluntly, *Capital* is severely impeded in its ability to study interest in its "pure form free of all distorting and obfuscating irrelevancies" by the development of money-dealing capital in Part 4 preceding the theory of interest in Part 5, which results in the development of loan capital being based on the practical development of the banking business that "... consists of concentrating large amounts of the loanable money capital in the bankers' hands, so that, in place of the individual money lender, the bankers confront the industrial and commercial capitalists as representatives of all money lenders. They become the general managers of money capital. On the other hand by borrowing for the entire world of commerce, they concentrate all the borrowers vis-à vis all the lenders."[24] The relationship in which money capitalist A's £100 have been loaned to

[21] [Ibid., p. 480.]

[22] [Ibid., p. 481. In Marx's manuscript, "the utmost exertion of its reproductive power" is written as "the utmost employment of the latent reproductive power." (MEGA, II-4.2, S. 539; *Marx's Economic Manuscript of 1864–1865*, p. 575) It can be assumed that Marx did not mean the "utmost exertion of its reproductive power" is "realized" here, since it is only "latent."]

[23] [MECW, Vol. 37, p. 400.]

[24] [Ibid.]

functioning capitalist B having been abstracted does not mean that this relationship is being "studied in its pure form."

This point, even if the situation differs as has already been pointed out, is very different when it comes to the development of a theory of rent that is carried out without relation to existing landed property, and in which, on the contrary, a capitalist form of landed property is established. In that case, the process by which the old landed property is transformed into capitalist landed property itself is not considered, but this must be described as natural in the development of a fundamental theory. Theoretically, it arises only as a form the capitalist mode of production "first creates for itself ... by subordinating agriculture to capital." This does not deny that capitalist landed property is a "form *transformed* through the influence of capital and of the capitalist mode of production, either of feudal landownership, or of small-peasant agriculture as a means of livelihood."

When Marx considers "pre-capitalist" interest-bearing capital in Chapter 36, he writes, "What distinguishes interest-bearing capital—in so far as it is an essential element of the capitalist mode of production—from usurer's capital is by no means the nature or character of this capital itself. It is merely the altered conditions under which it operates, and consequently also the totally transformed character of the borrower who confronts the money lender."[25] Citing circumstances in which in general "a man without fortune but possessing energy, solidity, ability and business acumen may become a capitalist," including cases in which "a man without fortune receives credit in his capacity of industrialist or merchant,"[26] he points out that capitalism, like the Catholic church in the middle ages, possesses the ability "to assimilate the foremost minds of a ruled class."[27] But while this may be acknowledged as something that actually occurs, can it be said to be a foundation capable of developing "interest-bearing capital—in so far as it is an essential element of the capitalist mode of production"? At very least, among the "altered conditions" in question, is it not indeed necessary to clarify not only the "character of the borrower who confronts the money lender" but also the changes in the "money lenders" themselves? Funds in the case of loan capital,

[25] [Ibid., p. 595.]

[26] [Ibid.]

[27] [Ibid.]

unlike land in the case of landed property, are something possessed by capitalists themselves, and changes in the "borrowers" cannot be said to reveal all of the "altered conditions." On the other hand, it can be said that they do not make "money capitalists" form a class, while "landowners" do. Here, theoretically at least, "money lenders" must themselves be industrial capitalists as owners of funds that become the money that can be loaned out who inevitably emerge out of the capitalist reproduction process. The banking business, too, is first described on the foundation of the capitalist reproduction process as an intermediary in lending and borrowing. It is only with both lenders and borrowers, represented by bankers, as industrial capitalists in this way that "interest-bearing capital—in so far as it is an essential element of the capitalist mode of production" can be developed and the fact that interest is determined based on the movement of the capitalist reproduction process can be elucidated. This is not simply [for interest—trans.] to receive a definition of quantitative change in which [it is—trans.] "just another name, or special term, for a part of the profit given up by capital in the process of functioning to the owner of the capital, instead of putting it into its own pocket," but for the funds that are loaned out themselves to become something that, while being formed within the capital reproduction process, also realize the "utmost exertion of industrial capital's reproductive power" through capitalist society-type lending. Even if the rate of interest does not necessarily conform to the fluctuations in the rate of profit of industrial capital within the cyclical movement in which the social reproduction of capital develops, at times expanding and at other times contracting, the fact that it undergoes a certain movement can only be explained based on this relationship. Loan capital being given its own, independent existence while being based on industrial capital cannot be explained by loan capital being placed exclusively in the hands of "money capitalists" who are outside of industrial capital. On the contrary, merging it with the funds of "money capitalists" has a "distorting and obfuscating" effect on this relationship, and can even be thought of as opening the door to approaches that find a mysterious power in the credit system.

Marx's "externalization of the relations of capital," in which, in the form of interest-bearing capital, "Capital appears as a mysterious and self-creating source of interest—the source of its own increase,"[28] is

[28] [Ibid., p. 389.]

fundamentally based on the capitalist society nature of loan capital in regard to each instance of industrial capital, but it cannot be thought of as something that is fully completed with loan capital. Here interest is determined by supply and demand of funds that are generally regulated by the movement of the capital reproduction process, and this "mysteriousness" does not obtain. As long as the expansion of the capital reproduction process, using, for example, the expansion of commercial credit, is realized while the reflux of capital is conducted in an easy and regular manner, increases in the interest rate are avoided. When this period of favorable conditions ends and we enter a period of crisis, if demand for loan funds increases in spite of a decline in the formation of funds (the supply), the interest rate increases drastically. In a period of unfavorable conditions, in contrast, interest rates go down even though the formation of funds is declining because demand is also going down. This is determined by supply and demand. To the extent that how supply and demand are formed is not made clear there is a degree of "mysteriousness," but this is not the mysteriousness of the "externalization of the relations of capital."

In Section 5 "The Externalization of Surplus Value" of Chapter 7 of Volume 3 of *Theories of Surplus Value*, Marx considers the process of the "reification of capital"[29] in the relationship of rent to profit and writes as follows:

> In the final state in which profit, assumed as something given, appears in capitalist production, the innumerable transformations and intervening stages through which it passes are obliterated and unrecognisable, and consequently the nature of capital is also obliterated and unrecognisable. This state becomes even more rigid owing to the fact that the same process which gives it its final FINISH causes part of the profit to confront it as *rent*, thus transforming profit into a *particular* aspect of surplus value, an aspect based on capital as a special material instrument of production, in

[29] [The original Japanese term is "*shihon no bukka.*" *Bukka* corresponds to the German term, "*Verdinglichung.*" Reification is usually used for the term "*Versachlichung*." However, it is difficult to identify which Marx discusses here. Marx states, "Und in dieser ganz entfremdeten Form des Profits,—und in demselben Grade, wie die Gestalt des Profits seinen inneren Kren versteckt, erhält das Capital mehre und mehr eine sachliche Gestalt, wird aus Verhältniß immer mehr Ding." (MEGA, II-3.4, S. 1482,3 English translation is on MECW, Vol. 32, p. 484, but it does not distinguish the two terms, "*Ding*" and "*Sache.*" Uno's usage of *Bukka* is close to the meaning of "*Versachlichung*" rather than "*Verdinglichung.*" See also Kōzō Uno, *Principles of Political Economy*, Sussex: Harvester, 1980, pp. 115–7.]

> exactly the same way as rent is based on land; thus this state, separated from its inner essence by a mass of invisible intermediate links, reaches an even more *externalised* form, or rather the form of absolute *externalisation*, in interest-bearing capital, in the separation of interest from profit, in interest-bearing capital as the simple form of capital, the form in which capital is antecedent to its own reproduction process.[30]

As I have already mentioned, if funds in loan capital, like land, were something external to capital that could not themselves produce, then "interest-bearing capital" could perhaps be described as already having completed this externalizing process through funds in the hands of "money capitalists" as loan capital. But when in fact funds in loan capital are nothing other than the funds of industrial capitalists, and their social use conducted through banks is carried out by industrial capital itself, this is merely the process that gives profit its "final FINISH." In reality, funds loaned to industrial capitalists are something that increases the rate of profit of their own capital, and ultimately are nothing more than a capitalist structure for averaging profit. Even if industrial capital obtains interest by giving over loanable funds in hand to social use via banks, this too becomes a factor that evens out the rate of profit of industrial capital. As payment for this capitalist social function, the so-called "margin" that bank capital obtains as its profit can indeed be described as a step toward transforming the concept of profit into entrepreneurial profit, but it is still merely a passive phenomenon that realizes the social use of the funds of industrial capital itself. Even if it represents an economization of circulation costs, it is still merely the appropriation of idle funds, not something that actively assumes the functioning of industrial capitalists itself. It is only in commercial capital that the functioning of capitalists is made purely independent, and moreover through the economization of circulation costs receives the distribution of profit—not as the production of surplus value, but as something that apparently increases it as though it were actively produced as a result of capitalistically inverted recognition. The work of capitalists in industrial capital, such as economizing the means of production, reducing wages, and making full use of

[30] [MECW, Vol. 32, pp. 486,7. Uno uses the Japanese edition of *Theories of Surplus Value*, Vol. 3 that was published in 1929 by Kaizo-sha Publisher. This is a translation of Kautsky's edition, which consists of seven chapters. The final chapter is titled "Profit, Zins und Vulgärökonomie" ("Profit, Interest, and Vulgar Economy"). The quotation here is taken from the chapter "Revenue and Its Sources" in MECW.]

labor power, does not appear as the functioning of capitalists when profits are being averaged. To put it another way, the averaging of profit rates is realized under the conditions of the means of production and labor power both being employed on the basis of averaged social standards, along with the averaging of labor wages, all of which are accompanied by the development of capitalism. This averaging of profit rates, owing to differences in capital composition and turnover, facilitates the transformation of commodity value into production prices and is supported by the social accommodation of idle funds. So-called "pure circulation costs" of the buying and selling of products within circulation costs more broadly defined that are included in the turnover period of capital, however, insofar as they do not depend on a specific form of capital as commercial capital that is differentiated from and independent of industrial capital, do not receive this averaging. Moreover, this differentiation is conducted through the economizing of circulation costs by concentrating buying and selling. It is only here that capitalists demonstrate their unique function of forming profit through their own activities—albeit, as previously noted, in a capitalistically inverted form. It is here, it seems to me, that the active foundation of entrepreneurial profit may be given. In practice, Marx's above-quoted idea that "a man without fortune but possessing energy, solidity, ability and business acumen may become a capitalist" can also perhaps be said to first manifest in this sector. It can indeed be conjectured that "the functioning capitalist as a non-owner of capital" who makes heavy use of industrial capital's idle funds could emerge in this sector as well. In terms of fundamental theory, this kind of "functioning capitalist as a non-owner of capital" is not yet supposed to be posited here, and it is not as though the types Marx describes when he says that in a certain period "those cavaliers who work without any reserve capital or without any capital at all and who thus operate completely on a money credit basis begin to appear for the first time in considerable numbers"[31] are limited to the sector of commerce. In the case in which capital is independent as commercial capital, however, it is conceivable that it could make use of bank credit more than industrial capital through the movement of this capital simplifying its reflux as M—C—M'.

Of course, a complete division of profit into interest and entrepreneurial profits is not undertaken here. And this alone does not

[31] [MECW, Vol. 37, p. 487.]

make loan capital into what I have called "capital as an automatically interest-bearing force."[32] It may seem obvious, since loan capital, fundamentally, is nothing other than the social accommodation of funds that have become idle in the hands of industrial capitalists. It is the "functioning" of capitalists in commercial capital that actively grounds the "externalization of the relations of capital," and "capital as an automatically interest-bearing force," as being not simply loan capital, turns all capital, including of course the funds invested in the buying and selling of land as well as the capital of capitalists who actually conduct their business with their own capital,—into capital as something that generates a certain amount of interest. The form of the incorporated joint-stock company (*kabushiki kaisha*) completes the reification of this kind of capital and can be thought of as the commodification of capital itself.

5 Conclusion

Is it not the case that the theory of interest in *Capital* having directly developed commercial profit as something that corrects the general profit rate in the theory of profit led to a consideration of money-dealing capital along with commercial capital, and furthermore to a consideration of loan capital as the loaning of funds accumulated in the hands of "money capitalists" being contrasted with "functioning capitalists" as "non-owners of capital"? And is it not perhaps also the case that this significantly impeded the development of the theory of interest in a pure form like the theories of profit and rent? Is Part 4 of Volume 3 of *Capital* taking up complex issues just as they arise in reality, too, not perhaps owing to this circumstance? As I have already mentioned, one can imagine that if he had published Volumes 2 and 3 Marx himself might have rearranged this part, but the problem comes down to the fact that along with the connection from Part 4, there seems to be room for reconsidering the method of abstraction employed in Part 5 itself. To me, at least, the method of considering loan capital in the form of A loaning £100 as a "money capitalist" to B as a "functioning capitalist," like small farmers selling their own products as commodities alone being extracted and considered as so-called "simple commodity producers," can only be thought of as a mechanical abstraction.

[32] Kōzō Uno, *Principles of Political Economy*, Vol. 2, Tokyo: Iwanami Shoten, 1952, Section 3 of Chapter 3.

Interest-Bearing Capital: Response to the Explanation of Kōzō Uno

Yoshio Miyake

In the previous section that considered the theory of Ichirō Kawai, I wrote the following:

> However, the sort of mistake shown by Kawai regarding interest-bearing capital is not unique to him. A similar case can be seen in the views of Tomoyoshi Fujitsuka. Commonalities can also be seen in the theory of

---

Translated by Michael Schauerte.
[This essay was first published in Japanese in *Rikkyo Economic Review*, Vol. 6, No. 2, 1953. This is a continuation of the essay appeared in the same journal, Vol. 6, No. 1, 1952, where Miyake criticizes the arguments of Ichirō Kawai and Tomoyoshi Fujitsuka. The translation is based on *Studies on the Theory of Money and Credit*, Tokyo: Miraisha Publisher, 1956, pp. 292–324—editor. All additions in the square brackets ([ ]) in this volume are made by the editor (Kei Ehara) unless otherwise noted.]

Y. Miyake (Deceased) (✉)
Rikkyo University, Tokyo, Japan

K. Ehara (ed.), *Japanese Discourses on the Marxian Theory of Finance*, Marx, Engels, and Marxisms,
https://doi.org/10.1007/978-3-030-83324-4_3

Professor Kōzō Uno in the second volume of his new work *Keizai Genron* (*Principles of Political Economy*; Iwanami Shoten, 1952), albeit developed in a slightly different form.

Here I want to consider that theory of Uno.

1 ["Loan Capital"]

Let's begin by taking a look at what Uno has to say. In that second volume ("Theory of Distribution"), he writes the following as a sort of prefatory remark:

> Loan capital, as will be made clear later, is not capital as something that is loaned out. Loaning out money that can function as capital at any time is not the loaning out of capital itself. It is the lending of money and the earning of interest thereon that makes it capital to the owner of such money. Therefore, the interest obtained from that lending is not the "value of capital" but merely a compensation for the use of money during a certain period of time. Here money itself becomes a commodity, but capital does not yet do so. On this point I differ from Marx's explanation (in Volume 3 of *Capital*), but here I will merely indicate this without going into further detail.[1]

It seems to me that almost no one reading the passage above just once or twice would be able to grasp the meaning. We need to begin, then, by confirming the meaning of what is written here. If we take the "therefore" in the middle of the passage as the dividing point between its first and latter half, we can begin by considering the first half.

First there is the line, "loan capital … is not capital as something that is loaned out." On its own this is a puzzling sentence that is extremely hard to understand, so let's set it aside for now and move on. Uno writes that "later" this will be "clarified" but I can come across nothing subsequently that provides a clearer explanation. However, I will try to single out places in his work where he is saying a similar thing to aid our understanding. Next, there is the line: "Loaning out money that can function as capital at any time is not the loaning out of capital itself." It seems to

[1] Kōzō Uno, *Principles of Political Economy*, Vol. 2, Tokyo: Iwanami Shoten, 1952, p. 8. [The two volumes are republished in 1977. We also refer to the page number in the 1977 edition, which is more available today. Uno, *Principles 1977*, p. 259.]

me that this means that money that is lent can function as capital in the hands of the functioning capitalist, but it only first functions as capital, i.e., is capitalized, when it is in that functioning capitalist's hands, so that the money itself is not capital and thus even if one can lend money it cannot be described as the "lending of capital." Uno later emphasizes the following:

> Commonly speaking, capital is thought of as something concrete that we might grasp as money, or as the means of production such as machinery, or as a commodity, but capital is not merely that ... It is value in motion that takes various forms such as money, means of production, commodity, etc., as well as the form of labor power. Therefore, even if this is commodified it cannot occur in a simple form.[2]

We will look later at this part regarding commodification, but from this passage cited one could posit that Uno, in saying that one cannot speak of the "lending of capital," considers it the "common" view to assume capital "as something concrete that we might grasp" such as money since capital is "value in motion." In other words, Professor Uno thinks that because money itself is not capital, the loaning of money does not amount to the loaning of capital. Next is the line: "It is the lending of money and the earning of interest thereon that makes it capital to the owner of such money," but this can be easily known from the fact that although the loan capitalist as noted above is lending money not capital, by obtaining interest for lending it that money becomes capital for the possessor of money, i.e., the loan capitalist. In addition, in the case of capital in the two senses, with regard to the "capital" that cannot be considered the lending of capital, and the "capital" in the case of "the money that becomes capital," the former is industrial or commercial capital, while the latter is loan capital.

If we now return to the line that I set aside earlier about "loan capital is not capital as something that is loaned out," its meaning can be imagined to be as follows.[3] A loan capitalist is loaning money, not capital,

[2] p. 292 [Uno, *Principles 1977*, p. 511].

[3] If you have an understanding of Professor Uno's way of thinking this can be read without a sense of puzzlement, but surely the feeling of "getting it" once you know the answer is indeed the mark of a puzzle; or some may read it once and immediately observe, "Professor Uno has misunderstood that point," but this is not because of the quality of his writing itself.

because money only first functions as capital in the hands of the functioning capitalist because capital is "value in motion" and money itself is not capital, so that loan capital is capital, or the loan capitalist is a capitalist, because of the ability to earn interest from lending money, and this does not mean that it is capital or he is a capitalist because capital is being lent. And this is also the meaning of the first half of what Professor Uno wrote at the beginning of his volume. As a matter of fact, this puzzling opening sentence might be understood in a different way—such as the idea that on the basis of capitalist production money takes on the use value of functioning as capital and is traded as a commodity with this use value, but the money that can be lent does not necessarily have to function as capital for its possessor, so that "loan capital is not capital as something that is loaned out"—but I'm afraid that I can only understand this line as explained above.

Now I think we can move on to consider the meaning of the latter half of the quotation, but before doing so I would like to deepen the understanding of the first half by explaining other parts of his book. Uno writes the following:

> [The industrial capital who receives funds from a bank—Miyake] in the case of directly receiving a loan[4] is also not a loan as capital itself. He is

[4] This term "direct loan" seems to have been coined as a neologism by Professor Uno, so we can note that he seems to be using it in juxtaposition to the "case of lending through discounting bills" (p. 245 [Uno, *Principles 1977*, p. 470]). Moreover, in quoting a passage from the third volume of *Capital* ["those cavaliers [of industry] who work without any reserve capital or without any capital at all and who thus operate completely on a money credit basis begin to appear for the first time in considerable numbers" (MECW, Vol. 37, p. 487)], Professor Uno writes the following with regard to the term *Geldkredit*. The term "money credit indicates a direct lending in distinction from commercial credit such as discounting bills" (p. 264 [Uno, *Principles 1977*, p. 486]). His equation of "discounting bills" with "commercial credit" is highly doubtful but setting that aside as some sort of error we can assume that a "direct lending" is the same as a "direct loan." And this is lending in "distinction" from the lending "such as discounting bills." And in the line right before the sentence quoted on page 245, he raises the example of the three following cases: "the case of receiving a loan of funds from discounting bills," "the case of receiving a loan from collateral of a commodity or other thing of value," and "the case of receiving a loan without collateral (although for banks such loaning could not be said to originally have an important role)" [Uno, *Principles 1977*, p. 469]. The meaning of "direct loan" seems to be the latter two cases.

Let me also note that Professor Uno, as we have seen, adds the explanation that "for banks originally this loaning does not have an important role," but why does he go to the trouble to insert this superfluous remark? What banks the expression "banks originally"

> being loaned funds that can be used as capital,[5] and the interest paid for this loan is because through these funds the power of capital is advanced and more surplus value is produced through a certain quantity of his equity capital.[6]

As can be seen above, according to Uno, earning interest from lending money makes that money capital. In other words, what makes money

is referring to is not clear, but this would not change the fact that it has become the norm among banks in Japan's large urban areas to provide more non-collateralized than collateralized loans, so that "important" lending is almost all non-collateralized. In the case of foreign countries as well, it certainly could not be said that unsecured loans or *ungedeckte Kredite* do "not have an important role." Moreover, for bank transactions, it can even be said that uncollateralized loans are more reliable than collateralized ones all over the world—although I will not go into the reason here to avoid too much of a digression. Incidentally, Professor Uno on the very next page notes that "it is not without meaning to distinguish between discounting bills and lending, especially in the case of bank management," (p. 246 [Uno, *Principles 1977*, p. 470]) but even from a banker's perspective, while discounting and loans are distinguished in their handling, this mainly arises out of factors such as safety of collection or duration, or the possibility of rediscounting. Also, in some cases—as is often so in Japan—discounting is a method to loan to the person requesting the discounting, where the discounting is usually done while considering that person's credit, so that the "distinction" between discounting and lending for "those involved in banking" is quite different from that in the realm of "credit theory," and the former is not so much significant as the latter. In the previous sentence the matter should have been put rather conversely as "Although it is not without meaning to distinguish between discounting bills and lending, especially with regard to the realm of credit." Professor Uno expresses himself as if he had a profound understanding of banking operations, but it is remarkably lacking in correctness, and generally there are quite a few people who share his way of understanding uncollateralized lending and distinguishing between discounting and lending, so it seemed necessary to include the comments above as an addition.

Furthermore, it should be noted that Professor Uno's understanding of the term "money credit" as indicating lending that is not the discounting of bills is a misconception. This should be immediately apparent from the passage where Marx writes: "in addition to this commercial credit we have actual money credit. The advances of the industrialists and merchants among one another are amalgamated with the money advances made to them by the bankers and money lenders" [MECW, Vol. 37, p. 483]. A detailed discussion of "money credit" can be found in my previous paper [in Yoshio Miyake, *Studies on the Theory of Money and Credit*, Tokyo: Miraisha, 1956, pp. 259–92. This is not included in this volume.].

[5] This expression "funds that can be used as capital" can likely be understood as having the same meaning as the expression "money that can function as capital" in the opening passage. In addition, the manner in which Professor Uno is using the term "funds" will be discussed again later.

[6] p. 245 [Uno, *Principles 1977*, p. 470].

capital—or what makes money into loan capital, if to avoid ambiguity we speak here of capital as loan capital—is the payment of interest. In response to this explanation, the question that must be immediately posed is why that interest is paid, but in the passage cited above the basis for paying interest is explained. It is said that interest is paid because "through these funds the power of capital is advanced and more surplus value is produced through a certain quantity of his equity capital." The expression "through a certain quantity of his equity capital" is extremely doubtful. This is because the surplus value increased here should be seen as what is produced and obtained through the functioning of industrial or commercial capital through the money borrowed, not what is produced through one's equity capital, which is not borrowed from others. But to avoid complicating the matter—and assuming that Professor Uno will not object to this usage—I will address this part while setting aside that expression.[7] Thus, it could be said that for Professor Uno the basis for the payment of interest is that "through these funds the power of capital is advanced and more surplus value is produced."

But another question must be posed in turn. Namely, what would be the case if the person who has borrowed the money does not intend to use it to produce surplus value or is unable to use it to expand the production of surplus value? In this case, is there no need to pay interest? Professor

[7] This explanation of "direct loaning" is made along with the explanation of discounting bills, and right before the passage quoted above Professor Uno writes the following: "In case of financing through discounting bills, this is merely the changing of a capital that is already in the form of a commodity into money; however … The acceleration of this process of transformation from commodity form to money form itself serves as an enhancement of capital power for capital." (p. 245 [Uno, *Principles 1977*, p. 470]) Following this, he speaks of "also in the case of receiving a direct loan …" and if we compare the two explanations we can interpret him as saying that the discounting of bills as well as "direct loaning" are not different insofar as "enhancing the power of capital" and increasing the production of surplus value. Thus, in his explanation of "direct loaning" his reason for adding the odd expression about "a certain quantity of one's equity capital" could be interpreted as being made in order to be in step with the case of discounting bills. Thus, this addition was not some sort of careless mistake but can be seen as a conscious error that was committed. However, as was indicated in the note at the end of the previous article [not included in this volume], in this short essay the discussion of the distinction between "direct loaning" and the discounting of bills is not of direct relevance to the main topic and is thus set aside, and this is why to avoid confusion I am not discussing that point here.

Uno could only answer as follows to this question that seems rather stupid at first glance. He would say that he is not discussing such an exceptional case and that in capitalist society money can be transformed into capital to generate profit (i.e., surplus value), and thus money with such a quality is what is loaned, so that even if a particular borrower does not use it to transform into capital to generate profit, that is the individual's affair but it does not change the fact that the handing over of money from the lender to the borrower—in the form of a loan—is to handle money with that character in terms of generating profit. It is precisely because something with that character and power to generate profit is handed over that the borrower must always pay interest for it. That would be the likely response of Professor Uno. In other words, money is here treated as a commodity that possesses the use value of functioning as capital. That is the answer he would have to give but to do so would be to place himself in trouble. For now, I will simply indicate this and next return to consider the meaning of the latter half of the passage initially quoted.

2 ["Value of Capital"]

With regard to the latter half of the passage, first let's look at the following line: "Therefore, the interest obtained from that lending is not the 'value of capital' but merely a compensation for the use of money during a certain period of time." Attention first needs to be directed to the expression in quotation marks "value of capital." The implication here seems to be that someone is insisting that interest is the value of capital whereas Professor Uno is saying that this is not the case, but it is not immediately apparent why he feels obliged to introduce such a manner of expression here. The next point to note is that this line begins with the word "Therefore." This word would have to be seen as referring to the directly preceding explanation with regard to how money only first functions as capital in the hands of the functioning capitalist and that because capital is "value in motion" it has to be said that the loan capitalist loans money and does not loan capital, but if one were to pose the opinion opposing that of Professor Uno it would be something like the question of why interest can become the value of capital, which makes little sense. If we look to another part of his book, we find the following:

> For banks, funds as such become a commodity. Interest is what can be considered the value of that commodity, but that of course does not have

> its value determined as in the case of general commodities. It is merely an allotment of a portion of the surplus value produced through the capitalization for the funds and thus its value is determined simply by supply and demand.[8]

In this way, it can first be understood that Professor Uno is saying that interest is what might be called the value of the funds as a commodity, and therefore in stating in the passage quoted earlier that interest is not the "value of capital" he is saying that it is the "value of funds" instead. In other words, in order to think that what is loaned is money not capital, he says that it is not the "value of capital" but the "value of the funds" (or value of money in the preceding terminology). In saying that interest is merely "compensation for the use of money during a certain period of time," he is thinking in terms of the "value of funds (money)" not something else.[9]

I think that the meaning of what Professor Uno is saying in the passage should be clear. The line can be abridged to say: "Therefore, the interest obtained from that lending is not the 'value of capital' but merely the value of money (funds)." But who does he imagine to be thinking that interest is the value of capital? The following passage seems to be the response to that question, but it is rather astounding: "Here money itself becomes a commodity, but capital does not yet do so. On this point I differ from Marx's explanation." Here "this point," judging from the page of *Capital* cited [*Marx Engels Collected Works*, Vol. 37, London: Lawrence & Wishart, 2010, pp. 336,7. *Marx Engels Collected Works* are hereafter abbreviated as MECW in this book], can be seen as relating to being a commodity, but if we look at the passage that says interest is not the "value of capital" but simply the value of money (or funds), and here money itself becomes a commodity and capital does not, Professor Uno having written "value of capital" was no doubt a result of his having viewed Marx as having asserted this. However, if one looks at what he is

[8] p. 248 [Uno, *Principles 1977*, p. 472].

[9] Incidentally, Marx writes the following: "We have seen that interest-bearing capital, although a category which differs absolutely from a commodity, becomes a commodity *sui generis*, so that interest becomes its price, fixed at all times by supply and demand like the market price of an ordinary commodity" [MECW, Vol. 37, p. 364]. And he also writes: "It is not until capital is money capital that it becomes a commodity, whose capacity for self-expansion has a definite price quoted in every prevailing rate of interest" [MECW, Vol. 37, p. 390].

saying here and trace what he has said up to that point, one realizes that far from the sense of surprise being exhausted it is just the beginning. This is because it can only be understood as meaning that he is saying that Marx (!) is insisting on what Professor Uno kept insisting could not be the case.

In other words, the following can be said. Whereas up to that point Professor Uno had repeatedly made the strange claim that money that functions as capital can be lent but capital itself is not lent, according to him Marx said that capital itself was lent, whereas Professor Uno opposes that view and insists it cannot be said and that what is lent is money. The reason he gives for this is that the money lent only first functions as capital in the hands of the functioning capitalist and that capital is "value in motion" and that money itself is not capital. He interprets this as meaning that apparently Marx did not know this, or he must have known it but completely forgotten it when it came to explaining interest-bearing capital. Thus, Professor Uno says that the interest obtained from lending is not the "value of capital" but the "value of money (funds)," and that here money itself becomes a commodity but capital does not.

3 [The So-called "Funds"]

I think that this should be enough already to have confirmed the meaning of what Professor Uno is saying, so that we can now enter into a full consideration of his argument, but before doing so I would like to look at the meaning of the term "funds" that he employed and is fond of using.

The term appears in the sentence quoted above, which is from page 245 of his book [Uno, *Principles 1977*, p. 470], and in his book *Principles of Political Economy*—particularly the chapter on "interest"—the vulgar term "funds" is commonly used. In that chapter on interest, he inserts a footnote where he explains the term in the following sort of way. Here I will quote the note in its entirety because it is a quite interesting explanation:

> The term funds is often used in general, but it is not given a clear definition. In this book as well, it is used with giving it almost any determination whatsoever, and also *in my own case it cannot be said that it is clearly defined*, but I generally understand it as referring to *what Marx describes as money as such, that is,* independent money, separate from the direct process

> of circulation and different from money as a means of circulation, *that can be put into circulation at any time as something that purchases commodities.* In any case, for original hoarded money the *fundamental character is that it is withdrawn from circulation*, so there are doubts about whether or not this can be considered as funds. Certainly, such money can be useful as funds, but it seems best to say that its character as funds is not clear, so money as such was not immediately treated as funds.
>
> But what we need to be careful to note is that whereas money as the means of circulation merely circulates within the realm of circulation without anyone producing and therefore consuming it, money as funds is in a relation where it is produced on the one hand and consumed on the other. Having said that it is produced does not necessarily mean produced as gold, but that it takes a form that is merely withdrawn from circulation, and being consumed means that it takes a form where it purchases a commodity thrown into circulation or is used for payments. Moreover, this comes to play the function of regulating the quantity of the means of circulation, but with regard to this point, unlike money as a means of circulation, it becomes itself the object of demand and supply, and as will be elucidated later becomes the object of sale and purchase from being commodified [although Professor Uno says he will elucidate this "later" he only says that "funds themselves become commodities" without "elucidating" the circumstances for this—Miyake]; this is basically how I understand the thing that becomes funds, but I think that these points can be examined from a variety of angles.[10]

According to this, we can see that Professor Uno defines the term "funds" first of all "generally … as referring to … money as such." But considered more closely what he means by this does not seem clear by any means. To begin with, he seems to suggest that his explanation of "money as such" in terms of being "independent money, separate from the direct process of circulation and different from money as a means of circulation, that *can be put* into circulation at any time as something that purchases commodities" is a definition shared by Marx, but even if it is said that "money can be put into circulation," this is the movement taken by money and is not something Marx would label "money as such." Such an expression would be inaccurate without being replaced with, for example, "independent money … in a form that can be put into circulation." Next, Professor Uno writes that, "for original hoarded money the fundamental

[10] pp. 231,2 [Uno, *Principles 1977*, p. 457]. The emphases are added by Miyake.

character is that it is withdrawn from circulation," but this is also an odd turn of expression. All money that is withdrawn from circulation takes the form of hoarded money, and all money that is a suspension of the metamorphoses of the commodity is in the form of hoarded money (setting apart the money that forms the so-called *Münzreserve* or "reserve funds of coin"), but what can be "*withdrawn* from circulation" is the money hoard, and the fact that the money is in the form of hoarded money is that it is in the form of *being* withdrawn from circulation. At first sight, this might seem to be quibbling, but these are the points that first must be clearly grasped here.

Leaving aside those issues of terminology (although I will return to them later), we can see that in the passage quoted, Professor Uno is using "money as such" and "original hoarded money" as nearly synonymous, but the former is something that concerns the movement of money "that can be put into circulation at any time as something that purchases commodities" (or in the sense of money in the form of that movement), whereas the latter has the "fundamental character of being withdrawn from circulation." This can be summed up as follows. "The term funds ... is generally understood as referring to ... money as such," and "money as such" is in the form "that can be put into circulation at any time," and "original hoarded money has the "fundamental character" of "being withdrawn from circulation," *so that* "money as such is not immediately funds." Professor Uno says to begin with the explanatory note that "in my own case it cannot be said that it is clearly defined," but the logic itself of the sentences within his explanation cannot be said to be "clear" or to make any sense.

But let's "examine" the problem more closely. The money hoard differs in its purpose and the role it plays depending on whether it exists on a capitalist or a pre-capitalist basis. On a pre-capitalist basis, money is also hoarded according to the needs of the exchange process, but on that basis, the characteristic is the "hoarding, as a distinct mode of acquiring riches"[11] that is manifested as a desire for gold, so that one seeks without limit to store it. In contrast, the money hoard on a capitalist basis that is founded on the necessity of the exchange process is increased under a wide array of forms that constitute the reserve fund, but at the same time, the limitless to desire to hoard money gradually disappears. This is because

[11] [MECW, Vol. 35, pp. 152,3.]

the capitalist by nature is augmenting value by means of throwing money constantly into circulation. When Professor Uno says that "for original hoarded money the fundamental character is that it is withdrawn from circulation," he probably has in mind the money hoard as it is characteristically manifested on a pre-capitalist basis. And he seems to be saying that the original hoarded money is stockpiled through the so-called original money hoard, whose principal character is constituted by such saving up of money.—Marx calls this *Schatz schlechthin* (original hoards) or *Schatz als solcher* (hoards as such).[12] In other words, this sentence seems at first glance to be a general explanation of the money hoard or hoarded money, but it certainly is not. As noted earlier, Professor Uno nonchalantly inserts the term "original" (*honrai*), but this is the characteristic of the money hoard and hoarded money on a pre-capitalist basis that gradually disappears under capitalism, and cannot be considered the dominant form of hoarded money on a capitalistic basis. It seems to me that he has failed to understand the following, or if he has understood it, it is unclear why he would raise the issue of that type of hoarded money if the problem he is posing precisely concerns money on a capitalist basis. In other words, the money hoard on a capitalist basis and that on a pre-capitalist basis differ in their aim and function, and yet the process of hoarding money itself, in which when the continuing supplementation through M—C is stopped the M that is a result of C—M becomes hoarded money, is common to all types of commodity production, and fully grasping this point is the cornerstone of an understanding of the form of hoarded money.[13]

It seems that Professor Uno has in mind the money in the form of being withdrawn from circulation in order to be thrown back into it, which he calls "funds," rather than money that is stockpiled in the manner of "original hoarded money." This seems to be the intention behind his definition of "the term funds," setting aside whether it is "often used in general." If that is indeed the case, there is no difference between the term "funds" he uses and the dominant form of hoarded money on the

[12] [MECW, Vol. 29, p. 383. This volume is *A Contribution to the Critique of Political Economy*.]

[13] For more regarding this point, readers can consult my essay "Money" ("A Short Essay on Money," [in Yoshio Miyake, *Studies on the Theory of Money and Credit*, Tokyo: Miraisha, 1956, pp. 7–42]). I also intend to attempt to write a more detailed paper on the form of hoarded money on the basis of capitalist production.

basis of capitalism. Thus, there is little need to use the term "funds" in the first place. Professor Uno also speaks of "what Marx describes as money as such," and this would seem to indicate the content of an April 2 letter Marx wrote to Engels, in which he speaks of "2. Money" in terms of "a) money as a measure," "b) money as a means of exchange," and "c) money as such,"[14] and if that is so, it is the same as section three within the chapter on money in *A Contribution* and *Capital* divided into "measure of value," "means of circulation," and "money." Money examined in that third section is money in distinction from the means of circulation, as money with the independent determinate being as exchange value, and the "money as such" referred to by Professor Uno is money in that sense. And money first of all does not indicate money in the determination as means of circulation—money in that determination is usually indicated by such terms as *currency, circulation*, and *Zirkulation*, setting aside how those terms are used by the advocates of the quantity theory of money who only grasp money in its function as means of circulation—and this generally indicates money in the same sense as discussed under the heading "Money" in that chapter, and since the chapter also includes the third section "money," there is no particular need to speak of "money as such."[15] Thus, it can be said that although Professor Uno uses the term "funds," his intended meaning in doing so is not different at all from the term "money."[16] Moreover, not only is there no difference between the

[14] [MECW, Vol. 40, pp. 301–2. There "c) money as such" is translated as "*money qua money*," but the original German term is the same, "Geld als Geld." See *Marx Engels Gesamtausgabe* (hereafter MEGA), III-9, S. 124.]

[15] Marx also uses, for example, the following sort of expression: "The first distinction we notice between money that is money only, and money that is capital, is nothing more than a difference in their form of circulation" [MECW, Vol. 35, p. 158.]. In this case, it is used in distinction from money as capital, so it is a bit different from money as such spoken of in the letter mentioned above.

[16] In a passage quoted above, Professor Uno himself uses the expression "being loaned funds that can be used as capital" on page 245 [Uno, *Principles 1977*, p. 470], but then speaks of "loaning out money that can function as capital" on page 8 [Uno, *Principles 1977*, p. 259]; in addition, on page 248 [Uno, *Principles 1977*, p. 472] he speaks of "funds as such become a commodity," while on page 8 [Uno, *Principles 1977*, p. 259] he writes in terms of "money itself becomes a commodity." It seems that he does this in order either to use the term funds more precisely (?) when he enters the chapter on interest or because he thought it was inadequate to only speak of money. As seen a bit earlier, Professor Uno defines the term "funds" as "generally ... referring to ... 'money as such'," but he also uses the term in the following sort of sentence, for example:

two but by introducing such a term with an unclear definition, through which he attempts to offer a new explanation of the "commodification of funds," objectively speaking the sentence as a whole becomes unclear in meaning so as to totally deceive himself and others (and this method seems to be Professor Uno's dislike of academia), so the use of the term must be said to be pointlessly harmful and useless. The terms funds and *money* are commonly used, so there is no reason to oppose them being brought into a theoretical explanation, but in this case the result has been to coin a new term or concept that does not have a clear definition.

Up to now, we have looked at the first half of Professor Uno's note on the term "funds," and the consideration above seems sufficient for the moment, so now we can enter into the consideration of the latter half to some extent. First of all, Professor Uno here says that "money as funds" is on the one hand "produced" and also "withdrawn from circulation," and on the other hand "consumed" by being "thrown into circulation to purchase commodities or to be used for payments." And he distinguishes this from "money as the means of circulation," which is "not produced and therefore not consumed."[17]

Professor Uno's so-called "production" of "money as funds" is carried out through the transformation of C' into M' in M—C—Mp/Lp....P ... C'—M' or P ... C'—M'—C ... P. If the M—C is said to be composed of a sequence of purchases or payments, then one part of the M is immediately expended as M—C, and another part is temporarily withdrawn from circulation and expended subsequently as M—C. Professor Uno seems to be saying that all of M' is "withdrawn from circulation," but of course that cannot be the case. The transformation of C' into M' is for the person

"interest that arises from the relation of loaning money as such as funds, based on the employment of the idle money capital that emerges from the process of the movement of industrial capital as additional capital for other industrial capital." (p. 7 [Uno, *Principles 1977*, p. 258]) What would happen if we view the term "funds" as having the meaning as in the sentence just quoted? This would be: "interest that arises from the relation of loaning money as such generally as money as such"!

[17] Professor Uno offers the following sort of explanation: "As for the reproduction process of capital, funds are capitalized to purchase and consume commodities within the circular movement wherein means of production and labor power are purchased with money to produce new commodities that are sold to realize money, but the new commodities are sold to form the new funds as money. As capital value, in this movement process, the self-value is kept while also augmenting through the production of new surplus value, but as funds it is in the relation of consumption on the one hand and production on the other" [Uno, *Principles 1977*, p. 469].

on the other side the transformation of M into C, and if this M is then transformed into C, it is clear that this M is functioning as a means of circulation, but if we think in terms of "production" and "consumption" as Professor Uno does, how can it be said that this M is not "produced" by the capitalist? This M is what the capitalist obtains through selling the commodity produced, and in terms of this point there is no difference from the other part of the M obtained through C'—M'. Similarly, why can it not be said that this M is "consumed" by the capitalist? The other part of M that is temporarily withdrawn from circulation is also employed as a means of purchase or means of payment when it is subsequently expended, so even if it is said to be "consumed" it is not in terms of being expended in a particular way. Therefore, we cannot be convinced at all by making the distinction that Professor Uno draws in saying that "money as funds" is "produced" and "consumed," "whereas money as the means of circulation merely circulates ... without anyone producing and therefore consuming it."

It can be additionally noted that Professor Uno also says that "money as funds" in this way is "produced" and "consumed" and this regulates the quantity of the means of circulation, so that "with regard to this point, ... it becomes itself the object of demand and supply, and ... becomes the object of sale and purchase from being commodified," but this raises the following sort of doubt immediately. Namely, how should we distinguish between the demand for these "funds" and the demand for the means of purchase, for example? Furthermore, if we consider that he says that it "becomes an object of sale and purchase," and assume sale to be C—M and purchase M—C, how can it be said that "generally money as such," or money with the determination as money, is sold? In other words, wouldn't it be a fruitless endeavor for money to be transformed into money, and to purchase money with money? How pointless this "objectification" is!

Now that we have basically dealt with his use of the term "funds,"[18] let's turn to his main explanation.

[18] The issue of the circulation of money in the circulation process of capital is significant and difficult issue that can be thought to merit a more adequate investigation.

4 [Lacking the Concept of Capital Fetish]

I think that from the preceding lengthy effort to verify Professor Uno's use of terminology it should basically be clear to the careful reader how he mistakenly understood the key point regarding the concept of interest-bearing capital, but in saying that the outward appearance of my manuscript as an academic paper would be lost. In relation to this I want to note the following.

The first key reason for why Professor Uno says that Marx is mistaken, which becomes the basis for the following, is that the loan capitalist who lends money cannot be said to be lending capital because it only first functions as capital when it is in the hands of the functioning capitalist, and because capital is "value in motion" and that the money itself is not capital. At issue is whether Marx was indeed unaware of this and completely forgot about it when it came to explaining this interest-bearing capital, as Professor Uno supposes. Certainly, it is no exaggeration on my part to say that Marx neither was unaware nor forget about such a thing. Rather, it must be said that it is exceedingly odd for Professor Uno himself to imagine that he had.

In the following sentences, we shall discuss with quoting what Marx writes as possible.

First of all, can it truly be said that Marx could not discern that money only first functions as capital in the hands of the functioning capitalist, and instead thought that money itself was capital and that the loan capitalist was in fact lending capital?

And can it in fact be said that Marx did not know that capital is "value in motion" and instead "vulgarly" considered it as "something that we can concretely grasp," such as "money," and that by lending money one is lending capital?

Marx writes the following:

> But in interest-bearing capital the first time M changes hands is by no means a phase either of the commodity metamorphosis, or of reproduction of capital. It first becomes one when it is expended a second time, in the hands of the functioning capitalist who carries on trade with it, or transforms it into productive capital. M's first change of hands does not

> express anything here, beyond its transfer from A to B—a transfer which usually takes place under certain legal forms and stipulations.[19]

As we can see, in explaining the independent circulation of interest-bearing capital, Marx is saying that the loaned money only first functions as commercial capital or industrial capital in the hands of the functioning capitalist, and indeed he draws attention to the fact that the first change in position of the M from the loan capitalist to functioning capitalist is merely the transfer of money.

Marx also writes:

> At no time during the metamorphosis, viewed by itself, does the capitalist sell his commodities as *capital* to the buyer, although to him they represent capital; nor does he give up money as capital to the seller. In both cases he gives up his commodities simply as commodities, and money simply as money, as a means of purchasing commodities. It is only in connection with the entire process, at the moment where the point of departure appears simultaneously as the point of return, in M—M' or C—C, that capital in the process of circulation appears as capital (whereas in the process of production it appears as capital through the subordination of the labourer to the capitalist and the production of surplus value). ... Commodities and money are here [in the process of circulation—Miyake] capital not because commodities change into money, or money into commodities, not in their actual relations to sellers or buyers, but only in their ideal relations to the capitalist himself (subjectively speaking), or as phases in the process of reproduction (objectively speaking). Capital exists as capital in actual movement, not in the process of circulation, but only in the process of production, in the process by which labour power is exploited.[20]

Here Marx is explaining that "capital in the process of circulation functions as commodity capital and money capital but in both cases capital does not become a commodity as capital," and it should already be clear without any doubt that this has nothing to do with Professor Uno's concern that "Commonly speaking, capital is thought of as something concrete that we might grasp as money, or as the means of production such as machinery, or as a commodity, but capital is not merely that,"

[19] [MECW, Vol. 37, p. 339.]

[20] [MECW, Vol. 37, p. 341.]

which notably must be interpreted as being directed against Marx's explanation of interest-bearing capital. That point is absolutely a matter of course for Marx, who first elucidated the value-*form* to strike at the fundamental defect of Classical political economy, showing that the commodity, money, and capital are not natural but historical things.[21]

But it seems that Professor Uno does not dare to read *Capital* broadly and rapidly to find fault with Marx. But why did he end up doing this? One reason can be explained from the circumstance explained earlier. This is the fact that he does not understand that the form of interest-bearing capital is the highest degree of fetishism of production relations, namely, the "capital fetish" (*Kapitalfetisch*). He did not understand that in the form of interest-bearing "capital assumes its pure fetish form, M–M' being the subject, the saleable thing."[22] Moreover, needless to say, this understanding itself is fundamentally important for grasping the category of interest-bearing capital, and therefore Marx took as his main task the theories of interest-bearing capital and interest in Chapters 21–24 in Part 5 of Volume 3 of *Capital*, and if this understanding is lacking then it will not be possible to understand interest-bearing capital either.

On the basis of capitalist production, money, in addition to its use value as such, comes to have the use value of generating profit, i.e., it takes on the use value of functioning as capital, and thus money with this use value is traded as a commodity. Although what is traded is certainly money, it is not disbursed merely as money but as money with that use value, so that it is from the outset traded as capital. This is the point that constitutes the independent character of interest-bearing capital, and it is necessary to firmly understand this.[23] Professor Uno thinks that capital is

[21] In "The Trinity Formula" the following description can also be found: "However, capital is not a thing, but rather a definite social production relation, belonging to a definite historical formation of society, which is manifested in a thing and lends this thing a specific social character. Capital is not the sum of the material and produced means of production. Capital is rather the means of production transformed into capital, which in themselves are no more capital than gold or silver in itself is money" [MECW, Vol. 37, pp. 801,2.].

[22] [MECW, Vol. 37, p. 390.]

[23] Some are likely to say in response to this that even if it has the use value to function as capital, it is merely as latent or possible capital at the moment the money is handed over from the lender to the borrower. In response to this, Marx wrote the following: "Interest-bearing capital remains as such only so long as the loaned money is actually converted into capital and a surplus is produced with it, of which interest is a part. But

not a thing. It was Marx himself who elucidated that fact, and so he is of course aware of this. But what is at issue here, constituting the crux of the theory of interest-bearing capital, is to expose and comprehend that the social relations, which are not things, are reified (*bukka*)[24] so as to manifest themselves as things, so that when all of the mediating processes vanish the results of the capitalistic production and circulation processes are all manifested as being the internal attributes of things. To elaborate even further, it is of course not possible for money to automatically generate money. This is why Marx, in concluding his theory of interest-bearing capital in the chapter titled "Externalisation of the Relations of Capital in the Form of Interest-Bearing Capital," refers to the theory of compound interest of Richard Price, which was a caricature arising from his bedazzlement by the upside-down phenomenon.[25]

In the previous article, we saw Ichirō Kawai and Tomoyoshi Fujitsuka saying that money is demanded by the borrower as capital and in the hands of the borrower is used as capital, and that only when it actually generates profit does the money become interest-bearing capital. We confirmed that this understanding of "loaning interest-bearing capital" was a mistake and that this misunderstanding stemmed from failing to grasp the reified appearance of capital involving the manifestation of social relations as things, which finds its completion in interesting-bearing capital; and the same lack of understanding can be seen in the case of Professor Uno who says that capital cannot be said to be commodified but money or funds becomes a commodity. In this sense, they all share a

this does not rule out that drawing interest, regardless of the process of production, is its organic property. So does labour power preserve its property of producing value only so long as it is employed and realised in the labour process; yet this does not argue against the fact that it is potentially, as a power, an activity which creates value, and that as such it does not spring from the process of production, but rather ***antecedes it***. It is bought as such a capacity for creating value. One might also buy it without setting it to work productively; for purely personal ends, for instance, for personal services, etc. The same applies to capital. It is the borrower's affair whether he employs it as capital, hence actually sets in motion its inherent property of producing surplus value. What he pays for, is in either case the potential surplus value inherently contained in capital as a commodity" [MECW, Vol. 37, p. 379. Emphases are added by Miyake.].

24 [The term "*bukka*" corresponds to the German word *Verdinglichung*. But Miyake is using this term to refer to the German word *Versachlichung*, which is usually translated in English reification, as Uno does. See fn. 29 in Chapter 2 of this book.]

25 [MECW, Vol. 37, pp. 392 ff.]

misunderstanding of the same character. One not insignificant difference, however, is that whereas Kawai says that this is what Marx said, Professor Uno says it is a point that "differs from Marx's explanation" and he holds the idea that what Marx had written was mistaken.

In addition, Kawai juxtaposes "demand from the outset for capital" and "loaning interest-bearing capital" that is "demanded as capital from the outset" with "loaning money merely as money"; he thinks that in the case of discounting bills, for example, this is the "loaning of money merely as money" and is not the "loaning of interest-bearing capital," but he explains that discounting "resembles the appearance of interest-baring capital in augmenting itself and is a legal fiction for the form of interest-bearing capital." In contrast, Professor Uno says that even when "directly loaned," it is "not capital itself that is loaned" but money or funds, so that it is explained in a unified way with the discounting of bills (!).[26] Thus the problem of "whether the cash that is loaned by a banker to his client is capital or money" is solved by Uno—or rather we should say the problem itself does not exist for him! In that way all of the problems are solved and disappear. At the same time, the category of interest-bearing capital itself disappears!

There are other points that should be raised with regard to verifying the meaning of the sentence at the outset of Professor Uno's paper, and therefore with regard to his grasp of interest-bearing capital, but that is the fundamental defect and the other issues are basically based upon it, so I will not delve further into that matter. Finally, in order to clarify just how important that defect is with regard to the overall understanding of *Capital*, we can consider the following passage from "The Trinity Formula":

> In the case of the simplest categories of the capitalist mode of production, and even of commodity production, in the case of commodities and money, we have already pointed out the mystifying character that transforms the

[26] With regard to this, Professor Uno writes the following: "Discounting bills ... becomes a sale that takes the form of M—C—M' but because of that it does not mean that it cannot be said to constitute the lending of funds. With regard to this point, the issue centered on whether the means of circulation is being lent or capital is being lent, but from my perspective neither the means of circulation nor capital are being lent. If funds are lent, they can be used as either means of circulation or means of payment, and this itself means that capital can be added." (p. 246 [Uno, *Principles 1977*, p. 470]) This essay will not touch more on this point.

> social relations, for which the material elements of wealth serve as bearers in production, into properties of these things themselves (commodities) and still more pronouncedly transforms the production relation itself into a thing (money). ... But under the capitalist mode of production and in the case of capital, which forms its dominant category, its determining production relation, this enchanted and perverted world develops still more. If one considers capital, to begin with, in the actual process of production as a means of extracting surplus labour, then this relationship is still very simple ... The division of profit into profit of enterprise and interest ... consummates the individualisation of the form of surplus value, the ossification of its form as opposed to its substance, its essence. One portion of profit, as opposed to the other, separates itself entirely from the relationship of capital as such and appears as arising not out of the function of exploiting wage labour, but out of the wage labour of the capitalist himself. In contrast thereto, interest then seems to be independent both of the labourer's wage labour and the capitalist's own labour, and to arise from capital as its own independent source. If capital originally appeared on the surface of circulation as a fetishism of capital, as a value-creating value, so it now appears again in the form of interest-bearing capital, as in its most estranged and characteristic form.[27]

5 ["Capital as an Automatically Interest-bearing Force"]

In Chapter 3 of Part 3 of *Principles of Political Economy* of Professor Uno, titled "Interest," there is the following problem in addition to his discussion of interest-bearing capital examined above. For example, there is the question of the order in which he proceeds from Chapter 2 on "Rent" to Chapter 3 on "Interest," especially since in Chapter 3, he deals with "Loan Capital" in section 1 and "Commercial Capital and Commercial Profit" in section 2, and "Capital as an Automatically Interest-Bearing Force" in section 3. Professor Uno writes the following: "The ability to demand a portion of the surplus value from the fact of possessing land is unprincipled as far as the capitalist is concerned unless the portion of surplus value is distributed for also being a possessor of capital."[28] He also speaks of "commercial capital that is manifested on the basis of the

[27] [MECW, Vol. 37, pp. 813–6.]

[28] pp. 6,7 [Uno, *Principles 1977*, p. 258].

formation of loan capital" and that "commercial capital rather assumes this loan capital."[29]

Professor Uno's thoughts on the first point call to mind the following passage of Marx: "Some writers, acting either as spokesmen of landed property and taking up the cudgels against the attacks of bourgeois economists, ... have tried to represent ground rent, the specific economic expression of landed property, as identical with interest. ... The opposite method was employed in the early stages of capitalist production. In those days, landed property was still regarded by popular conception as the pristine and respectable form of private property, while interest on capital was decried as usury. Dudley North, Locke and others, therefore, *represented interest on capital as a form analogous to ground rent*, just as Turgot deduced the justification for interest from the existence of ground rent."[30] However, the fact that economists in the early period of capitalism sought to justify interest was not made possible on the basis of "rent" being dealt with prior to "interest." The only basis that Professor Uno indicates in his book for reversing the order of "interest" and "rent" is the passage quoted earlier. Unless a more compelling basis is given, it

[29] p. 8 [Uno, *Principles 1977*, p. 259]. The position of this "rent" was to be dealt with by Marx according to his January 1863 plan—on "Rent (Illustration of the difference between value and price of production)—after production price and before law of the fall of the rate of profit and the division of profit into industrial profit and interest [see MECW, Vol. 33, p. 346], but in an April 30, 1868 letter to Engels Marx notes that he decided to treat rent—"transformation of surplus value into rent"—after dealing with interest, as is the case in the published edition of *Capital* [see MECW, Vol. 43, p. 25. To be precise, Marx mentions here "transformation of surplus *profit* into rent."]. In addition, with regard to commercial profit and interest, within the January 1863 plan, there is "8. Division of profit into industrial profit and interest. Mercantile capital. Money capital," [MECW, Vol. 33, p. 346. The original German word for "Mercantile capital" is *mercantile Capital*. See MEGA, II-3.5, S. 1861] but in the 1868 letter Marx writes: "IV. Until now we have only dealt with productive capital. Now there enters modification through merchant capital" and "V. We have now reduced profit to the form in which it appears in practice, according to our assumptions 16 2/3%. Next comes the division of this profit into entrepreneur's gain and interest. Interest-bearing capital. The credit system" [MECW, Vol. 43, pp. 24,5. The original German word for "merchant capital" here is *Kaufmannskapital*. See *Marx Engels Werke*, Bd. 32, S. 74]. In other words, *at first glance*, Professor Uno's classification of chapters seems to be in line with the plan that Marx had written down before writing the published version of *Capital*. However, he does not seem to have adopted this order of chapters and sections in order to suggest that the previous plan of Marx was better.

[30] [MECW, Vol. 37, p. 616. Emphases are added by Miyake.]

cannot be considered and the reversal would have to be seen as unjustified. Next, when it comes to the reversal of the order of description of loan capital and commercial capital, Professor Uno presents quite convoluted ideas about the relation between the two types of capital and how to grasp commercial profit, so that even if that part is re-read the crux of his point cannot be fully understood. Moreover, entering into a consideration of this is not directly related to the task of this paper. Therefore, I will only note the following two or three points.

The term loan capital means that when money has the use value of generating profit, and is thus traded as a commodity with the use value of functioning as capital, it is sold in a unique way that differs from the case of other commodities; in other words, instead of being completely handed over, it is handed over on the condition that it is returned after a certain period of time, which is to say, the focus is on it taking the form of being loaned, and this term can be called interest-bearing capital, so that there is no difference whether one speak of loan capital or interest-bearing capital. Oddly, though, according to Professor Uno, they each form a separate category. These separate categories can be received simply from the headings in Chapter 3 ("Interest") of Part 3; namely, section 1 on "Loan Capital" and section 3 on "Capital as an Automatically Interest-Bearing Force,"[31] and yet the nature of the distinction between them is not clearly noted.

For instance, Professor Uno writes: "Marx seems to explain that in the case of loan capital, capital becomes a commodity (Chapter 21 of Volume 3 of *Capital*), but my understanding is that capital is not yet commodified in this case. Capital is first commodified and sold as such when stock shares and land become fictitious capital insofar as they generate interest. That value ... stems from capitalization based on interest, but is not interest itself."[32] The meaning here of "that value [of stock shares and land—Miyake] ... is not interest itself" is not clear, but setting that aside, the fact that a stock dividend, for example, can be capitalized according to a calculation based on the rate of interest, is premised on a certain sum of money being able to generate a certain amount of interest, and thus is

[31] More precisely, it seems more appropriate to say that Professor Uno, who had not understood the category of interest-bearing capital, is using the term loan capital to designate a distorted and trivialized concept of interest-bearing capital, and further has created the long expression "capital as an automatically interest-bearing force."

[32] p. 248 [Uno, *Principles 1977*, p. 472].

premised on the fact that a revenue that regularly generates a certain sum of money being as the interest that should derive from the loaning of a certain quantity of money; in other words, this is premised on the generation of the category of interest-bearing capital. Nevertheless, Professor Uno does not attempt to correctly grasp this relation, and instead simply uses the term "loan capital" on the one side and "fictitious capital" and "capital as an automatically interest-bearing force" on the other hand as separate terms. Moreover, in relation to the sentence quoted above, he offers the following explanation: "... a dividend, conversely, fictionalized as interest on a sum of capital. Stock capital itself cannot become loan capital, but is seen as such.[33] As a result, capital itself is commodified."[34] In other words, Professor Uno is saying that through joint-stock capital being seen as loan capital, capital itself is commodified. Capital is not commodified in the case of loan capital, but it is commodified by being seen as loan capital! I doubt that anyone except Professor Uno would be able to understand the situation between the two.

Next, the following point also seems a bit strange. That is, within section 3, "Capital as an Automatically Interest-Bearing Force," the part A, "Division of Profit into Interest and Profit of Enterprise," has the subtitle "System of Joint-stock Capital," and this seems to be based on the idea that "Generally capital profit is divided into interest and profit of enterprise. The system of joint-stock companies is merely the concrete indication of this" (pp. 289,90 [Uno, *Principles 1977*, p. 509]), but he presents the core of this explanation in the following manner: "This form [of the joint-stock company—Miyake] is in fact concretely divided into the capitalist of an enterprise and the owner of the capital that is capitalized in the form of loan capital. However, the relationship in which the industrial capitalist views one portion of his own capital profit as the

[33] Here he inserts the following footnote: "Along with the development of the stock-company system regarding this capital...a trend toward corporate bonds emerges, but it is not as though it is completely transformed into loan capital." Is this a state of affairs in which transformation into loan capital means not being commodified, but since it has not yet been "completely" transformed into loan capital it is commodified? Meanwhile, if Professor Uno says that "joint-stock capital" is the "commodification of capital," why doesn't he consider the case of corporate bonds the "commodification of capital"? It should be able to be sold as a commodity according to the certainty and the calculation of the profit margin, but perhaps even the professor himself cannot explain why it does not become a commodity.

[34] p. 294 [Uno, *Principles 1977*, p. 513].

interest that capital itself generates and the rest as the profit of enterprise as the capitalist's compensation for his own business activities does not immediately correspond to the relation between the dividend received by the general shareholder capitalist and the compensation received by the main shareholder capitalist who controls the company."[35] In other words, while Professor Uno says that the joint-stock company system concretely divides capital profit into interest and profit of enterprise, "however" in this system this division "does not" appear "immediately"! But one should be able to easily perceive the following from that sentence. That is, even before the joint-stock company appears, he recognizes that there arises a relationship in which "the industrial capitalist views one portion of his own capital profit as the interest that capital itself generates," but how is this possible without establishing the category of what is called "capital as an automatically interest-bearing force" or interest-bearing capital? In addition, Professor Uno, as seen above, raises "capital as an automatically interest-bearing force" in distinction from loan capital, and explains that in relation to the former, profit is divided into interest and profit of enterprise, with the joint-stock company system pointed to as a concrete indication of this,[36] but why is it that he does not recognize interest obtained by the loan capitalist "as the interest that capital itself generates"? Why doesn't he, as is done in *Capital*, only premise two types of capitalists—money capitalist and industrial or commercial capitalists, i.e., functioning capitalists—and pursue the transformation of a portion of profit into interest, the establishment of the category of interest, and therefore the establishment of the category of profit of enterprise? I think that such a doubt must occur to anyone, but Professor Uno pays no mind to it at all. This is the cause of his failure to grasp the category of interest-bearing capital, and it is incomprehensible that he did not reflect upon it in the course of constructing his original theory, especially when we think

[35] p. 290 [Uno, *Principles 1977*, pp. 509,10].

[36] Let me add here incidentally that the joint-stock company system rather acts to conceal and obscure the division of profit into interest and entrepreneurial gain and the relation between the loan capitalist and the functioning capitalist, which is why up to this day the definition of dividends and the nature of stocks have not been adequately clarified. This issue must be considered historically and to some extent typologically. Particular attention needs to be drawn to the fact that Hilferding in his work *Finance Capital* posited a *fundamentally* mistaken definition—and contrary to popular opinion it is certainly not a good book in terms of its own value.

of the result of construction based on the failure to grasp the category is quite coarse and lacks fineness.

Next, the following point is also strange. The part B in section 3, "Capital as an Automatically Interest-Bearing Force" is titled "Commodification of Capital." Professor Uno insists that, on the one hand, what Marx mentions does not occur in the cases Marx raises, and on the other hand, that what Marx says can be observed in the cases Professor Uno himself raises. Professor Uno, who failed to understand money to be traded in the determination of having use value of functioning as capital, pompously declares the following sort of "commodification of capital." "Joint-stock capitalists are now able to freely transfer the ownership of capital, which is at this point merely a right to request dividend, through the sales of stock certificates. This is an only method to commodify capital as it is, as value in motion that repeats the circular movements."[37] Literally, ***parturiunt montes nascetur ridiculus mus!*** Since capital is "value in motion" direct commodification as motion is impossible, but here there are paper copies and ownership titles of value that are moving, and, to the extent they are sold, these are commodities. Professor Uno finally finds here "commodification of capital." "It [Capital—Miyake] is value in motion that takes various forms such as money, means of production, commodity, etc., as well as the form of labor power. Therefore, even if this is commodified it cannot occur in a simple form. … This is because capital … does not exist simply as a thing."[38] "Stock certificates" are indeed paper, and thus "things"! What can one say about the vulgarity of this making into "things," this "commodification of capital," that Professor Uno proposes after claiming, in regard to Marx's explanation in which in interest-bearing capital the relationships of production are maximally inverted and capital relationships emerge as a single entity, "capital is not yet commodified in this case"!?

Let me also add that Professor Uno in raising the issue of the "commodification of capital" mentions "stock certificates" and "land." It is a bit forced to include the commodification of land with the commodification of stock shares as the same sort of "commodification of *capital*," but setting that aside, the "capital" that he speaks of with regard to the "commodification of capital" is the imaginary capital formed through the

[37] p. 293 [Uno, *Principles 1977*, p. 512].

[38] p. 292 [Uno, *Principles 1977*, p. 511].

capitalization of dividends and rent. I have already touched on the lack of "logic" explaining fictitious capital, created on the basis of the formation of the category of interest-bearing capital, while negating the formation of interest-bearing capital, but be that as it may, what is his point in positing the "capital" in the "commodification of capital" that he speaks of thusly as imaginary capital? And given this, why exactly does he not include national bonds and the like therein? And why does the "commodification of capital" not also include company bonds and other interest-bearing certificates? I cannot understand these points and I suspect that Professor Uno himself would not be able to explain them.

As we have seen above, in Professor Uno's new work *Principles of Political Economy*—in whose "Afterword" he says that he had "pondered for quite some time" and that his book "reveals the limitations of [his] understanding of *Capital* up to now"[39]—his view of interest-bearing capital has an extremely *broad* and *fundamental* defect, and this part of his book can be said to be more "creative" and at the same time more fragile than its other parts. I should note though that unlike the frequent cases of superficial "research" that seeks to conceal an insufficient understanding—and is not always even aware of doing so—the frankness shown by Professor Uno is a scholarly attitude quite worthy of respect.

As a follow-up to considering the views of Ichirō Kawai and Tomoyoshi Fujitsuka in the previous paper, this paper has examined the views of Professor Uno, but as indicated in that earlier paper, the aim of considering these views has merely been to more precisely grasp the category of interest-bearing capital. Once we can locate the errors of their views through that examination and understand why they occur, I think we will be able to basically avoid major errors when grasping interest-bearing capital.

[39] [Uno, *Principles 1977*, p. 523.]

How a Theory of Interest Should Be Developed: Answering Yoshio Miyake's Critique of the Theory of Interest in My *Principles of Political Economy*

Kōzō Uno

Part 5 of Volume 3 of *Capital* develops a theory of interest, but in Japan, this has not been discussed and debated like the theories of profit and rent, and expository scholarship has not been conducted on it the way it has on other parts of *Capital*. Regardless of its quality, the fact that recently research on this part of the text has at last begun to be seen here and there can be said to demonstrate progress in the study of

Translated by Robert Chapeskie.
[This essay was first published in Japanese in *Rikkyo Economic Review*, Vol. 7, No. 1, 1953. The translation is based on *Kōzō Uno Collected Works*, Vol. 4, Tokyo: Iwanami-Shoten, 1974, pp. 206–9—editor. All additions in the square brackets ([ ]) in this volume are made by the editor (Kei Ehara) unless otherwise noted.]

K. Uno (Deceased) (✉)
University of Tokyo, Tokyo, Japan

K. Ehara (ed.), *Japanese Discourses on the Marxian Theory of Finance*, Marx, Engels, and Marxisms,
https://doi.org/10.1007/978-3-030-83324-4_4

Capital. However, this part—to me at least—includes elements that are quite problematic and cannot be dealt with simply through direct exposition. I myself have attempted an explanatory study of it once or twice in the past, but I concluded that I could not make any progress in interpretation without considering its connection to other parts of *Capital*, and in *Principles of Political Economy* I developed my own view—albeit, of course, relying on *Capital*—based on the theories of profit and rent. There were many places in which I adopted my own approach, and from the start I did not believe this would solve every problem. But I had my reasons for what I did, and I proceeded with the hope that later critiques would correct my errors. Recently, Yoshio Miyake's "Essay on Interest-Bearing Capital," begun in *Rikkyo Economic Review* Vol. 6, No. 1 and continued in Vol. 6, No. 2,[1] has presented a critique that fundamentally rejects my approach and can be said to require me to reexamine my own view. Mr. Miyake's essay will continue, but—as Mr. Miyake has almost no understanding of my approach—I thought I would save wasted effort on both our parts if I were to respond to the aspects concerning myself right away and endeavor to clear up his misunderstandings regarding my views.

1 [The Method of Marx's Theory of Interest]

Readers of Volume 3 of *Capital*, if they are somewhat attentive, should not fail to notice that there is a difference between the development from Part 1 to Part 3 and the development from Part 4 to 5. Particularly if we look at it in comparison to the theory of rent in Part 6 and general summary in Part 7, which, like Parts 1 to 3, are for the most part argued on the basis of a "pure capitalist society," it cannot be denied that the section from Part 4 to Part 5 gets into more practical, realistic issues. This may be connected to the nature of the manuscript of Volume 3 of *Capital*, but while this is indeed not inconceivable based on Engels's prefaces to Volumes 1 and 2, I do not want to get into this kind of interpretation here. The fact is that this difference is undeniable. I discussed what can be thought of as a problematic aspect of Marx's theory regarding commercial capital that arises as a result of this in the essay "Commercial Capital and Commercial Profit" in the recently published

[1] [The latter part of this article, in which Uno is criticized, is included as chapter "Interest-Bearing Capital: Response to the Explanation of Kōzō Uno" of this book.]

collection commemorating the 60th birthday of Dr. Hyoue Ōuchi (Part 1) in *Marxian Economics Studies*,[2] but this point emerges even more clearly in the theory of interest in Part 5.

In Chapter 21 of Part 5 "Interest-Bearing Capital," after stipulating to begin with that "Money ... may be converted into capital on the basis of capitalist production, and may thereby be transformed from a given value to a self-expanding, or increasing, value. It produces profit, i.e., it enables the capitalist to extract a certain quantity of unpaid labour, surplus product and surplus value, from the labourers, and to appropriate it. In this way, aside from its use value as money, it acquires an additional use value, namely that of serving as capital. Its use value then consists precisely in the profit it produces when converted into capital. In this capacity of potential capital, of a means of producing profit, it becomes a commodity, but a commodity *sui generis*. Or, what amounts to the same, capital as capital becomes a commodity,"[3] Marx then continues as follows:

> Suppose the annual average rate of profit is 20%. In that case a machine valued at £100, employed as capital under average conditions and an average amount of intelligence and purposive effort, would yield a profit of £20. A man in possession of £100, therefore, possesses the power to make £120 out of £100, or to produce a profit of £20. He possesses a potential capital of £100. If he gives these £100 to another for one year, so the latter may use them as real capital, he gives him the power to produce a profit of £20 — a surplus value which costs this other nothing, and for which he pays no equivalent. If this other should pay, say, £5 at the close of the year to the owner of the £100 out of the profit produced, he would thereby pay the use value of the £100 — the use value of its function as capital, the function of producing a profit of £20. The part of the profit paid to the owner is called interest, which is just another name, or special term, for a part of the profit given up by capital in the process of functioning to the owner of the capital, instead of putting it into its own pocket.[4]

I've quoted at considerable length, but this is the starting point of Marx's explanation of interest-bearing capital and can also be described as its fundamental definition. There is nothing particularly difficult to grasp about this

[2] [Published in 1953 by Iwanami-Shoten Publisher.]

[3] [*Marx Engels Collected Works* (hereafter MECW), Vol. 37, London: Lawrence & Wishart, 2010, pp. 336,7.]

[4] Ibid., p. 337.

definition itself, but when you view it in the context of the society posited in the process of developing the theory of profit up to Part 3, as I mentioned above, it is not so easy to say that you understand it. How are we to theoretically understand the emergence of the contrast between functioning capitalists and owners of capital spoken of here? Is our not finding Marx's definition difficult to understand not the result of our having imported here the so-called entrepreneurial capitalists and money-lending capitalists, or so-called "general investors," with whom we are already familiar as a matter of common sense? Of course, a capitalist society based on interest-bearing capital, both conceptually and in actuality, separates profit into interest and entrepreneurial gains, but theoretically this is not something that can be assumed from the start. In Part 4, after the theory of profit in general is developed, "merchant's capital" is already presented as commodity capital and money capital transformed into commercial capital and money-dealing capital in advance; this perhaps amounts to an acceptance of this assumption by Marx. At the same time, however, does this not also make it impossible to avoid the gradual insertion of things that are systematically external to the capitalist society maintained up to Part 3?[5] Part 5 clearly brings in relations of a concrete nature not considered in the theory of profit developed on the

[5] In the development of commercial capital and commercial profit in Chapters 16–18 of Part 4, commercial capital is often thought of as being the same as the old merchant's capital. On this point, please see my essay mentioned above. In fact, developing commercial capital simply from the aspect in which independent capital conducts the buying and selling of products as commodities in their process of circulation as Marx does makes it difficult to give this a definition within a capitalist society that differs from merchant's capital. It has to be given the following definition later on: "In so far as commercial capital is not, therefore, just a form of industrial capital in the merchant's hands as commodity capital or money capital, it is nothing but that portion of [social] money capital which belongs to the merchant himself and circulates in the purchase and sale of commodities." [MECW, Vol. 37, pp. 277,8. An insertion ["social"] is added by a Japanese translator, Fumio Hasebe, as Uno indicates as follows.] In my view this is the fundamental point that distinguishes commercial capital from merchant capital. I think Fumio Hasabe's addition of "social" in his Japanese translation is appropriate.

Even if in reality the development of capital has been conducted with traditional merchant capital and money-lending capital functioning within it as something that has played quite a large role, that does not mean this can be directly reflected in theoretical development. This on the contrary can only be incorporated as one aspect of the general definition of capital when money is transformed into capital. Commercial capital must be explained not simply as something that has arisen through the transformation of traditional merchant capital in this way, but as something that has developed out of industrial capital itself—at least in theoretical development as I understand it, if this is not done it will not be considered consistent from start to finish.

basis of a pure capitalist society. And this cannot simply be seen as theoretical progress rising to more concrete elements, because from Part 6 onwards Marx does not follow this method.

I will add one more comment on this point, which also relates to Mr. Miyake's criticism, before moving on. Here Marx says of money, "aside from its use value as money, it acquires an additional use value, namely that of serving as capital," defines this as it becoming "a commodity, but a commodity *sui generis*," and immediately offers a rephrasing: "Or, what amounts to the same, capital as capital becomes a commodity." Is it right to directly equate money becoming a commodity and capital becoming a commodity based on money transforming into capital in a capitalist society and in doing so accruing some portion of surplus value? Is there no contradiction between this and Marx's definition of capital? Or here must capital already be something that is reified (*bukka*)?[6] Does this not make it simply a given as something external to the movement of industrial capital? To me, this is a fundamental issue.

But enough about my doubts concerning Marx's theory of interest. I will now turn to Mr. Miyake's critique.

2 ["Loan Capital"]

Mr. Miyake begins by quoting me as follows. "Loan capital, as will be made clear later, is not capital as something that is loaned out. Loaning out money that can function as capital at any time is not the loaning out of capital itself. It is the lending of money and the earning of interest thereon that makes it capital to the owner of such money. Therefore, the interest obtained from that lending is not the 'value of capital' but merely a compensation for the use of money during a certain period of time. Here money itself becomes a commodity, but capital does not yet do so. On this point I differ from Marx's explanation, but here I will merely indicate this without going into further detail."[7] He then says, "It

[6] [Regarding the term "*bukka*," see fn. 29 in Chapter 2 of this book.]

[7] [Kōzō Uno, *Principles of Political Economy*, Vol. 2, Tokyo: Iwanami Shoten, 1952, p. 8. The two volumes are republished in 1977. We also refer to the page number in the 1977 edition, which is more available today (hereafter Uno, *Principles 1977*). Uno, *Principles 1977*, p. 259.]

seems to me that almost no one reading the passage above just once or twice would be able to grasp the meaning"[8] and complains of my saying "loan capital is not capital as something that is loaned out" that "on its own this is a puzzling sentence that is extremely hard to understand."

I am loath to take up and refute such trivial matters one by one, but since such things are repeated constantly in Mr. Miyake's critique I will try to get them out of the way here. The passage quoted above is taken from the Introduction to Part 3 "the theory of distribution" of my *Principles of Political Economy*,[9] and moreover from a note in which I discuss the explanation in which commercial capital is developed on the assumption of the form of loan capital. This not being understood after being read "once or twice" may perhaps be owing to my awkward phrasing, but the words "loan capital is not capital as something that is loaned out" themselves not having a clear meaning is quite a surprise. Being capital as something that lends money is clear to everyone, as can even be seen from the continuation of the quoted passage. What makes him write so pretentiously? If we look at how Mr. Miyake then continues we get a good sense of his capacity for understanding. He writes that although I said "as will be made clear later," "I can come across nothing subsequently that provides a clearer explanation." What exactly is it he needs to have "clarified"? If we are talking about capital that lends money and obtains interest, there will of course be no "'later' explanation that 'clarifies'" this beyond what is stated here. This is not the issue. The issue is how this form of capital arises. To have ignored this point is no different from having looked up "loan capital" in a dictionary and sought a definition. When I said it would be "made clear later," I was referring to this point being clarified in the bank credit that developed based on commercial credit. I did not write *Principles of Political Economy* as a dictionary of economic jargon, so the "similar thing"[10] appearing more than once cannot be helped.

Regarding capital not being loaned, Mr. Miyake says that he does not understand what this means, so he seeks a definition of capital among my writings on the "theory of interest," eventually discovers that capital is "value in motion," and uses this definition to decipher this "puzzling sentence." If he had read what I wrote from the beginning, however, there would have been no need to look for such things in the theory of

[8] Miyake, p. 64. [p. 60 of this book]

[9] [Uno, *Principles 1977*, p. 259 ff.]

[10] [Miyake, p. 64. (p. 60 of this book)]

interest, and no cause to consider this phrase "puzzling."[11] That capital is "value in motion" is something even Mr. Miyake has known for a long time, so I don't think this phrase was "puzzling" to him, but if so why he had to pretend not to understand it and then decipher it is indeed "puzzling" to me. What matters is clarifying how this capital as value in motion becomes a commodity.

Mr. Miyake expends great effort interpreting this simple definition of mine, but, perhaps because as I have noted he is pursuing this interpretation in the manner of looking something up in a dictionary, he completely bypasses the crucial issue. For him, perhaps because that is how it is in *Capital*, or because of the influence of what we take as common sense, my definition of loan capital is understood from the start in terms of the contraposition of "functioning capitalists" and "loan capitalists." Of course, it is not that the names "loan capitalists" and "functioning capitalists" cannot be given to those who lend money and those who borrow it and incorporate it into their management of industry, but I believe these two kinds of capitalists cannot be so easily understood in contraposition to one another. It is for precisely this reason that I have started from an explanation of the commercial credit that is implemented within industrial capital and clarified the "transformation of money into loan capital as funds in banks." It seems to me that there are aspects of separating "functioning capitalists" as those who do not own capital and "loan capitalists" as those who loan "capital" to them from the start and holding them in contraposition to each other that obscure the process of formation of loan capital along with its definition.

This point clearly emerges in the next volley of criticism. Regarding my assertion that interest being paid on money that has been loaned occurs "because through these funds the power of capital is advanced, and more surplus value is produced through a certain quantity of his equity capital," Mr. Miyake says this is "extremely doubtful" and dogmatically asserts that this occurs "because the surplus value increased here should be seen as

[11] In a note on page 66 of this essay, Mr. Miyake himself reflects, "If you have an understanding of Professor Uno's way of thinking this can be read without a sense of puzzlement, but surely the feeling of 'getting it' once you know the answer is indeed the mark of a puzzle." [fn. 3 on p. 61 of this book] This inane statement may be a confession that he did not read my writings from the beginning, but what comes next is more interesting. I quote it here for our amusement. "Or some may read it once and immediately observe, 'Professor Uno has misunderstood that point,' but this is not because of the quality of his writing itself." This can indeed only be described as a "puzzling sentence."

what is produced and obtained through the functioning of industrial or commercial capital through the money borrowed, not what is produced through one's equity capital, which is not borrowed from others."[12] One cannot critique what another person has written like this. Rather than say such inane things, he should try to think about why I said, "more surplus value is produced through a certain quantity of his equity capital." For him, it is as though lending to people who possess their own equity capital, whether in large or small amounts and who engage in capitalist business is fundamentally inconceivable. As a result, he cannot understand the meaning of an increase in the rate of profit of equity capital through these loaned funds. What happens, he asks, if the capitalist "is unable to use it [loaned money—trans.] to expand the production of surplus value? In this case, is there no need to pay interest?"[13] He claims I must presumably say that "money is here treated as a commodity that possesses the use value of functioning as capital" and then I, as someone who believes it is money and not capital that becomes a commodity, would place myself "in trouble,"[14] but I am not the least bit troubled. He himself says, "money is treated as a commodity that possesses the use value of functioning as capital," and is it not clear here that under a certain definition money is being bought and sold as a commodity? Indeed, wouldn't it be stranger if we asserted there would be absolutely no instances where "the capitalist tries to increase the production of surplus value but fails" insofar as the money "possesses the use value of functioning as capital"? When capitalist operations in which some amount of equity capital is possessed and managed "try to increase the production of surplus value" with borrowed capital "but fail," interest must be paid from the surplus value produced by equity capital or by converting equity capital into money. This is the case because interest is the price of a purchased commodity. Why should it be that just because this commodity has the "use value of functioning as capital" its price must be paid out of increased surplus value obtained by using the borrowed funds as capital? To say that it "functions as capital" does not mean that it alone "functions as capital" and produces surplus value, but in general capitalists add these borrowed funds to their

[12] Miyake, p. 67. [p. 64 of this book]

[13] Ibid.

[14] Ibid., p. 68. [p. 65 of this book]

own capital and make them "function as capital." Such things should not require explanation.[15]

[15] Regarding the previous quote, Mr. Miyake adds a note suggesting he believes that my reference to the word "direct loan," which I contrast with the concept of "discounting of bills," is some kind of "neologism." [Miyake, pp. 68,9. (p. 62 of this book)] He imagines that this "direct loan" refers both to "the case of receiving a loan from collateral of a commodity or other thing of value" and "the case of receiving a loan without collateral" in contrast to "the case of receiving a loan of funds from discounting bills," but just because I have contrasted the two extremes of these three cases does not mean that the two latter cases are included in a "direct loan." This distinction was originally made by Marx himself—that is not to say that it has to be made by Marx in particular—but a "direct loan" is described as though it were my own "neologism." It is presented as though I made this distinction out of ignorance, but in *Capital*, which presumably Mr. Miyake has read, Marx writes as follows: "The loan is made (we refer here strictly to commercial credit (as Mr. Miyake notes, in this case the original term used by Marx differs from what is normally translated as "commercial credit" [the original German term here is "Handelskredit," not "kommerzieller Kredit," which is usually translated as "commercial credit." See *Marx Engels Werke*, Bd. 25, S. 416. The same word is used in Marx's manuscript. See *Marx Engels Gesamtausgabe* (hereafter MEGA), II-4.2, S. 472])) by discounting bills of exchange—by converting bills of exchange into money before they come due—and by advances of various kinds: direct advances on personal credit, loans against securities, such as interest-bearing paper, government paper, stocks of all sorts, and, notably, overdrafts against bills of lading, DOCK WARRANTS, and other certified titles of ownership of commodities and overdrawing deposits, etc." [MECW, Vol. 37, p. 401] This is also repeated by Engels (see ibid., p.453. [This addition by Engels is in answer to the following question: "To what extent, now, shall the bank's advance to A be regarded as an advance of capital, or as a mere advance of means of payment?" (MECW, Vol. 37, p. 452). It is now known that this question was actually not raised by Marx, but by Engels himself. See fn. 8 in chapter "Theorizing Bank Capital: Neo-Unoist Approach" of this book.]).

His problem seems to lie primarily in the note regarding my assertion that when it comes to "cases of receiving a loan without collateral...for banks such loaning could not be said to originally have an important role." [Uno, *Principles 1977*, p. 469] Complaining that it is not clear what my phrase "banks originally" refers to, he criticizes my assertion that "it has become the norm among banks in Japan's large urban areas to provide more non-collateralized than collateralized loans." What I mean by "banks originally" is clear if you read "(1) Loan Capital (B) The Establishment of the Credit System through Bank Credit" in Chapter 3 "Interest" of my *Principles of Political Economy* And I at least think that we cannot say loans without collateral are important for "banks originally" merely because "it has become the norm among banks in Japan's large urban areas to provide more non-collateralized than collateralized loans." Regarding "commercial paper or bills of exchange," in the chapter entitled "Component Parts of Bank Capital" Marx says that their "discounting constitutes the essential business of the banker." [MECW, Vol. 37, p. 461] For my own part, I thought that understanding the development of bank credit on the basis of commercial credit clarified its essential function, and this being the case

I naturally focused primarily on discounting bills. I find *Capital*'s having placed great emphasis on it as well to be quite natural for the same reason.

I think this kind of misunderstanding would not have occurred if I had explicitly stated that "direct loans" were loans without collateral. More significantly, however, the issue is whether or not to clearly distinguish between banks that are explicated by fundamental theory and the kinds of things that are explicated by what is referred to as "financial theory." I think questions such as what kinds of loans occupy important positions in the actual banking industry and what percentage of total advances they make up, and how this has changed with the development of capitalism, should be explicated by "financial theory." Of course, fundamental theory must also be based on these changes that accompany the development of capitalism, but what is especially important to note is the fact that actual banks display phenomena particular to the recent era of "finance capital" without ever becoming something explained by fundamental theory. This point is the same as with other phenomena, but in all cases essential definitions must be sought in fundamental theory.

Regarding my statement, "it is not without meaning to distinguish between discounting bills and lending, especially in the case of bank management," [Uno, *Principles 1977*, p. 470] Mr. Miyake says, "even from a banker's perspective, while discounting and loans are distinguished in their handling, this mainly arises out of factors such as safety of collection or duration, or the possibility of rediscounting. Also, in some cases—as is often so in Japan—discounting is a method to loan to the person requesting the discounting, where the discounting is usually done while considering that person's credit" and states that distinguishing between the two does not have as much meaning for "those involved in banking" as it does for "credit theory." [Miyake, p. 69. (p. 63 of this book)] But what are we to make of his not considering "factors such as safety of collection or duration" to be significant criteria for making this distinction? According to Mr. Miyake, everything seems to boil down to individual credit, and while I don't know on what that which serves as this credit then depends, and whether banks can manage this, without hearing more details from Mr. Miyake, "who speaks as though he had a profound understanding of banks," it will not do to discard "distinguishing in general between loans without collateral and discounting (on the part of banks.)" [ibid.]. My words quoted here mean nothing more than when it comes to the comparison of discounting and loans, regarding the view in which in the case of discounting capital in the form of commodities is simply converted into capital in the form of money, insofar as discounting also lends funds it does not differ at all from direct loans.

Finally, one last point is that Mr. Miyake says that my having added a note that "this refers to a direct lending in distinction from commercial credit such as discounting bills" [Uno, *Principles 1977*, p. 486] to "money credit" when I quote Marx's assertion, regarding rising interest rates in periods of prosperity, that "those cavaliers [of industry] who work without any reserve capital or without any capital at all and who thus operate completely on a money credit basis begin to appear for the first time in considerable numbers" [MECW, Vol. 37, p. 487] was a misunderstanding of what Marx means by "money credit." This may indeed be a misunderstanding. In the passage I quoted, however, it is "cavaliers of industry" who are "without any capital at all" much

3 ["Value of Capital"]

Next, Mr. Miyake addresses the latter half of the quote cited above: "Therefore, the interest obtained from that lending is not the 'value of capital' but merely a compensation for the use of money during a certain period of time ..."

He begins by saying, "This word would have to be seen as referring to the directly preceding explanation with regard to how money only first functions as capital in the hands of the functional capitalist and that because capital is 'value in motion' it has to be said that the loan capitalist loans money and does not loan capital, but if one were to pose the opinion opposing that of Professor Uno it would be something like the question of why interest can become the value of capital, which makes little sense."[16] He then clarifies that elsewhere in my book the commodification of funds is contraposed with the commodification of capital. Once again, however, is there actually anything that "makes little sense" here? If capital is commodified, then there is nothing to stand in the way of considering interest to be the price of this commodity as the "value of capital." It is thus natural to reject this when capital is not commodified. It is important to note that here too I, unlike Mr. Miyake, do not dichotomously restrict capitalists who borrow funds to being "functioning capitalists." This point not being understood seems to be fundamental.

As is clear from Mr. Miyake's quote, Marx also said, "It is not until capital is money capital that it becomes a commodity, whose capacity for self-expansion has a definite price quoted in every prevailing rate of interest."[17] For Mr. Miyake, however, the problem seems to lie in who has used unreasonable terms such as "value of capital." Here my words "money itself becomes a commodity, but capital does not yet do so.

less "reserve capital" who are being addressed, so I considered it important to grasp direct loans distinct from loans via methods such as discounting bills that have developed on the basis of commercial credit among general industrial capitalists. In this case, saying "commercial credit such as discounting bills" was clearly my mistake. However, what Marx is trying to say in the case of "actual money credit" in the passage quoted by Mr. Miyake cannot be clearly understood as Mr. Miyake portrays it if we read what Marx goes on to say following this quote, beginning with "In discounting bills of exchange the advance is only nominal." [ibid., p. 483] Elsewhere Marx also uses the phrase "speculators, who count on the credit capital of other people." [ibid., p. 493]

16 Miyake, pp. 70,1. [p. 65 of this book]

17 [MECW, Vol. 37, p. 390.]

On this point I differ from Marx's explanation" are said to be "rather astounding."[18] He presses the issue at length, writing, "This 'this point,' judging from the page of *Capital* cited [MECW, Vol. 37, pp. 336,7], can be seen as relating to being a commodity, but if we look at the passage that says interest is not the 'value of capital' but simply the value of money (or funds), and here money itself becomes a commodity and capital does not, Professor Uno having written 'value of capital' was no doubt a result of his having viewed Marx as having asserted this."[19] Mr. Miyake, who is not "astounded" when it is said that capital is a commodity and interest is its price, is flabbergasted when it is said that interest is the "value of capital." Whether capital or money, when either is commodified to speak of either its price or its value is an exaggerated expression. If this point is made clear there is no reason to be so surprised by such terms.

However, as I put the words "value of capital" in quotation marks and later said that they differ from what Marx explains, it appears that Mr. Miyake looked at the page in *Capital* I referenced in relation to the commodification of capital and, having not found the phrase "value of capital" on it, therefore concluded that I had somehow slandered Marx. But it is not the case that the phrase "value of capital" is not used at all in *Capital*, which Mr. Miyake has presumably read. Whether this phrase is used appropriately as Marx's own words is a separate issue, but it cannot be said that it is not used. For example, in Chapter 26 "Accumulation of Money Capital. Its Influence on the Interest Rate" Marx writes as follows in a note addressing the testimony of Lord Overstone: "Value of capital, generally speaking, signifies precisely the rate of interest! … 'Value of capital', as we have shown elsewhere, is never conceived otherwise in theory."[20] Of course, here Marx is taking up Lord Overstone's words, but elsewhere, not only in direct reference to Lord Overstone, Marx also says things like "this depreciation of the money capital"[21] regarding declines in the rate of interest and "value of money capital, i.e., the interest rate."[22] Why is my using the phrase "value of capital,"

[18] [Miyake, p. 72. (p. 66 of this book)]

[19] Miyake, p. 72. [p. 66 of this book]

[20] MECW, Vol. 37, p. 417.

[21] Ibid., p. 501.

[22] Ibid., p. 575.

which Marx himself uses both with and without quotation marks, in relation to Marx "astounding"? As long as capital becomes a commodity, if we are aware of the exaggeratedness of this term as noted above there is nothing wrong with having used it in this way. The issue is whether or not capital becomes a commodity here.

Incidentally, the manner of Mr. Miyake's surprise is perfectly extraordinary. He says the following about the passage just discussed. "However, if one looks at what he is saying here and traces what he has said up to that point, one realizes that far from the sense of surprise being exhausted it is just the beginning. This is because it can only be understood as meaning that he is saying that Marx (!) is insisting on what Professor Uno kept insisting could not be the case."[23] There are many aspects of this passage that are hard to understand, but he seems to think I had gone out of my way to hide my differences from Marx all along and only revealed them at the end, and takes exception to this. As can be seen if one reads the quoted passage, however, I state this in just a few lines. It is Mr. Miyake who makes it a difficult-to-understand "puzzling sentence" and goes on about it at length. The question is whether capital becomes a commodity or not when it comes to loan capital. As is clear in the passages of mine that Mr. Miyake himself has quoted, I understand Marx as "insisting" that "capital ... becomes a commodity," and on this point disagree with him—that is all. There is no reason for surprise.

What Mr. Miyake says surprises him, however, is that since for me the reason capital is not yet a commodity here is "that capital is 'value in motion' and that money itself is not capital,"[24] and that in my view "apparently Marx did not know this, or he must have known it but completely forgotten it when it came to explaining interest-bearing capital."[25] To not only add his own delusions to what he read in another's work, but to go so far as to criticize these writings based on these delusions makes him seem quite full of himself. How can he say things like "apparently Marx did not know" that capital is "value in motion"? I myself learned this from Marx, and in *Principles of Political Economy*, I have repeatedly stated this from the theory of the forms of capital. That my *Principles* were learned from Marx is clearly stated in the foreword,

[23] Miyake, p. 72. [pp. 66,7 of this book]

[24] Ibid., p. 73. [p. 67 of this book]

[25] Ibid.

and at the same time, I also state that there are points on which I cannot follow him. I learned so many things from him that I cannot say of each "I learned this from Marx," but I am not so senile as to have forgotten the source of my understanding. His remarks are beyond inane. And to go so far as to suggest that I thought "[Marx] must have known, but completely forgotten" cannot be seen as anything other than poking fun. Marx examines this point in Chapter 21, as is well-known. I merely said that I could not unreservedly accept his conclusions. For example, when explaining the specific form of the movement of loan capital in contrast to the general definition of the movement of capital, Marx says, "A gives away his money not as money, but as capital. No transformation occurs in the capital. It merely changes hands. Its real transformation into capital does not take place until it is in the hands of B. But for A it becomes capital as soon as he gives it to B. The actual reflux of capital from the processes of production and circulation takes place only for B. But for A the reflux assumes the same form as the alienation. The capital returns from B to A. Giving away, i.e., loaning money for a certain time and receiving it back with interest (surplus value) is the complete form of the movement peculiar to interest-bearing capital as such."[26] In this case, why can't capital be money as funds to A, the lender? Why must the money that is given away or loaned for a certain time itself be handed over from A to B as capital? Is it correct to simply say, "It merely changes hands"? Why must it be said of the relationship between what is money for A becoming capital simply because it is given away and the actual transformation of money into capital only occurring once it is in the hands of B that money is given away as capital? What is wrong with understanding the ownership of the capital itself as remaining with A even here when the money is given away? Why must we say, as Marx does, that regarding A's ownership in relation to this capital he "had never ceased being its legal owner"?[27]

Regarding this point, while Mr. Miyake has presumably read it, in my *Principles* the development of bank credit based on commercial credit is developed with capital still not having completed the externalization of "capital as an automatically interest-bearing force." That is to say that it does not directly develop a relationship in which "loan capitalists" lend

[26] [MECW, Vol. 37, p. 347.]

[27] Ibid., p. 339.

"capital" to "functioning capitalists." I myself acknowledge that on this point I disagree with Marx's explanation. Criticism must be conducted by showing that there is some kind of failing in my own theoretical development.

But Mr. Miyake, who does not understand this point, believes that I mistakenly take Marx to have a "conventional" view of capital in which money is loaned as capital, and declares that I do not understand Marx's fetishism of capital—or if I do understand it do so with "vulgarity."[28] I would like to consider whether or not this is ultimately the case, but first I would like to examine his criticism regarding what I say about "funds."

4 [The So-called "Funds"]

Mr. Miyake makes much of my having used the commonplace term "funds," but it is not as though I too were not aware of the conceptual ambiguity that comes with such an ordinary term. I nevertheless think it can be convenient to use this word, and as long it is not greatly mistaken there is nothing standing in the way of doing so. I even think it can be unexpectedly beneficial. In the same way, vagueness can be said to remain in the case of "currency" as an ordinary term. In actuality, calling the money that is handed over from the lender to the borrower in loan capital simply "money" does not clarify its distinction from money as a means of circulation, nor does calling it "capital" clarify the movement of loan capital itself and thus its relationship of ownership to the lender's capital. Even in the case of loan capital, I do not understand its movement as being capital handed over from A to B. If the lender is viewed as handing over funds to the borrower, then the ownership of the loan capital itself does not move, nor does it constitute handing over as a means of circulation. Is it not acceptable to refer to money that has the "use value of functioning (according to Mr. Miyake's view, precisely speaking I suppose I should say 'possibility of functioning') as capital" as "funds"? It is evident that this itself is neither capital nor something handed over as a means of circulation.

For Mr. Miyake, the problem seems to be that regarding this term "funds" I "generally understand it as referring to what Marx describes as money as such, that is, independent money, separate from the direct

[28] Miyake, pp. 84, 95. [pp. 76 and 84 of this book]

process of circulation and different from money as a means of circulation, that can be put into circulation at any time as something that purchases commodities. In any case, for original hoarded money the fundamental character is that it is withdrawn from circulation, so there are doubts about whether or not this can be considered as funds."[29]

To begin with, regarding my wording Mr. Miyake points out that "can be put into circulation" must be phrased as "in a form that can be put into circulation" and "withdrawn from circulation" must be phrased as "in a form withdrawn from circulation." His corrections seem relevant, but in the case of "funds" what I wanted to say was indeed that this has a slightly more limited meaning than "what Marx called 'money as such.'"[30] What I wanted to express was not simply that it was something in a certain form, but that it was something in a certain form that already had an orientation toward circulation. "Original hoarded money" can be understood as having the opposite orientation while also being "money as such." In both cases, however, as Mr. Miyake points out, "form" is confused with "movement," and this point should indeed be corrected. It is nevertheless difficult to endorse Mr. Miyake's overly formal definition of "hoarded money" when he says that "all money that is a suspension of the metamorphoses of the commodity is in the form of hoarded money."[31] In the case of "original hoarded money," as Mr. Miyake puts it, this is money that has been "stockpiled,"[32] but even if this of course "is characteristically manifested on a pre-capitalist basis,"[33] I do not think this means that regarding "money on a capitalist basis" it must not be "raised."[34]

[29] [Uno, *Principles* 1977, p. 457.]

[30] Regarding my having said "what Marx describes as 'money as such,'" he writes that this "would seem to indicate the content of a letter Marx wrote to Engels, in which he speaks of ... 'c) money as such'" (Miyake, p. 77. [pp. 70,1 of this book]) but there is no need to have conducted such an arduous search for this reference; the phrase in question is often used right there in Part 5 of Volume 3 of *Capital*, the part of the text in question. I am simply referring to this usage. Let me give one or two examples: "The urge to obtain money as such consists always in the wish to convert value from the form of commodities or creditor's claims into the form of money" [MECW, Vol. 37, p. 425]; "What is sought from the owner of a hoard is not capital, but money as such" [ibid., p. 593].

[31] Miyake, p. 75. [p. 68 of this book]

[32] Ibid., p. 76. [p. 70 of this book]

[33] Ibid.

[34] See ibid., p. 77. [p. 70 of this book]

Mr. Miyake seems to understand the hoarding of money only from the perspective of the form in which "the process of hoarding money itself, in which when the continuing supplementation through M—C is stopped the M that is a result of C—M becomes hoarded money, is common to all types of commodity production,"[35] but as Marx put it, "Among the effects of the gold drain, then, the fact that production as social production is not really subject to social control, is strikingly emphasized by the existence of the social form of wealth as a *thing* external to it. The capitalist system of production, in fact, has this feature in common with earlier systems of production, in so far as they are based on trade in commodities and private exchange."[36]

Regarding my having said that money as funds, unlike money as a means of circulation, is produced and consumed and therefore an object of supply and demand to be commodified, Mr. Miyake understands this as holding that funds being produced "through the transformation of C' to M'" in the capital movement process M—C ... P ... C'—M' somehow constitutes the entirety of the production of funds, but if he had continued to read the passage immediately following those he quotes there would have been no room for doubt. "Of course, when it comes to funds that are truly newly produced, these never differ from what corresponds to the portion of surplus value, but the making into funds of money as something separated from the movement of capital is not necessarily limited to this portion of value. These are funds separable from the capital movement process as money."[37] If he had read this passage, the question of money as a means of circulation in the processes of C'—M' and M—C also having to be understood as "produced" and "consumed" like funds would presumably never have arisen. Funds being "produced" is of course not simply money itself being produced and increased. They increase and decrease independently of the amount of money in circulation.

As for why he does not understand that money as something that can be used at any time to buy commodities, or for all manner of payments, arises as something separated from the capital movement process, I have nothing to say. Mr. Miyake asks, "how should we distinguish between the

[35] Ibid.

[36] [MECW, Vol. 37, p. 569.]

[37] Uno, *Principles 1977*, p. 469.

demand for these 'funds' and the demand for the means of purchase, for example?"[38] But when he says, "demand for the means of payment," who exactly has this demand in regard to whom? Interrupting the C—M—C' circulation of commodities at the first stage and using M as a means of payment is merely to assign money drawn from the circulation process as payment. If to do so is to specifically demand money as a means of payment, isn't this nothing other than to borrow money that has in some form been drawn from the circulation process and turned into funds in the hands of other people? For the lender, this is neither the supply of a means of payment nor the supply of capital. It is nothing other than the supply of funds. The problem does not lie in whether money sold as funds is used as a means of payment or serves as capital to purchase the means of production or labor power, as long as repayment is secured. On the contrary, it would be problematic if the likes of demand for a means of payment, demand for capital, or simply demand for a means of circulation were distinguished according to the aims of the demander. Mr. Miyake makes claims such as that the commodification of funds ultimately results in "a fruitless endeavor ... to purchase money with money."[39] I am dismayed by this attitude. I cannot help doubting whether he is worthy of discussing the theory of interest.

5 [Reification and Capital as an Automatically Interest-bearing Force]

The problem is that in what Marx defines as "interest-bearing capital" the development from "loan capital" to what I call "capital as an automatically interest-bearing force" is done in a single stroke. From the fact that in the case of loan capital the reification of capital has not yet occurred, Mr. Miyake concludes that I do not understand the reification of capital. He then asserts that what I call loan capital is "a distorted and trivialized concept of interest-bearing capital,"[40] and asserts that what I call the "commodification of capital" is hardly worthy of being addressed, asking,

[38] Miyake, p. 81 [p. 73 of this book].

[39] Ibid.

[40] Ibid., p. 91. [p. 81 of this book]

"What can one say about the vulgarity of this!?"[41] But is it right to think the issue has been resolved with this hyperbolic expression?

It goes without saying that the reification of capital is completed by capital becoming something that automatically bears interest. Of course, even in industrial capital as such, capital must distribute its surplus value among all capital as something produced not only through variable capital but also constant capital, and not only production capital but also circulation capital, and already has a tendency toward reification, but if this reification does not have a basis, and if this basis is moreover not given by something external, then it cannot be completed. The reason reification is still not complete in the case of loan capital is that while interest constitutes part of surplus value, its rate is given based directly on the supply of and demand for funds. When this relationship uses commercial capital as an intermediary and all kinds of capital are made into loan capital, despite the interest rate being set by loan capital, in general it transforms into something that emerges externally for each instance of individual capital; here everything up to equity capital is uniformly reified as "capital as an automatically interest-bearing force" and thought of as though it were borrowing a part of the total capital of society.

Regarding my having said that the "commodification of capital" is realized through joint-stock companies, Mr. Miyake says, "Literally, *parturiunt montes nascetur ridiculus mus*! Since capital is 'value in motion' direct commodification as motion is impossible, but here there are paper copies and ownership titles of value that are moving, and, to the extent they are sold, these are commodities. ... 'Stock certificates' are indeed paper, and thus 'things'! What can one say about the vulgarity of this making into 'things,' this 'commodification of capital,' that Professor Uno proposes after claiming, in regard to Marx's explanation in which in interest-bearing capital the relationships of production are maximally inverted and capital relationships emerge as a single entity, 'capital is not yet commodified in this case'!?"[42] He seems to have understood my approach as stock certificates simply realizing the making into a "thing" of capital as pieces of "paper." Indeed, "What can one say about the vulgarity" of *this*!? It is as though he has no knowledge of the role being played by the buying and selling of "paper copies and ownership titles"

[41] Ibid., p. 95. [p. 84 of this book]

[42] Ibid.

as "things." Moreover, by merely saying "Literally, *parturiunt montes nascetur ridiculus mus*" without refuting my definition of what can be described as the only way of commodifying capital as value in motion, he cannot be said to have caught the "*mus*." The "*montes*" can only be thought of as having remained "*parturiunt*." Mr. Miyake says, "I have already touched on the lack of 'logic' explaining fictitious capital, created on the basis of the formation of the category of interest-bearing capital, while negating the formation of interest-bearing capital, but be that as it may, what is his point in positing the 'capital' in the 'commodification of capital' that he speaks of thusly as imaginary capital?",[43] and seems to think that asserting that "the formation of the category of interest-bearing capital" is not completed in loan capital is "negating" this formation. This is presumably because he thinks of fictitious capital as "imaginary" capital, but even if the capital itself is "imaginary," the fact that ownership of capital as "value in motion" moves through its being bought and sold is not. Capital emerging as "an automatically interest-bearing force" is "imaginary" from the beginning. It nevertheless cannot be dealt with simply by considering it "imaginary." This is an "imaginariness" that is unavoidable for the capitalist method of production. It is precisely because of this fact that if it takes this form capital itself can be bought and sold as a commodity. Discussing joint-stock companies, Mr. Miyake immediately says, "given this, why exactly does he not include national bonds and the like therein? And why does the 'commodification of capital' not also include company bonds and other interest-bearing certificates? I cannot understand these points"[44] but this is merely the banking industry conception of interest-bearing capital. Just because national and corporate bonds are interest-bearing securities, the question of why their being bought and sold is the transfer of real capital as "value in motion" is one that should be examined.[45] Even as the "value

[43] Ibid. [pp. 84,5 of this book]

[44] Ibid., pp. 95,6. [p. 85 of this book]

[45] Regarding my words, "Along with the development of the joint-stock company system, regarding this capital … a trend toward corporate bonds emerges, but it is not as though it is completely transformed into loan capital," he raises the following question: "Is this a state of affairs in which transformation into loan capital means not being commodified, but since it has not yet been 'completely' transformed into loan capital it is commodified?" (Miyake, p. 92 [p. 82 of this book]) These are the words of someone who is in incapable of understanding the development of theory. The "commodification of capital" not yet being describable in loan capital in no way prevents the right of

in motion" of M . . M', this is merely the movement of loan capital that has already been separated from the movement of real capital. Is it right for these things to be addressed together? "What can one say about" his inability to conceive of such simple things while saying, "I suspect that Professor Uno himself would not be able to explain them"?[46]

The issue lies in my having developed capital as an automatically interest-bearing force out of loan capital through the intermediary of commercial capital, whereas Marx explains interest-bearing capital through loan capital directly. Criticism of my approach boils down to clarifying what sort of gaps exist in this logic. His saying "Professor Uno presents quite convoluted ideas about the relation between the two types of capital," viz. loan capital and commercial capital, "and how to grasp commercial profit, so that even if that part is re-read the crux of his point cannot be fully understood. Moreover, entering into a consideration of this is not directly related to the task of this paper"[47] shows that Mr. Miyake does not even know where the issue is to be found. Whether this is something worthy of such "entering into consideration" to begin with is a separate question. It is nonsense to say that someone who asserts that

claim of an interest-bearing obligation such as a corporate or government bond being fictitiously made into capital on the basis of "capital as an automatically interest-bearing force." Considering these to be the same as stock certificates is impossible, however, even if they are both fictitious capital. In relation to this point, I cannot endorse the language Marx uses regarding national bonds when he says, "The capital itself has been consumed, i.e., expended by the state." [MECW, Vol. 37, p. 462] It is presumably correct to say that to the buyer of national bonds "his capital is invested, from his individual point of view, as interest-bearing capital," [ibid., p. 463] but it goes without saying that money loaned to the state is not itself capital. Mr. Miyake saying "since it [a stock certificate] has not yet been 'completely' transformed into loan capital it is commodified" can only mean that he does not understand the relationship between loan capital and capital as an automatically interest-bearing force. He does not seem to understand stocks that are not loan capital being transformed into loan capital and commodified. The reification of capital is completed when what is not loan capital is transformed into loan capital.

In Mr. Miyake's theory there is no shortage of what can only be described as formal games the point of which is unclear: if I assume funds can generally be described as corresponding to what Marx calls "money as such," he directly replaces the word "funds" with the phrase "money as such" (Miyake, p. 79. [fn. 16 in Chapter 3 of this book]); if I say that loan capital cannot describe the commodification of capital, he then concludes that this means securities cannot become commodities. I wish he would consider these things a bit more carefully—I cannot be expected to answer each and every question of this sort.

[46] Miyake, pp. 95,6. [p. 85 of this book]

[47] Ibid., p. 90. [pp. 80,1 of this book]

so-called "interest-bearing capital" is not fully explained in loan capital does not understand loan capital because interest-bearing capital is not explained in it. I do not by any means cling to my own assertions. If there are errors, I want them to be corrected. I would simply prefer to receive criticism based on a reading less encumbered by preconceptions.

Development After Uno

A Systematic Approach to Marxian Credit Theory Based on the Uno Theory

Shigekatsu Yamaguchi

Marx left several outlines of his "systematic critique of political economy." We can put them into the following table, which could be assumed as summarizing Marx's ideas approximately from 1853 to 1863.

I. Capital

1. Capital in General
   (1) Commodity

Translated by Kei Ehara.
[This essay is first published in Japanese in T. Sakurai, S. Yamaguchi, M. Takumi, and M. Itoh eds., *Economics* (Part I), Tokyo: Yuhikaku Publisher, 1980. The translation is based on S. Yamaguchi, *The Theory of Financial Systems*, Tokyo: The University of Tokyo Press, 1984, pp. 19–47—editor. All additions in the square brackets ([ ]) in this volume are made by the editor (Kei Ehara) unless otherwise noted.]

S. Yamaguchi (✉)
University of Tokyo, Tokyo, Japan

K. Ehara (ed.), *Japanese Discourses on the Marxian Theory of Finance*, Marx, Engels, and Marxisms,
https://doi.org/10.1007/978-3-030-83324-4_5

(2) Money
(3) Capital
(a) The Process of Production of Capital
(b) The Process of Circulation of Capital
(c) The Integration of the Above Two (or Capital and Profit, Interest)
2. Competition
3. Credit
4. Joint-stock Capital

II. Landed Property
III. Wage Labor
IV. The State
V. Foreign Trade
VI. The World Market (and Crisis).

By comparing this plan and the current edition of *Capital*, we find that *Capital* is based on "Capital in General," which has three parts: "The Process of Production of Capital," "The Process of Circulation of Capital," and "The Integration (Profit, Interest)," and that the external items such as "Competition," "Credit," "Joint-stock Capital," "Landed Property," and "Crisis" are added to it. We could therefore conclude that Marx had abandoned the older plan, yet he did not ever admit that he had changed it. In *Capital*, Marx investigates the topics excluded from "Capital in General," but he left many notes saying that he would leave detailed analyses of "Competition" and "Credit" for later books. It seems that the plan was on the way of changing, yet the change was not sufficiently clarified.

The theory of interest is in Part 5, Volume 3 of *Capital*. The manuscript here was not well written and Engels had difficulty editing it. As a result, it is particularly difficult here to know what Marx was thinking about the plan. It appears that he simply combined the manuscript of the theory of interest in "Capital in General" and that of "Credit." A general explanation of interest-bearing capital in Chapters 21–24 is radically different from the explanations in Chapters 25–36, which are dedicated to a study of the credit system. It is very difficult to comprehend how these two parts are related and why Marx put them in this order. Besides, whereas the contents up to Chapter 24 are relatively well arranged, the theory of credit in Chapter 25 thereafter contains a large bulk of rough texts compiled from excerpts of parliamentary documents and fragmentary notes, making it nearly impossible to understand the logic of each chapter and to trace the theoretical connections between chapters.

Kōzō Uno reorganized the theory of interest in *Capital* and presented a new systematic theory in his *Principles of Political Economy* (originally published in 1950 and 1952, then republished in 1977 in the combined version. Hereafter, abbreviated as *Principles 1977*. All quotations are from 1977 edition). We discuss the theoretical significance of Uno's reorganization in the next section. Here, we briefly contrast the two theories and see how the theory of interest in *Capital* was reorganized. The main points are as follows:

1. The theory of interest in *Capital* is placed between the theory of commercial profit in Part 4 and the theory of ground rent in Part 6. Meanwhile, in Uno's theory of distribution [the third and last part of *Principles 1977*], the theory of ground rent is in Chapter 2, just after the theory of profit in Chapter 1, and his theory of interest is in the last chapter, Chapter 3. Also, Uno's theory of commercial profit is included as one section in the theory of interest.
2. As we have noted above, the theory of interest in *Capital* explores two issues: the theory of interest-bearing capital in the former part and the theory of credit in the latter. In Uno's *Principles 1977*, however, the theory of credit is followed by the theory of interest-bearing capital, which presumes the development of the credit system.
3. In *Capital*, the theory of credit is not well presented. In Uno's *Principles 1977*, however, we find the theoretical development from commercial credit to bank credit, which evolves into the centralized issuance of banknotes by a central bank. After covering the establishment of the credit system and the money market, Uno discusses the role of credit in the real process of accumulation of industrial capital, with special attention to the moment of crisis.

4. On the one hand, in Parts 4 and 5 of *Capital*, we find the contents in this order: commercial capital, interest-bearing capital, and the credit system. On the other hand, in Uno's *Principles 1977*, the credit system comes first, followed by commercial capital and capital as an automatically interest-bearing force. The interest-bearing capital in *Capital* is divided into two in Uno's *Principles 1977*: one is the loan capital conceptualized in the theory of credit and the other is the capital as an automatically interest-bearing force that is mediated by the commercial capital.
5. Joint-stock company in *Capital* is just mentioned in "the Role of Credit in Capitalist Production," Chapter 27 of Part 5. Uno studied it in the last part of the theory of interest and its analysis concludes the systematic theory of the principles of political economy.

Why were these reorganizations necessary in Uno's *Principles 1977*? What is their theoretical meaning? In this chapter, we answer these questions in Sect. 1. The last two sections will introduce Uno's theory of credit.

1 Kōzō Uno's Problematics

1.1 The Introduction to the Theory of Interest

The starting point of the development of the theory of interest was the central question of Uno regarding the method of the theory of interest in *Capital*. In developing the theory of interest in Part 5, Marx made the initial assumption that two types of capitalists have completely different roles in the process of social reproduction: the money capitalist who only lends capital, and the functioning capitalist who productively employs the capital borrowed from the former. Here, the same capital makes a dual motion in the hands of two different capitalists: it separates into two aspects, property and function, which are represented, respectively, by the two separate capitalists. The first four chapters in Part 5 are based on this relationship and explain issues like the formation of interest, the division of profit, and the externalization of the relations of capital.

Uno questioned Marx's method and assumed that the starting point of the theory of interest should be the relation of commercial credit mutually developed among individual industrial capitals. The most significant point of the reasons and implications would be that Uno eventually proposed a sort of differentiation and development method. In *Capital*, the relations of money-lending and earning interests are the relations between the property of capital and the function of capital. This method severs the logical connection between loaning and the preceding theory of profit, consequently rendering loan relations abstract and formalistic. If this starting point is taken, the loan relations are assumed to be an external condition of industrial capital, a conflicting relation with industrial capital, as it were. The relation between loaning and industrial capital will not be sufficiently elucidated. Indeed, money loaning historically preceded industrial capital so the latter presumed and utilized the former externally, as it were. However, industrial capital subjugated it as a historical result of winning the struggles with money-lending capital and transformed it into the system as a subordinate condition. Hence, the relation between the two should not be regarded as a simple conflict, but an internal one.

Uno tried to explain this internal relation by taking the method of differentiation. He took as a starting point the commercial credit, which is internally developed as the system for profit augmentation within the process of competition among individual industrial capitals; then the systematic limitations are overcome by the bank credit, in which money-lending relations are established among the industrial capitals, viz. the lenders and borrowers are both industrial capitals. The money-lending relations, which are consummated as the money market system with the bank capital at its core, are generated from the relations inside the industrial capitals. This allows us to understand the systematic relations of the two three-dimensionally and organically, as they in reality coexist with and confront each other. This is the most important theoretical achievement of this method.

Marx describes money-lending and the formation of interest in terms of the relations between the property of capital and the function of capital. Actually, the same description holds not only for money-lending but also for the relations where those who have shares of capital demand the dividend as an income based on the property. Indeed, Marx himself apparently does not always distinguish the two. Since money-lending is a relationship in which the right to use the money for a certain period is transferred to others and the interest is paid as its price, the use value of the money in that period is sold here; hence it could be said that the money is commodified. Nevertheless, this is far from the relation where the capital is commodified. The capital is commodified when the shares of capital are separated from its function and sold, viz. the securities of capital are commodified. However, as Marx maintains at the beginning of his theory of interest that his assumption includes the commodification of capital, the two types of commodification are confused and the commodification of capital as such becomes difficult to conceptualize.

Uno's problematics was to solve these problems in *Capital*: it clearly separated what Marx called the interest-bearing capital into two: the one in the money market and the other in the capital market, focusing on the issues of the former rather than the latter at the beginning of the theory of interest.

1.2 The Fetishism of Capital

The problem at the starting point in *Capital* clouds its analysis of the fetishism of capital. Marx titles Chapter 24 of Part 5 "Externalisation of the Relations of Capital in the Form of Interest-bearing Capital" and argues that the self-valorization is purely achieved in the form of interest-bearing capital and the capital relation is mystified and fetishized. We summarize his explanation as follows.

In Chapter 22, Marx discusses the division of profit in the payment of interest. He then turns to the establishment of new categories in Chapter 23, investigating the transformation of the quantitative division of profit into a qualitative one and studying interest and profit of enterprise. In this process, Marx argues that the establishment of the idea of capitalist fetishism adopts a two-step approach. In the first step, as a functioning capitalist borrows capital and pays interest to a money capitalist, gross profit is qualitatively divided into interest and profit of enterprise, gain from a mere property of capital and gain from functions of capital. In the second step, this qualitative division is applied to the capital owned by those who do not borrow capital from others and use their owned capital, consequently turning the profit of enterprise into wages for supervisory work. In this process, capital relation reaches its most external, most fetishistic form.

Nevertheless, this qualitative division results from the fact that Marx has assumed in the first place the two qualitatively different types of capitalist, a money capitalist representing its property and a functioning capitalist representing its function. This cannot be considered a logical development of the idea of capitalist fetishism. It presupposes the externality of the interest-bearing capital to the actual ground for valorization, failing to analyze the reality of this idea.

Meanwhile, Uno explains the formation of interest in his theory of the money market, which evolves internally from the actual competitive process of accumulation of industrial capital. The issue of capitalist fetishism is separated from that of loans in the money market: it is established by his original concept, capital as an automatically interest-bearing force, which presumes the concepts of loan capital and interest and is mediated by the formation of the idea of entrepreneurial profit based on the capitalist activity of commercial capital. Although Uno's argument is here somewhat ambiguous, his reorganization of Marx's theory of interest intends to reexamine the logic of establishing capitalist fetishism by clearly distinguishing the money market from the capital market and developing the former as the inner relations of industrial capital, thereby solving the problems of the externalization of the relations of capital in *Capital*.

1.3 Conceptualizing the Rate of Interest

As we have seen above, Marx's starting point of the theory of interest raised several questions. This method of Marx is closely related to his understanding of the functions and roles of money loaning. Uno's critique of Marx, therefore, derives from and is grounded on Uno's understanding of money loaning. The difference between Marx and Uno can be observed in their views about the nature and role of the interest rate.

Marx discusses the rate of interest in Chapter 22, insisting that its movement has no law and lacks such a thing like a natural rate that regulates competition, as the rate of interest is determined totally by accident in the midst of competition. According to Marx, this is because it is a purely empirical, accidental matter how the profit generated by capital is allocated to the money capitalist and the functioning capitalist in accordance with the dual aspects of capital. This understanding is evidently based on his method of starting the theory of interest.

Uno attributes Marx's understanding to his view that the category of interest is external to the motion of industrial capital. He believes that it led Marx to the conclusion that the rate of interest is determined exclusively by the two types of competing capitalists. As Uno explains, money loaning represents the externalization of the mutual relations of industrial capital; the supply of and demand for money loaning is determined by the inner logic of the process of social reproduction managed by industrial capital. Thereby Uno tried to discover the law governing the movements of the interest rate. His main arguments are as follows.

The moneylender gains interest as a portion of surplus value on the basis of the fact that the idle money capital, which is necessarily generated within the process of reproduction of capital, is financed to the process of production of other capital and thereby enhances the production of surplus value. The level of interest is not determined by mere relations of supply of and demand for the loan external to the social production of capital. Behind supply and demand, there lies the production of surplus value enhanced by the loan, which governs the relations of lenders and borrowers and consequently determines the rate of interest. In Sect. 2.3, we discuss the necessity of the generation of idle money capital.

1.4 The Roles of Money Loaning to the Capitalist Production

Uno understands the function of money loaning as above and analyzes its fundamental role in capitalist production and the foundation of the regulated movements of the interest rate from the two viewpoints. First, he takes a vantage point of horizontal regulation of capital allocation, as it were. Marx points out at the beginning of Chapter 27, "the Role of Credit in Capitalist Production," "its[the credit system] necessary development to effect the equalisation of the rate of profit, or the movements of this equalisation, upon which the entire capitalist production rests,"[1] yet this chapter does not go into further detail. In Chapter 36, the last chapter of Part 5, Marx argues that the credit system is "an immanent form of the capitalist mode of production" and touches upon this issue. Here he maintains "this social character of capital," such as the ability to appropriate the average profit, "is first promoted and wholly realised through the full development of the credit and banking system,"[2] yet does not go into any detail.

In contrast, Uno discusses this issue in the concluding part of his theory of interest in *Principles 1977*, "Loan Capital as an Intermediary of Profit Rate Equalization":

[1] *Marx Engels Collected Works* (hereafter MECW), Vol. 37, London: Lawrence & Wishart, 2010, pp. 432,3.

[2] Ibid., pp. 601,2.

> Though the competition between capitals mediating profit rate equalization could be regarded in principle as the process of withdrawing capital from the branch of production with a lower rate of profit and investing it to the branch with a higher rate, this is not the exact description. ... In the end, each capital is subject to this tendency, but the tendency must be continuously hampered by newly emerging relations. The idle funds, which are generated from the process of movements of individual capitals, turn into loan capital and mediate the social process that cannot possibly be managed by individual capitals.[3]
>
> The relation of bank credit to industrial capital is to equalize the unevenness, so to speak, of the funds that appears on the surface of the production process of industrial capital to fulfill the demands generated in the activities of industrial capitals seeking for the surplus profit. The industrial capital with additional profit utilizes loan capital and expands its production process. ... Then this results in the direction of equalizing the difference in the profit rate among industrial branches.[4]

Second, there is an analysis of vertical regulation of capital allocation, as it were. Uno maintains that the above equalization of the profit rate of industrial capital is realized in the changes of the rate in the business cycles, in which the profit rate is regulated by the changes in the interest rate; he studies the relation between the two rates in the process of business cycles. Here Uno considers the feature of loan capital as common and social capital for capitalists, which is seemingly independent of and confronted with the entire industrial capital.

It is true that Marx also often mentions the peculiarity of the movements of interest rate in business cycles in some chapters in Part 5 where he examines the relation between money capital and real capital. In Chapter 36, after the abovementioned passage, he writes "banking and credit thus become the most potent means of driving capitalist production beyond its own limits, and one of the most effective vehicles of crises and swindle."[5] Nevertheless, Marx could not clarify the method of considering the accumulation of money capital purely as that within the immanent movements of industrial capital because, in the theory of

[3] *Principles 1977*, p. 492.

[4] Ibid., p. 493.

[5] MECW, Vol. 37, p. 602.

interest, he generally fails to strictly employ the method of pure capitalism as adopted in the theory of profit and that of ground rent. As a result, Marx ends up with regarding the character of loan capital clashing with industrial capital as that of mundane external conflicts seen in historical events.

Regarding this issue, Uno states:

> Although Marx recognized in *Capital* the relationship between the changes of interest rate and the business cycles, he failed to grasp its inner relation because he generally took loan capital as money held by money capitalists outside the reproduction process. As a result, Marx failed to clarify the roles of interest rate in the outbreak of the crisis. This also prevented him from completing the theory of crisis. The fundamental problem was that the theory of interest ... was not based on the assumption of pure capitalist society.[6]

Uno's opinion was that the theory of interest should be included among the topics of the principles of political economy, the object of which would be the pure capitalist society, and that the methodology of the theory of interest must be determined accordingly. Uno then studied loan capital as externalized from the immanent relations of industrial capitals themselves and clarified the fundamental relation between the interest rate and the profit rate. This methodology finally has defined the term of the absolute surplus of capital, where the excessive accumulation of capital induces wage increases and decreases in the general rate of profit, while causing the interest rate to surge. The relations immanent in the accumulation of industrial capital are thus externalized as social regulation. Based on this mechanism, the necessity of credit crisis is proved at the level of the principles of political economy. Here, we highlight the theoretical significance of this methodology.[7]

[6] K. Uno, *The Methodology of Economics*, Tokyo: The University of Tokyo Press, 1962, p. 284.

[7] For detailed explanations of Uno's problematics, see K. Uno, *The Study of the Principles of Marxian Political Economy*, Tokyo: Iwanami-Shoten, 1959, Part 4.

2 Industrial Capital and Credit System

We have reviewed the theoretical significance of Uno's theory of interest in comparison with that in *Capital*. We now examine the details of Uno's theory of credit, which is the starting point of his theory of interest and is at the same time systematically arranged as the main issue therein.

2.1 Saving Costs of Circulation

As discussed above, Uno saw commercial credit as fundamental to bank credit. In other words, he considered bank credit as the developed relation of commercial credit. By making commercial credit the starting point of the theory of interest, Uno established the method of developing the money market or the relation of so-called loan capital as the system inherent in industrial capital. In what sense, then, can the money market or loan capital be regarded as the immanent system of industrial capital? How is the theory of interest connected systematically with the preceding sphere, the theory of profit?

Uno answers these questions by explaining that the credit system, or the money market, is saving the costs of circulation of industrial capital, especially the circulation capital. Commercial credit is regarded as the most fundamental system of the money market while the bank credit is more developed.

In *Capital*, we can certainly find passages in which the saving of circulation costs is described as one of the roles of the credit system. For instance, in Chapter 27, Marx enumerates the roles of credit system under "Reduction of the Costs of Circulation": saving money, accelerating currency or reducing circulation period, promoting turnover, and reducing reserve funds or idle money capital.[8] Other chapters explain these issues, though in rudimentary forms. Nonetheless, Marx does not seem to have a particular theoretical interest in the point that the credit system is immanent in industrial capital, thus he is not concerned with the theoretical significance from this point of view.

Meanwhile, it is not accurate to assert that *Capital* makes no reference to the relation between commercial and bank credit, the former being fundamental to the latter. The example is the beginning of Chapter 25: "Just as these mutual advances of producers and merchants make up the

[8] MECW, Vol. 37, p. 433.

real foundation of credit, so does the instrument of their circulation, the bill of exchange, form the basis of credit money proper, of banknotes, etc."[9] However, even if we read this chapter, or all of Part 5, we cannot determine what "the basis" exactly means. In Chapter 30, while Marx writes that commercial credit "forms the basis of the credit system," he maintains in the nearby sentence that bank credit "constitutes an entirely different sphere."[10] Marx was far from considering the problem of how commercial credit plays the role in saving circulation costs and becomes the basis of the credit system.

2.2 Complementing the Theory of Profit

Uno considered the credit system as the saving system of circulation costs, especially of circulation capital, and took the commercial credit as fundamental, thereby developing the theory of credit by a method of differentiation. This development could be seen as the internal logic of capitalist production in the following two senses.

First, his theory of credit complements the preceding theory of profit by taking up the relation between the moments in the circulation process and the competition. This problem is not yet explored in the theory of profit, where a general concept of competition is introduced. Although it goes without saying that the circulation process is indispensable for the valorization of industrial capital, the circulation process is a restriction on valorization in a sense, for industrial capital has the production process with the fixed part of invested capital inside its motion. Since the moments in the circulation process, such as the circulation period, the purchase price of the means of production, and the selling price of the products, are subject to indeterminate fluctuations, a certain amount of the reserve capital is necessary to maintain the continual production of some scale. At the same time, it has a negative effect on the profit rate. Another problem is that the needed amount of the reserve capital is indeterminate and constantly changing. As a result, in the motion of a certain amount of capital, idle money capital arises in some cases, or a shortage of the reserve capital when one tries to minimize the idle capital in others, leading to other problems such as a change in the scale of

[9] Ibid., pp. 397,8.

[10] Ibid., p. 478.

production and the idle fixed equipment. Industrial capital therefore has an incentive to remove this restriction on the valorization in some way and thereby increase its rate of profit. Hence, the study of the activities with that purpose must follow the theory of profit, which concentrates on a general concept of profit without taking them into account. The credit system, along with commercial capital, is developed as the system of lifting the restriction of the circulation process. Both are necessary and function to save circulation costs amidst the activities of profit rate augmentation of individual industrial capitals. The development results in, as an unintended consequence, the function of intermediary of profit rate equalization as depicted above. In this sense, the theory of interest has an inner relation to the theory of profit, but this is not the only meaning of developing the internal logic of capitalist production.

2.3 Idle Money Capital

As we have seen above, the demand for saving the circulation cost originates in the motion of industrial capital. In addition, Uno explains that the condition of the relations of credit meeting this demand rests in the inevitable generation of idle money capital inside the motion of industrial capital. This is the second reason that credit relations are intrinsic to capitalist production.

Part 2 of *Capital* Vol. 2, "The Process of Circulation of Capital," is "The Turnover of Capital," where Marx discusses idle money capital generated by various reasons. He also mentions in some passages that idle money capital is the basis of the credit system. Uno's basic idea in his theory of credit discussed above actually derives from these passages in *Capital* Vol. 2.

There are three main sources of idle money for this credit system.

1. Idle money capital generated in the turnover process of circulating capital, when (i) the money in bulk must be separately invested; or (ii) the investment must be large while the money inflow is sporadic; or (iii) the reserve money is needed to maintain some scale of production as the circulation period and commodity prices are constantly and indeterminately fluctuating.
2. The depreciated fixed capital that returns in money form and accumulated for the replacement.

3. The accumulated portion of profit in money form that has not yet reached the appropriate amount, or that waits for the appropriate time, to be invested.

The idleness of money for these reasons is, on the one hand, an inevitable cost in that it must arise in the motion of industrial capital. At the same time, it is in an idle state because it can be separated from the motion of industrial capital itself during the period of accumulation and be temporarily used for other purposes. When the use value of the idle money, or its monetary function, can be freely exercised during a certain period, the money is called idle funds (*shikin*). Industrial capital has a motivation for effectively diverting this idle money, if possible, to other temporary purposes and making it contribute to the rise of profit rate.

However, if there were no such stagnation of capital in a money form, the scale of production under the given amount of capital would be larger. It would lead to an increase in the number of products and transactions, hence the rise in the rate of profit. In this sense, stagnant money represents the idleness of capital. Industrial capital therefore wants to eliminate it and minimize the idle money as much as possible, yet too much saving would create the shortage of the reserve and the resultant reduction in the production, as we have noted above, since the necessary amount of reserve is indeterminate. Provided one could get short-term financing in some way when faced with a temporary shortage, the reserves could be reduced to the least amount and the rate of profit could be raised. This creates a demand for temporary finance from other capitals.

Therefore, on the one hand, industrial capital reduces the idle money capital as much as possible and compensates for the resultant shortage of the reserves by obtaining financing from others. On the other hand, there remains the idle money capital inevitably in the process of its motion as the surplus reserves, as it were, which are financed to others in seeking for higher profitability as possible. Each capital thus finances and uses idle money with each other under its circumstances, which are innate in the motion of the capital itself. Stimulated by the descriptions in *Capital* Vol. 2, Uno theoretically developed the credit system as the intermediary of this mutual finance of idle money between industrial capitals themselves.

3 The Basic Structure of the Credit System

3.1 Commercial Credit

As we have argued, the capitalist form of money loaning could be developed as a mutual relation of loaning between industrial capitals, not as an external relation to industrial capital. According to Uno, this development is the appropriate way to study it in the principles of political economy, viz. to theorize it. Since commercial credit is posited as a starting point of the theory of credit systems as such, Uno takes commercial credit as the embryonic or fundamental form of mutual finance of idle money. Marx defines commercial credit as "the credit which the capitalists engaged in reproduction give to one another"[11] and Uno also sees it as a "mutual help relationship, as it were, between industrial capitals who finance various idle funds to one another."[12] To Uno, the entire system of credit, or the capitalist relations of loaning money themselves, is regarded as this "mutual help relationship" beginning with commercial credit.

Then, how is the commercial credit conceptualized in Uno's theory of credit? Uno cites an example of Marx, the trade relations among three capitals—the weaver capital, the spinner capital, and the cotton planter capital—illustrating the basis, the advantages, and the limitation of commercial credit.

First, in terms of the basis of commercial credit, Uno maintains that on the side of the seller, capital must be held as commodity or money for a certain period; in other words, a product as a commodity must be turned into money in a certain period and the money must be spent to purchase the means of production at another time. Uno considers it as the basis of the seller being able to sell his/her product to other capitalists with the payment deferred, viz. to give credit to other industrial capitals. On the side of the buyer, Uno states that this relationship is based on the prospect of the product of buyer's capital being turned into a certain amount of money by a certain time.[13]

Second, Uno explains the advantages or the meanings of this relation by raising the following points. This credit relation makes buyer's capital finance the additional capital of the seller. Meanwhile, the seller succeeds

[11] Ibid.

[12] *Principles 1977*, p. 465.

[13] Ibid., pp. 461,2.

in selling his/her commodity that would not be purchased immediately in cash. The buyer can save some of the circulation capital thanks to the funds of the seller and maintain production, while turning circulation capital into production capital, which would be needed if the funds were not financed through the credit. This saving of circulation capital allows expansion of the production process under a given amount of capital.

Lastly, as saving by means of commercial credit is not widely available, Uno points out the limitation of commercial credit. Firstly, the money has to be paid as wages for labor and the portion of surplus value that corresponds to the individual consumption of capitalists. Drafts cannot replace money in these payments. Secondly, the amount and/or usance of the bill of the seller do not always fit the amount and/or period of credit given by the buyer. These conditions are determined by the individual circumstances of the reproduction process. Consequently, while some trades are conducted by commercial credit, others must be done in cash. Thirdly, not all the exchange relations can be formed by the credit, as commercial credit is based on the mutual social relationship between the reproduction processes of capitals invested in various productions. Fourthly, the credit relation individually and partly replaces the organic relation of the social reproduction process of capitals subject to price fluctuations. Hence it cannot help being a passive moment restrained in the social relation of the entire economy. As a result, credit transactions become impossible or unnecessary in some phases of business cycles.[14]

It should be noted here that the idle money in the hands of industrial capital who gives credit is not directly financed to the industrial capital who will be a debtor, though the commercial credit is a basic form of the mutual relation of idle funds between industrial capitals. Let us go into the details of this point to capture the essence of credit.

The example is as follows: the weaver capital, B, purchases cotton yarn from the spinner capital, A, by draft, issuing a promissory note of £100 with a usance of three months. When this commercial credit relation is formed, the buyer, B, can save the reserves of money capital, or the addition of it, that are necessary for maintaining, or expanding, the production process. This relation presumes that the seller, A, has the reserves of money capital, say £40, that are necessary for maintaining three months of production without selling the yarn by cash for now, which means that

[14] Ibid., pp. 464,5.

the cash sale would result in the surplus reserves that would otherwise be left idle. In this example, A successfully sells his/her product on credit, which B could not buy in cash, yet it is not necessarily true that A would not be able to sell to any other capitals in cash. A's product would be bought for £80 in cash by B' or B'', yet A chooses credit sales to B.

This credit relationship thus allows the seller, A, to sell by draft and earn £100 of money in three months instead of selling the product for £80 in cash and leaving the money idle. Meanwhile, the buyer, B, gets £80 of additional purchasing power financed by this relation and pays £100 after three months. This relation is similar to the one in which the money is lent and repaid with the interest. However, it is by no means formed by the direct finance of money that is left temporarily idle. A chooses £100 that B gets in future and will be paid to A, rather than £80 that would be idle in cash sales, on the basis of the allowance of reserve capital of £40. The £100 become additional purchasing power for B. The essence of the credit relation is that future money functions as the current additional purchasing power. It should be borne in mind that the mutual finance of idle money does not mean the direct finance of the existing idle money of £40 in the above illustration.

3.2 *Bank Credit*

We will now take a look at how Uno elucidates bank credit.

Commercial credit has the abovementioned limitations, which certainly restrict the purchasing power and circulation of the drafts. Commercial credit is the general foundation of credit money. In the aforementioned example, the spinner, A, is sometimes able to purchase raw cotton from the cotton planter, C, by the note received from the weaver, B. Nevertheless, this note is not money that circulates generally. Uno maintains that the scope and period of circulation of the drafts are limited by the credit founded on the relations of reproduction of individual industrial capitalists. Both the creditors and debtors are, according to Uno, fettered by the property of commodities and their individual circumstances. These restrictions on commercial credit are removed by the development of bank credit. Uno explains the bank credit from the relations of financing the funds to A for purchasing cotton from C by what is called the discount, in which the bank buys the note issued in the commercial credit between A and B with a certain amount of interest charged. The commercial credit between industrial capitals is thus replaced by the bank credit between the bank and industrial capital and thereby the limitations of the former are overcome.[15]

Uno's explanation of this bank credit consists of two steps. In the first step, the idle funds of each industrial capital are collected into the bank. When the credit is grounded upon these collected funds, according to Uno, the bank credit removes the limitations of commercial credit. Here the bank functions as a common vault for many industrial capitals, as it were. The collection of idle funds allows the bank to replace the commercial credit that each industrial capital has given to the others. The bank is regarded as an intermediary, as it were. The individual circumstances of industrial capital average out, as it were, through the bank, thereby transformed into the general relations of capitalist society. This is the significance of bank credit in Uno's formulation.

In the second step, the bank not only directly finances the idle funds of industrial capital collected in the bank but can also discount the commercial notes of individual industrial capitalists by issuing the banknotes promising ready payments based on the funds. The spinner, A, could purchase raw cotton by handing to C the commercial note that was issued when A sold the cotton yarn. This note is now replaced by the banknote, a kind of bill of the bank. Uno considers that this relation arises on the basis of the social collection of idle funds of individual industrial capital in the first step and that the banknote circulates as general credit money because it is based on the idle funds socially collected from industrial capital.

In sum, Uno regards the practical significance of bank credit as its function of collection and distribution of funds of industrial capital that are laid idle in various periods. This elucidation consists of the above two steps. Uno certainly mentions that the bank is not to lend the idle funds of industrial capital as such but is to lend funds of its own: in the second step, particularly, the bank is supposed to issue its banknotes, the idle funds of industrial capital taken as the reserves. Even here, however, Uno emphasizes that the banknotes are not issued arbitrarily since the issuance must reflect the social relations of the reproduction process of individual industrial capitals.[16]

[15] Ibid., p. 467.

[16] Ibid., pp. 468,9.

In Uno's elucidation, the bank loan has its limitations since it is just the relation financing idle funds; the relation between deposits and loans must not be neglected; the request for conversion restricts the issuance of banknotes as the banknotes are the sight bills promising ready payment of money. In addition, we must notice the following third point in Uno's formulation. As the banknotes are loaned, "the loan must be repaid. One who has consumed the funds loaned, viz. who has purchased a commodity by spending them in the circulation process, must make a repayment by the funds newly gained from the circulation through the sales of commodities."[17] Regardless of methods of loan (e.g., bill discounting, collateral loan, and non-collateral loan), "all repayments to the loan of funds must be made by the funds newly raised through the process of reproduction of capital."[18] Hence the issuance of banknotes is fundamentally restricted by the relations of the new formation and the reflux of payment of the funds. This is the third point. Here the essential aspect of credit is clear: the credit is to create current purchasing power in expectation of future payment, or reflux of money. Though Uno's theory of bank credit basically illustrates the mediated relation of loaning money, at the same time, it touches upon the aspect of credit creation in the sense that the purchasing power is formed in the bank credit.

3.3 Central Banking

Uno asserts that the bank credit transforms commercial credit into the general relation in capitalist society, hence banking is essentially social in a capitalist sense. This is of course not to say that capitalist society has only one bank. Many banks compete with each other as private capitals, developing complicated transactions amid this competition. The result is the formation of the bank of banks.

We assume that Uno was the first to try to theorize this problem of banking organization and central banking. Uno's illustration includes the following points.[19]

[17] Ibid., p. 469.

[18] Ibid.

[19] Ibid., p. 477.

1. The supply of and demand for the funds between individual industrial capitals differ widely in industrial branches, in regions, and in seasons. The banks constantly conduct transactions with other banks in order to maintain the balance of supply and demand. In the meantime, the bank in the central city will perform a maintenance role.
2. At the same time, banks commonly make transactions with the bank in the center (or in the central city) and use its banknotes to settle the transactions. The reserve funds of each bank will be accumulated in this central bank. Just as the commercial notes are replaced with the bills of the banks (i.e., the banknotes), individual banknotes are replaced with the central banknotes. From the viewpoints of these banks, the central banknote occupies the position of the money.
3. At the same time, the so-called credit on the book using a deposit account serves as a replacement for issuing banknotes. Each industrial capital who gets funds in its deposit account from the bank makes every payment by check. When a drawee deposits the check in another bank, the settlement is made by the exchange between the banks. This exchange is made with the central banknotes or the deposits in the central bank.
4. As the issuance of the banknote is centralized, the bank centering on the issuance becomes what Marx called "a peculiar mixture,"[20] a quasi-public enterprise. The banknote now occupies the important position of the means of circulation and payment. The gold is accumulated as the reserves of the central bank and the circulation of gold money almost disappears.

The point 1 is maintaining that the idle funds in some branches or in some regions are deposited in the banks in other branches or regions where the demand for the funds is strong and thus utilized there and that the central bank is to control and regulate this relation. In the point 2, though somewhat in an unclear way, it is noticed that the reserve funds for interbank transactions are deposited in the central bank and the central banknotes are issued on that basis. The point 3 pertains to the loan in the deposit account and the circulation of so-called deposit currency and check, which undermine the meanings of issuing banknotes of individual

[20] MECW, Vol. 37, p. 401.

banks. While the first three points are in relation to the central bank as the bank of banks, the point 4 concerns the central bank as the one that centralizes and monopolizes the issue of banknotes.

Though Uno gave all issues that should be discussed in the theory of central banking, neither the developmental order nor the contents were well arranged theoretically. The point 4, the problem of monopolized issuance, is particularly difficult: it is a methodological question whether it can be logically proved or not. Also, in the theory of banking organization, we cannot yet settle the dispute about whether we can find out the ranking among the banks, especially the fixed one, in the sphere of the principles. Hence we here refrain from going into the details of the above issues of central banking, yet the following point should be kept in mind.

Uno's basic understanding is that the central bank mediates the mutual finance or loaning of ready money between individual banks. Also, when he considers that the central banknotes and the deposits of individual banks to the central bank are used to settle the transactions between banks, it is regarded as a somewhat technical problem of saving money in clearing balance between banks in the payments of various banknotes and checks. However, clearing balance changes the amount of reserves in individual banks, consequently forcing banks with a deteriorating rate of reserves to form credit relations with the central bank. In other words, when the balance in credit-debt relations is cleared, the central bank as the bank of banks is required to finance banks that are short of the funds for the settlement by rediscounting their bills. In this process, the central bank offers credits by issuing its banknotes or creating deposits, which are used for the settlements between banks. Therefore, the central bank is not just receiving surplus funds on the one hand and sending them to the other: it is creating the current funds in expectation of future formation of funds, thereby regulating the supply of and the demand for the funds between banks. This point must not be overlooked concerning the bank of banks.

3.4 Credit Creation

It has recently become common practice among Marxian economists to use the term "credit creation" even in academic writing. Yet scholars understand the term in different ways: the theoretical definition remains to be provided. Generally, however, it means creating debts as purchasing power without reserves. The credit creation of this meaning is usually regarded as one of the banking activities: the increase in loans by issuing debts of the bank (banknotes and deposits) exceeding the amount of the reserves of ready money (or, in some cases, primary deposits). This is considered as unique to the bank credit, thus scholars have seldom studied the inner relation to the commercial credit.

When this credit creation is discussed, people seem to think it important how much the loans exceed the reserves: it is not considered as the credit creation when the deposited cash is sent for loans with some part left as the reserves, nor is it when the deposited cash is all left as the reserves and the corresponding amount of banknotes are issued for loans; the credit is created in this common understanding only when the bank issues its debts for loans exceeding the deposited cash all left as the reserves. However, even in the former cases, some of the deposits or the debts of the bank have no reserves. Meanwhile, the creation of banknotes and deposits exceeding the reserves in the latter case is the result of the loans by discounting bills, etc. These debts are certainly not backed by the cash reserves, but by the claims of the bank. The debts turn into purchasing power based on the repayment of loans by a certain period. The essence of the term "creation" lies, therefore, not in the formalistic and ambiguous point that the credit exceeds the reserves, but in the practical function of creating the current funds in expectation of future formation of funds in the background.

In this essential meaning, credit creation could be observed even in the relation of commercial credit, thereby we could clarify the inner relation to the commercial credit. The bank credit replaces the commercial credit so that the former removes the limitation of credit creation in the latter. In this sense, commercial credit is regarded as the fundamental form of credit creation. Rather, the commercial credit is a direct way of credit creation in expectation of future formation of funds, while the bank credit is an indirect way, as it appears to be directly supported by the reserves but is essentially backed by the future expectation. This might be why people have understood that the meaning of credit creation is that the credit exceeds the reserves.

We have studied in the above that Uno clarified the character of credit system or money loaning as the system innate in capitalist production and considered it as the topic in the principles of political economy. The internal character of the credit system for Uno means that it is a mutual financing relation of idle funds necessarily generated within the motion of industrial capital. Indeed, Uno's theory of bank credit actually includes credit creation, but the main function is deemed as an intermediate of money loaning. However, describing the credit system as the internal one does not necessarily follow that it must theoretically be regarded as mediating money loaning. Also, credit creation is not a moment that is totally separate from and essentially independent of commercial credit. It is certainly possible to theoretically discuss the creation of the current purchasing power in expectation of future formation of funds within the system intrinsic to capitalist reproduction. It would be natural to consider this aspect as the essence of credit if the commercial credit is set as a starting point. Uno's development was epoch-making in Marxian credit theory; now we must advance its unique theory of credit creation as discussed above.

Bank Capital and Credit System

Masashi Shimizu

As recent studies on this topic have stated, the importance of bank credit is rooted not in its deposit-based lending function for the purchase and sale of existing funds, but in its debt-based lending ability to create additional purchasing power in the present by anticipating the formation of future funds. Also, this anticipation of future funds formation is regarded as the credit creation function of an increasingly sophisticated credit system that extends from commercial to bank-based lending. Accordingly, the substantive grounds for calculating bank debt liquidity no longer require on-hand cash currency holdings to equal reserves, but are now based on the certainty of future return payments and the soundness of current bank assets. Nonetheless, even in the above view—which can be referred to as the "*credit creation theory*"—the importance of reserves is not completely disavowed. Conversion reserves and refund reserves continue to be significant, because there is invariably a risk of payments being claimed in excess of the possible return of funds in a bank capital

M. Shimizu (✉)
Senshu University, Tokyo, Japan
e-mail: mshimizu@isc.senshu-u.ac.jp

K. Ehara (ed.), *Japanese Discourses on the Marxian Theory of Finance*, Marx, Engels, and Marxisms,
https://doi.org/10.1007/978-3-030-83324-4_6

that functions primarily to enable credit creation rather than to allocate funds. Some argue that this fact was first made clear by the *credit creation theory* itself. Because the actual basis for bank debt circulation is not cash reserves but uncertain future return payments, the only choice is to insist upon the existence of reserves as a supplement to payments to provide a formal basis for circulation.[1]

However, the above argument does present some problems. The first is that this argument is premised on an unreasonable view of the banker's equity capital. Much of the *credit creation theory* is based on the promise of future general acceptability, so it advocates for the issuance of banknotes as if it were possible *without* the initial reserves. This kind of issuance business gives rise to the pre-clearance of loans that should not have been cleared, resulting in the subsequent stagnation of return payments and the decrease in bank's receiving power and ultimately advocates for the existence of the reserves that were actually essential from the start. In this case, even if the banker has no equity capital other than the "circulation costs associated with credit,"[2] such as issuance costs, does this not lend itself to the lingering idea that solid banking operations based solely on ascertaining the amount of credit issuable without the currency losing its acceptability should be possible? If it is impossible to start an issuance business without a mechanism in place to stabilize the lender's receiving power, even when there are fluctuations in the bad debt rate, then the reserves that provide this buffering function should be considered essential bank capital assets from the beginning. The second and perhaps more important problem is that *credit creation theory* might possibly lead to a one-sided understanding of the essential function of the reserves. If the reserve requirements of bank capital are emphasized only from the perspective of providing for future claims, this would seem to deemphasize the importance of the valorization function of the main body of bank capital.

The aforementioned problems do not arise only in the bank capital theory, which may be called the first half of the foundation of the bank credit theory. Even in conventional credit theory research discusses the

[1] S. Yamaguchi, *The Theory of Financial Systems*, Tokyo: The University of Tokyo Press, 1984, p. 46, etc.

[2] H. Hidaka, *Commercial Credit and Bank Credit*, Tokyo: Aoki Shoten, 1966, p. 155.

inevitability of interest-bearing deposit institutions and interbank organizations functioning as a mechanism for reinforcing individual bank reserves and adjusting excessive or deficient reserves between multiple banks. Accordingly, the question of how best to understand the reserve function gives rise to the second half of the bank credit theory, which concerns the relationship between the bank capital and the money market. If we expand upon this point, it calls into question the relationship between the bank capital and the market systems other than the money market, although this goes beyond the scope of the basic bank credit theory in its narrowest sense.

1 Bank Capital and Reserves

One of the more well-known issues in the research on the subject of credit is the problem of defining bank capital (*Bankkapital*) as distinct from the bank credit and the loan capital (*Leihkapital*). This has given rise to debate regarding whether the bank capital should be considered "simply an empty point for the accumulation of social funds"[3] and if it can possibly exist in the absence of equity. This debate has become intertwined with fundamental conflicts at the foundation of the credit theory research, such as whether to emphasize the funds-mediating function or its credit-creating function regarding the bank capital. At the same time, however, attention has been primarily focused on the existence of bank capital as a form of individual capital, which has naturally brought to light the question of what are components of banker's equity capital, which is, as it were, the ontology of bank capital.

This paper takes the following position on the ontology of bank capital. Simply put, as a component of banker's equity capital, reserves are more difficult to ignore than the circulation costs associated with credit. This does not necessarily mean that the ratio of banker's equity capital to total reserves must be larger than the ratio of borrowed capital. These two ratios are in constant flux and reflect the profit rate of the bank and the in-bank retention rate of deposits at any given time. Moreover, mobilizing greater amounts of borrowed capital and allocating it to the reserves to expand credit activities should be considered an appropriate way for a bank to leverage its capital to increase its profit rate. Even so, some

[3] Ibid, p. 134.

portion of the reserves must certainly be invested as equity capital. This portion not only takes on the external reserve function of providing for future claims, but more importantly, it also serves the internal reserve function of providing a means for offsetting shortfalls in bank assets that might be caused by future bad debts. This internal preparatory function has a unique significance that cannot be replaced by the circulation costs associated with credit, because the past and present credit research is nullified by future bad debts.

In order to justify the above conclusions, we must consider two questions: why is the existence of the current reserves indispensable for bank capital? and why should a portion of the bank capital reserves be invested as equity capital? The first of these questions has already been definitively answered in the extant credit theory research; this is what was previously referred to as *credit creation theory*. Partial credit losses are unavoidable, even with thorough credit research, so bank capital must therefore carry the burden of risk of payment claims exceeding return payments, which, taken together, means that certain levels of reserves must continuously be secured. This requirement to maintain certain level of reserves is a feature of bank capital, which is especially emphasized by *credit creation theory*. Bank capital should remain keenly aware that the risk associated with future debt fulfillment is combined with the risk associated with the related debt collection, because bank capital relies on future return payments rather than the current cash reserves. The integration of these two types of risk is a special phenomenon that is unique to the bank capital and is not characteristic of money-lending capital, i.e., the capital who lends cash as it is. This means that, for the bank capital to bear the combined burden of these two types of risk, the reserves are especially essential. This can be considered the main reason for the existence of bank capital holding the reserves, a fact that was first clarified by *credit creation theory*.

Meanwhile, the "deposit-oriented view" highlights the significance of the reserves, while at the same time pointing out that they are not equity capital that is held as reserves by the banker, but rather borrowed capital that remains in the bank.[4] In this case, bankers' equity capital is invested in the circulation costs associated with credit (such as credit research, debt

[4] Deposit-oriented *credit creation theories* include those of Hiroshi Hidaka, *Theory of Bank Capital*, Tokyo: The University of Tokyo Press, 1968; Tsutomu Ouchi, *Credit and Bank Capital*, Tokyo: The University of Tokyo Press, 1978; and others.

collection, and bookkeeping costs specific to its credit business) or its general money handling costs, which cannot be regarded as specific to any particular credit, or both.[5] Of course, the capital used to lend equity capital as well as the portion of equity capital invested in the reserve funds and used to operate the issuance business does not exist from the perspective of the bank capital, which is a hallmark of pre-modern (*zenki-teki*) money-lending capital. This perspective appears to be gaining widespread support today. Therefore, we must examine the validity of such a deposit-oriented theory in relation to the second of the above two questions, especially given the fact that it demonstrates the ontology of bank capital.

We examine the issue in the following context. Put simply, how effective is the distinction between whether or not to invest equity capital for reserves as an indicator of the difference between the bank capital and the money-lending capital? First of all, the money-lending capital itself is not necessarily intended only for simple cash lending that uses equity capital as a source of funds, as has been previously assumed. Many theorists have pointed out that the managing banks of clearing houses, pre-modern money-lending capitals, and money-dealing capitals (such as money changers and goldsmiths) accepted a certain amount of deposits and issued their own self-addressed debts.[6] In addition, bank capital is often forced to reduce its total amount of cash lending in order to use part of the circulation costs associated with credit as reserves when the idle funds from the commodity market dry up, or when the in-bank retention rate of deposits and the in-market retention rate of banknotes deteriorate. However, this should not cause the bank capital to suddenly fall to the

[5] The three positions listed here are held by, in order, Hidaka, *Bank Capital*; I. Okamoto, *Currency and Credit*, Tokyo: Toyo Keizai Shinpo Sha, 1973; and Ouchi, *Credit and Bank Capital*. Kōzō Uno also stated, "Bank capital is not only used for the buildings, equipment, and labor costs necessary for bank management, but also forms part of the reserve." (*Economics Seminar/The Principles of Political Economy*, Tokyo: Seirin Shoin, 1955, p. 427).

[6] I. Kawai, *Capital and Credit*, Tokyo: Yuhikaku, 1954, p. 74; E. Ono, "Financial Functions," in E. Ono et al. eds., *Theory of Contemporary Finance*, Tokyo: Jichousha, 1971, pp. 46,7; K. Fumoto, *The Theory of Financial Economy*, Tokyo: Nippon Hyouron Shinsha, 1956, pp. 224–7; Hidaka, *Commercial Credit and Bank Credit*, pp. 121–4; Yamaguchi, *Financial Systems*, p. 75; A. Moriyama, *The Theory of Banking Organization*, Tokyo: Dobunkan Shuppan, 1994, pp. 65–81.

money-lending capital. The fact that the bank capital operates issuance business by using equity capital as the reserves and that retained deposits are maximized for issuance business means that, regardless of the ratio of banker's equity capital to the retained deposits in total reserves, one cannot argue that a particularly contradictory relationship exists between the two. The difference is that the retained deposits added to the reserves remain as monetary debts, no matter how much the in-bank retention rate of deposits increases, whereas the reserves funded by equity capital do not, and this remains irreversible. This can be assumed because deposits before yields require the bank capital to maintain the refund reserves that differ from the convertible reserves themselves, and any increase or decrease in the in-bank retention rate of deposits is synchronized with that of the currency market retention. Adding retained deposits to the reserves is not necessarily equivalent to reducing the overall amount of equity capital, even though it reduces the ratio of bankers' equity capital to total reserves.

In the first place, the reserves that support the credit creation function of bank capital should be recognized as having a function that is distinct from that of general credit reserves. With the development from the commercial credit to the bank credit, even if the substantial function of credit creation itself remains unchanged, the function of the reserves can be expected to change as the form given to this substantial functionality changes. For example, the primary significance of reserves in the bank credit is to cover the period of uncertainty between claims and debts, but the credit period is fixed in the commercial credit. The secondary significance is to secure the acceptability of the loaned, self-addressed debt, but in this respect, commercial credit issuers are also limited to converting the credit of themselves and others into purchasing power that can be used to procure commodities. The reserves in commercial credit are already linked to the past credit that has been given and received if the sales proceeds accumulated as part of the receiving capital after the beginning of the credit period are regarded as the reserves for payment. Conversely, the reserves in bank credit are linked to additional credit that will be given and received in the future, as is clear from the fact that the amount of banknotes issued is determined according to total reserves.

This also demonstrates that there is a special resistance in the savings used as the bank capital reserves. In fact, even with the industrial capital reserves that serve to avoid disruptions and reductions in the production process, or so-called "costs of circulation," there are uncertain costs that cannot be easily saved. It is entirely natural for capital released from the production process also to be released from these kinds of difficulties. For example, the commercial capital dealing with cash purchases is, as it were, used entirely for the "costs of circulation" and therefore does not have any special monetary reserves to avoid disruptions in the circulation process. The elasticity to accommodate equity capital presents the commercial capital with the possibility to store inventory intentionally. However, with the bank capital being released from the production process, the money reserves serve to prevent defaults in self-addressed debts, which are payable at sight, suspensions of cash conversions, and delayed-deposit refunds. In that sense, the reserves can be said to be a kind of fixed capital restriction for the bank capital. In fact, this restriction is inevitably strengthened to the extent that it is incomparable to the case of the industrial capital, as it arises due to the allocation of self-addressed debts to an unspecified number of creditors. While a single disruption or reduction in the production process does not always result in a loss that immediately leads to bankruptcy of the industrial capital, the default of any form of bank debts almost inevitably leads to bankruptcy of the bank capital. Of course, the bank capital is no different from the industrial capital in that the reserve rate is determined based on the forecasts for trends of return payments and payment claims, and the reserve rate is maintained at the so-called minimum required level to avoid losses caused by the excess reserves. However, the shortage of reserves represents an absolute loss to the bank capital that is not comparable to other types of losses. The reserve rate is kept at the minimum required level after the probability of avoiding this form of absolute loss has been increased to a level that can be considered definite in light of past experience. This does not mean that the reserves, which of course will be subject to uncertain increases and decreases, are easy for the bank capital to save. The actual reserve rate fluctuates daily, but it is not always easy to adjust its expected or empirically determined level in the face of uncertainties; nevertheless, there is no way to save reserves other than by lowering this difficult-to-move figure. Even in the event that it is saved, it is necessary to expand the credit activities themselves based on total reserves rather than just lending out the excess reserves. Losses caused by improper expansion are intertwined with all previous credit activities, unlike industrial capital, wherein only additional commodities are left unsold. Furthermore, at that time, unlike industrial capital, which requires additional means of production and labor that must be funded with cash, expanding credit activities in itself creates additional self-addressed debts and therefore greater risk of non-performing bank debts. In other words, the fixed capital restrictions on the reserves will be strengthened in the future.

2 The Two Types of Reserves and Their Functions

While discussing the deposit-oriented *credit creation theory* above, we examined the reason reserves under the bank capital cannot be entirely capitalized as borrowed capital. However, as we look further into this reasoning, we can realize that the reserves themselves have two subtly different functional aspects. One is the aspect of monetary reserves or payment reserves that are used to fulfill already drawn bank debts. The other is the aspect of asset reserves or non-payment reserves that are used to fill holes in bank receivables, meaning that the fulfillment of bank debts that have already been drawn down can be deferred, and further bank debts can be drawn down.[7] What is required for monetary reserves is the characteristic of cash monetary assets or, in other words, the attribute of cash, and what is required for asset reserves is the characteristic of equity capital or, in other words, certainty.

Of course, these two aspects are closely interrelated. Depending on the proportion of asset reserves allocated to cover late return payments, the credibility of bank capital and frequency of bank debt claims change, which ultimately determine the amount of monetary reserves that should be prepared. If the retention rate of bank debts deteriorates, the monetary reserves of bank capital will decline, which will eventually place increased pressure on the asset reserves. In the event of conversion claims that

[7] In this chapter, the term non-payment reserves is not limited to the literal allowance for doubtful accounts, but rather includes stocks and other financial assets held by the bank capital that appear in the assets section of the balance sheet, unlike the allowance for doubtful accounts. In the case of the allowance for doubtful accounts, even if it appears in the assets section, it is in a form that is deducted from specific monetary claims. In a broad sense, the *reserve requirements* exist on both the asset and liability sides of the bank capital, and depending on the difference in their reserve functions, a conceptual distinction between "monetary reserves = payment reserves" and "asset reserves = non-payment reserves" is given. In constructing these discussions, the distinction between specific items such as the allowances for doubtful accounts and the reserve requirements does not necessarily have a decisive meaning.

exceed the current amount of convertible reserves or refund requests that exceed the current amount of refund reserves, the bank capital might be forced to self-finance using its asset reserves, even if only temporarily. At its core, the asset reserves of bank capital exist to maintain the credibility of bank capital by mitigating the uncertainty around return payments, which is caused by the uncertainty of commodity circulation. Given that the asset reserves form the basis for the solvency of bank capital, they should actually be classified as the payment reserves. The bank capital creates the current purchasing power by drawing down self-addressed debts. The non-delivery rate of bank receivables, the reserve rate of bank capital, and the retention rate of bank debts are therefore inseparably interlinked, with the two types of reserves together forming in a broad sense the *reserve requirement*.

Nonetheless, this does not mean that it is meaningless to distinguish between the two types of reserves.[8] Even if return payments are made smoothly and the credibility of bank capital is not disturbed, with no need to draw on the asset reserves, the payments of the bank debts can still be required for external payments or settlements, because the circulation area of individual bank debts is subject to individual limits. By contrast, even if payments of bank debts are not requested and there is no need to draw on the monetary reserves, the asset reserves can become insufficient to cover return payments which are now or expected to deteriorate. The mixture of these two separate functions of the *reserve requirement* can also be demonstrated through some aspects of the money market.

These functional differences can be observed in the following examples. Since monetary reserves have the characteristic of debt fulfillment reserves from the viewpoint of bank capital as recipients, holding reserves at a level above the empirical minimum is regarded as disadvantageous.

[8] Tsutomu Ouchi argued as follows. When the bank capital suffers a loss due to the non-payment of bills, capital and profit must be utilized to compensate for the loss. It is therefore possible that the bank capital "prepare[s] loss compensation reserves in advance." However, he doubts the relationship between the *reserve requirement* and the non-payment reserves. According to Ouchi, non-performing loans do not immediately result in undermining the credibility of bank capital and ensuing conversion claims. Thus, Ouchi concludes that as long as the bank capital can keep the non-payment rate below a certain level, most of the *reserve requirements* can be covered by deposits (Ouchi, *Credit and Bank Capital*, pp. 201,2). It is clear that the reserves here were understood exclusively as the conversion reserves = monetary reserves. As a result, "loss compensation reserves" were disregarded as "unidentified non-payment reserves." (Ouchi, *Credit and Bank Capital*, p. 202).

Conversely, asset reserves do not necessarily have such a minimum level because they also have the characteristic of retained earnings to compensate for losses from the viewpoint of bank capital as a creditor. Rather, asset reserves, which are indispensable even in cash lending, should be regarded as a target for active valorization as a core part of the reserves that compose bankers' equity capital. Of course, bankers' equity capital can also take the form of monetary reserves, and it is naturally preferable to keep a small ratio of bankers' equity capital to bank profits, in light of the basic principle of increasing the profit rate. However, as previously discussed, in the case of bank capital, trying to reduce the proportion of the reserves held as equity capital forces bankers to expand their credit activities. Reducing the total amount of equity capital itself would mean that there is no choice but to reduce the balance of discounted bills in proportion to the decrease in the asset reserves, which would then reduce the scale of credit activities that generate bank profits.[9] Even attempting to reduce the ratio of bankers' equity capital to the conversion reserves by collecting more deposits would require increasing refund reserves, which would not necessarily lead to a reduction in total reserves (except in special cases in which the probability of refund request is clearly lower than that of conversion request). Could credit activities be extended to accommodate this? Doing so would accomplish more than simply increasing bank profits as margins. Any increase in bank profits increases surplus equity capital, boosts the asset reserves invested from equity capital, and ultimately strengthens the credibility of bank capital—as long as it is supplemented by the asset reserves. By strengthening the credibility of bank capital and thus increasing the retention rate of bank

[9] Hideaki Tanaka argued that while preparations for exceptional non-payments that exceed expectations are covered by banker's equity capital, preparations for other frequent non-payments are added to the discount fee and burdened by receivers who brought bills in the bank capital (H. Tanaka, "Bank Credit as a Market System," *The Bulletin of Japan Society of Political Economy,* No. 37, 2000, pp. 136–40). Of course, it is quite possible that the holes in bank assets created by the non-delivery of discounted bills can be filled by withdrawing the retained portion of bank profits. However, this does not immediately mean that non-payment reserves always have a source outside of the bank capital. According to Tanaka's argument, a discount fee paid from the receiving capital to the bank capital would significantly weaken its character as a reward for taking over the uncertainty associated with credit. In addition, there is some doubt about the theoretical validity of making a distinction between the inside and outside of the expected range for the non-payment of bills, given that this is a situation that could not be prevented by the credit research in any event.

debts, the bank capital can significantly preserve the monetary reserves, thereby offsetting the increase in asset reserves. Increasing asset reserves is a shortcut to reduce the ratio of bankers' equity capital to the *reserve requirement* in a broad sense and also increase the profit rate.

The same conclusion can be drawn by considering the relationship between the two functions. The smoothness of return payments that accompanies the collection of interest on loans first will appear as an increase in the asset reserves through an increase in the surplus that composes the net worth account of the bank capital. Secondly, the credibility of bank capital, which is supported by this smoothness of return payments, will be stronger than before, and as this occurs, a complementary increase in the asset reserves will arise. Accordingly, it is possible to save the monetary reserves in preparation for the payment claims and increase the issuance of bank debts. In terms of the monetary reserves, this means that the reserve rate of bank capital lowers more significantly than before. The inverse of this is that any stagnation of return payments will appear as a decrease in the asset reserves through the loss of the surplus as bank profits and the decrease in allowances for doubtful accounts. Any decrease in the asset reserves more or less weakens the credibility of bank capital. However, even in such cases, as long as the credit losses are limited to the extent that they can be countered by the asset reserves, this will not cause an excessive outflow of the monetary reserves. As long as the depletion of monetary reserves is avoided, the credit activities of bank capital can be continued on a reduced scale, and the asset reserves will soon be recovered. As a result of this connection, the asset reserves of bank capital not only form the *reserve requirement* by their combination with the monetary reserves, but save the monetary reserves. However, as will be described later, some payment claims are directly attributable to the external limits of the acceptability of bank debts itself, not to the undermined credibility of bank capital, so we cannot say that the function of the asset reserves to save the monetary reserves works under any condition. Nevertheless, it should not be overlooked that an individual bank capital has a built-in mechanism for independently saving the *reserve requirement* and that, as far as the asset reserves are concerned, it has a stronger demand to reinforce it rather than to reduce it.

The above understanding provides clarity regarding some difficult aspects of *credit creation theory*. As mentioned above, the significance of reserves is not downplayed by this theory. *Credit creation theory* is perhaps most explicit about the significance of reserves in bridging the time and monetary gap between return payments and payment claims. However, the distinction between the monetary and the asset reserves is not sufficiently clarified under this theory. Although credit research explains the necessity for the reserves due to the risk of bad debts that cannot be eliminated, the function of the reserves themselves is exclusively considered to exist in the aspect of the monetary reserves that cover conversion and refund claims. In addition, the claims for payments to the bank capital—whether due to fluctuations in the certainty of bank receivables or due to the external limits of the acceptability of bank debts—are treated equally as causes of outflows of the *reserve requirements* = *monetary reserves*. Naturally, the value-form of the reserves is narrowly interpreted as cash holdings or holding similar debts of other banks in the *credit creation theory*.

The following points should be emphasized in addition to the problems of the *credit creation theory* when considering the remainder of this chapter. Non-cash debts of other banks can be considered monetary assets if they have a strong relationship with future cash holdings. Furthermore, stocks, which are not monetary claims, can also be considered as asset reserves if they have a strong connection with their future capital value. Moreover, the value-form of these reserves can be further diversified on the basis of the favorable fund formation in the commodity market. When the commodity market is booming, corporate bonds and stocks that were previously not rated as proper assets can at this point be promoted to the reserves as future cash holdings or capital value. Nonetheless, this does not eliminate bank capital's need for cash holdings. Any decline in the commodity market highlights the fact that cash holdings exhibit special merits as the most solid type of asset. Furthermore, there are some types of bank debt claims that cannot be fulfilled in forms other than cash, regardless of the ups and downs of banking operations. As long as the commodity market extends beyond the circulation area of individual bank debt and as payments to other banks are unavoidable, it is difficult to tolerate a value-form other than cash for a certain portion of a bank's reserves. However, as will be described in greater detail in the following sections, this need for cash reserves is not easily met by the money market. In fact, in this regard, it is often more rational to solicit investments from other capitals in the capital market (i.e., issuing markets). An investment in bank capital, which does not operate the production process, cannot be used as a way to provide the production capital in motion, i.e., an in-kind investment, by the industrial capital, for example. In fact, an investment in the bank capital has no choice but to be a provision of idle money capital, which is cash investment. This remains true even when it is invested in bank debt. If the investment is made by using other bank's debts, it can be treated like a cash investment. If a bank receives investment in the form of its own debts, it can reduce its debt balance without reducing its asset balance, which, unlike the return payments of its own debt, reinforces its reserves as a form of equity capital. Indeed, the need to hold a portion of the reserves as cash holdings is not independent of the need to hold part of the reserves as bankers' equity capital. If cash holdings are temporarily increased by borrowed capital, the bank capital must still contend with unavoidable uncertainty regarding the depletion of its reserves. By contrast, if the investment is made in forms of capital other than cash, including a bank's own debt, it is not an investment in borrowed capital but in equity capital, with no fluctuations in uncertainty stemming from its payment obligations. The fact that the *reserve requirement* has two divergent functions and differing degrees of freedom in changing the value-form for each affects directly the relationship between the bank capital and the money market and also the relationship between the bank capital and other market systems.

3 Bank Capital and Interest-bearing Deposit System

As discussed in Sect. 1, the predominant theory of bank credit is that deposits accumulated by the bank capital should be the main component of the reserves. The narrow idea that the *reserve requirements* should be identical with the monetary reserves suppresses the function of the *reserve requirement*. By contrast, with the understanding of the function of the reserves presented in the previous section, a different view of the relationship between the bank capital and the money market in which the bank capital participates is also required. Firstly, we should examine the basis for considering the interest-bearing deposit system as a more primitive form of the money market.

The flow leading to the generation of an interest-bearing deposit system has been conventionally considered as follows. As a result of the agreement between the request for industrial capital to save money handling costs and the request for bank capital to obtain fees for money handling operations, the bank capital primarily opens checking deposit accounts in which she/he accepts the sales of industrial capital only on a temporary basis. Next, there is coincidentally a stagnant portion of cash holdings that accumulate as checking deposits that can potentially be converted into the *reserve requirement*. As a result, a new need to expand credit business arises in the bank capital, even if fees (for money handling operations) are surrendered. Because it is in line with the need of industrial capital to earn interest on deposits, fixed-term deposit accounts that are distinguished from checking deposits can be opened. In this way, the idle funds of industrial capital are ultimately bought and sold by the bank capital, and the *commodification of funds* in the interest-bearing deposit system can be socially fulfilled.[10]

The above argument is premised on the logic of "*unintended consequences*,"[11] the idea that the retention of checking deposits and their conversion into the reserves was not the intended purpose of the deposit business but merely a result. By contrast, this chapter posits that the aggressiveness of bank capital, who consistently requires additional preparations for issuance business, should form the core of the discussion. We believe that the deposit retention and its benefits to the credit business are simply the intended purpose of the deposit business from the perspective of the bank capital. The bank capital anticipates the additional issuance profit precipitated by the deposit retention and reduces fees, or pays interest on deposits as long as she/he does not lose the issuance profit, thus soliciting additional checking and time deposits. On the other hand, the industrial capital that either temporarily or on a regular basis deposits money also demands interest on deposits from the start and tries to use the interest-bearing deposit system for parasitic valorization. This view is also an inevitable consequence of this chapter's position, in which we raise doubts about the meaning of reserves in the traditional bank credit theory.

Could we suppose that, after accepting large checking deposits collected from various industrial capitals, the occurrence of deposit retention within a certain range of probability is only an *unintended consequence* for the bank capital who has already specialized in the credit subrogation business? We should consider this issue by conceiving the character of the money capital that forms the core of checking deposits.

[10] Yamaguchi, *Financial Systems*, p. 59, etc.

[11] S. Yamaguchi, *Problems with the Theory of Financial Systems*, Tokyo: Ochanomizu Shobo, 2000, p. 139.

The checking account of industrial capital includes not only the monetary capital that is paid and received very frequently and irregularly, such as that used for the purchases of the labor power and the means of production as well as the sales of its own products, but also the circulation capital that is necessarily left idle for a certain period. Of course, the total amount of this circulation capital increases or decreases uncertainly to some extent, while reflecting the price trends of the labor power and the means of production as well as the sales trends of the capital's own products. However, it also has a minimum level that must consciously be maintained; any reductions below this level become unsustainable. This is why the circulation capital can be used as a buffer to mitigate uncertainty in the circulation process during the circulation of industrial capital. Some portion of the money capital in the industrial capital must then be left idle, unless it could be included in a checking deposit. We can therefore state that it is quite probable that, from the perspective of bank capital, this money capital will stay idle, even when it takes the form of a checking deposit. In fact, this applies to forms of monetary capital other than the circulation capital—even forms such as coin reserves that exist in a certain scale—which are paid and received both very frequently and very irregularly. The amount of means of circulation tends to be predictable or fixed, to a greater or lesser extent, under the industrial capital, who could be considered a bundle of trading relationships, in comparison to that accumulated under the bank capital.

We should consider the fact that the grounds for generating the interest-bearing deposit system are first and foremost in their significance as a system of mobilizing the reserves that anticipates the deposit retention. When viewed in this manner, the interest-bearing deposit system certainly still has limitations, which often overlap with those of interbank organizations. The interest-bearing deposit system serves as a method of contracting bank debts. If the deposit business is performed in addition to the issuance business, the bank debts will tend to increase as the circulation area extends, and payments to the bank capital and deposits will be made more frequently through the use of bank debts. The deposit returns provide the bank capital's self-addressed debts with a new path for contraction in addition to the conversion returns and the payment returns. Even for the bank capital, to prevent an influx of payment claims that exceeds the reserves, it is necessary to maintain and strengthen the acceptability of bank debts, and payments and deposits in the form of bank debts cannot be refused. Accepting them also increases the in-bank retention rate of bank debts. Moreover, accepting payments in bank debts simultaneously reduces both the balance of discounted bills and the balance of banknotes, thereby increasing the reserve rate. In this sense, the interest-bearing deposit system seems to be versatile as a system of mobilizing the reserves, not only in terms of increasing the cash retained in the bank capital but also in terms of diversifying the methods of the contraction of bank debts. Nonetheless, accepting payments in bank debts is not the same as obtaining cash itself. The kind of *reserve requirement* = monetary reserves that must be held in the form of cash cannot always be reliably mobilized through the interest-bearing deposit system, even if the certainty of deposit retention increases. The same concept applies to deposits in bank debts. Acceptance of these will certainly reduce the balance of banknotes but will also increase the balance of deposits and therefore only serve to rearrange the composition of debt without reducing its total amount. The interest-bearing deposit system is mostly ineffective in mobilizing the reserves or increasing the reserve rate when the retention rate of bank debts is gradually declining, both in the market and within the bank, and the risk of depletion of the reserves becomes more serious. Moreover, for the industrial capital that seeks to save money handling costs, it is natural to select banknotes that bear less cost than cash as a means of depositing in the bank capital. Accordingly, the means of payment to the bank capital will also switch to bank debts, including deposit currency. In this regard, the mobilization of cash itself must also be restricted. We should question the idea in the conventional bank credit theory that the interest-bearing deposit system is used to mobilize borrowed capital in the form of cash (i.e., genuine currency), based on the assumption that the reserves represent borrowed capital.[12]

4 Bank Capital and Interbank Organization

For the bank capital, reserves should be invested as equity capital and should form the basis of the credit creation function as the return payments do. For the bank capital, it is desirable to reduce the ratio of bankers' equity capital to the monetary reserves and increase the ratio of

[12] For example, K. Uno, *The Principles of Political Economy*, Tokyo: Iwanami Shoten, 1952; K. Suzuki, *The Principles of Political Economy*, Tokyo: The University of Tokyo Press, 1962.

outstanding self-addressed debts to total equity capital. Even if the reserve rate temporarily deteriorates due to an increase in self-addressed debts, it will soon recover to its previous level, as the asset reserves are increased by raising the surplus. However, in this regard, the interest-bearing deposit system does not always produce the desired effect. In order to increase the ratio of borrowed capital to the reserves, the interest rate on deposits must be raised to attract more deposits, especially time deposits, which are more likely to be converted to the reserves. However, this drives down the margins acquired as the bank profits. Moreover, in the case of the interest-bearing deposits, as the deposit balance increases, increasing the refund reserves becomes necessary, which are nothing but monetary reserves. The limitations of interest-bearing deposit systems also remain when the credit business is downsized to secure the acceptability of self-addressed debts. The reserves are the go-to tool in situations in which the certainty of return payments is volatile, but the in-bank retention rate of deposits also significantly worsens during this critical phase. Then, from the perspective of bank capital, in order to prepare for a shortage in the reserves that cannot be fulfilled by the interest-bearing deposit system, some bills must be re-discounted by other banks as needed and be collected as cash or debts owed by other banks. In that sense, interbank organizations, along with return payments and reserves, form the third basis for the circulation of bank debts, as it were. The significance of the interbank organization to the bank capital should be considered not as a function of the efficiency created as a part of external competitive mechanisms, but essentially as an internal mechanism for the reserves.

However, the interbank organizations are not without limitations. A prototypical interbank organization is an individual business relationship of money accounting and bill exchange between bank capitals who dominate different commodity markets, yet such a business can operate only after the establishment of the business relationship between the various commodity markets. Moreover, the interbank organizations themselves can only be established by further consolidating the relationships between the money markets that ultimately become available after the relationships between the commodity markets have been established. There is a fairly big time lag between changes in the commodity market and the resultant changes in the money markets, which demonstrates the inherent passivity of the bank capital who can fulfill the credit creation function only after receiving demands in the commodity market arise. This time lag is increased by the fact that the interbank organizations require cooperation between multiple banks for "joint action,"[13] as is the case with a general equivalent in the commodity market. The structure of established interbank organizations does not necessarily fluctuate every time a new bank capital is added or when contact with other interbank organizations occurs. Nonetheless, this is no longer the case when contact with bank capitals outside the interbank organization becomes common and changes to the deposit destinations among banks become frequent. Established interbank organizations are then swallowed up in a vortex of restructuring, thereby creating competitive relationships with other interbank organizations over the rank in the money market. Integrating multiple interbank organizations also requires new forms of "joint action." In addition, the constant increases and decreases in the credibility of individual banks continually exert an internal transformative force on individual interbank organizations. Furthermore, despite such internal and external transformative forces, the determination of whether the structure of the interbank organizations can be stable is ultimately left to the trends in the commodity markets that influence the strength of the transformative forces. Given these instability factors—namely, the partiality of interbank organizations—, the business relationships between bank capitals, such as re-discounts and re-deposits, are difficult to be unilaterally centralized or irreversibly organized, as previously explained in the central banking theory.[14] Therefore, it is unlikely that the time lag between changes in the commodity and the money markets can be unilaterally or irreversibly shortened. Individual interbank organizations and the banks who belong to them are constantly forced to confront new externalities via the commodity markets.

The above is a short summary of the ex-post changes in the money markets that occur as a result of the uncertain change in the commodity markets, and the partiality this generates in the interbank organizations. However, and perhaps more importantly, there is another limitation of interbank organizations that becomes apparent when considering the reserves. As mentioned in Sect. 2, the limits of the acceptability of bank

[13] *Marx Engels Collected Works*, Vol. 35, London: Lawrence & Wishart, 2010, p. 77.

[14] A typical example of this is Koichiro Suzuki's theory of concentrated issuance, which positions lower-ranked banks as sub-contractors for bill discounts by the central bank (Suzuki, *Principles*, p. 377).

debts are divided into two categories: internal limits caused by the fluctuations in the credibility of bank capital and external limits due to the partiality of money market fluctuations. In order to mitigate the internal limits, the asset reserves should be invested as equity capital, but the value-form in which the asset reserves for certainty can appear is not limited to cash. In order to mitigate the external limits, the monetary reserves should be invested in the form of cash or as claims to other banks that can be cashed when needed, but the monetary reserves should not be necessarily invested as banker's equity capital to secure liquidity. Depending on the limits of the acceptability of bank debts, the required *reserve requirement* function can be divided into two types along with the required value-form. Therefore, we will now consider the limits of interbank organizations in terms of the mobilization of monetary and asset reserves.

First, we examine the limitations of interbank organizations as a system of mobilizing the monetary reserves by distinguishing between the following two aspects: maintaining the reserve rate and securing the monetary reserves.[15] Maintaining the reserve rate can be achieved through the contraction of bank debts via the return of payments in banknote or deposit currency as well as through requests for re-discount or credit by deposit creation to higher-ranked banks; it is not always necessary to mobilize cash itself. Conversely, even if the reserve rate is maintained, the absolute amount of monetary reserves might be insufficient for payment claims. The bank capital is involved in uncertainties that are not straightforward, even when it comes to the monetary reserves, and its resolution must be entrusted to some external systems.

It then becomes clear that interbank organizations can only respond to requests to maintain the reserve rate and not necessarily to requests to secure monetary reserves. Certainly, the demand for receiving credit that is covered by higher-ranked bank debts should be satisfied under reasonably stable conditions by the interbank organizations that operate in the multi-layered re-discount market. Also, credit research does not

[15] Shigekatsu Yamaguchi states that the reserve rate and loan-debt rate have the empirical standards of individual banks, which cannot be theoretically grounded, but it is necessary to analyze theoretically the function of the reserves intended to deal with the time lag and the monetary gap between the payment and collection of bank debts (Yamaguchi, *Problems*, pp. 130,1). See also Yamaguchi, *Financial Systems*, pp. 78, 92.

need large additional costs for second or additional discounts. The re-discount rate might increase significantly for underwater bills, but it would be unusual for the re-discount itself to be refused. On the lower-ranked bank side, if the recovery of the reserve rate is meant to prepare for the payment requests from other banks belonging to the same interbank organization, there is no inconvenience in receiving the debts of the higher-ranked bank. However, this is not the case when it comes to the demand for cash, because the cash collected by the higher-ranked banks through the re-deposit system, together with the monetary reserves of the higher-ranked banks, forms the absolute basis of the credit creation function of the entire interbank organization. Crediting that uses cash, which cannot be substituted, seems, at least superficially, to be identical to an outflow of the monetary reserves of the higher-ranked banks caused by the payment requests from outside the circulation area of the higher-ranked bank debts. Even if the bills brought into the re-discount are secure, the cash re-discount itself unreasonably undermines the credibility of the higher-ranked bank and can actually cause increases in the payment claims on the higher-ranked bank. On the other hand, the difference between the higher-ranked bank debt and cash is not significant, as long as it is the monetary debt payable at sight. Therefore, in a situation in which an increase in the demand for rediscounting is expected to require payment to those who are outside of the interbank organization (that is, it is expected that the conversion claims will be made immediately after the re-discount), it is deemed as high risk, and rediscounting by issuing the debts of the higher-ranked bank is not possible. In short, the interbank organizations cannot substantially overcome the limitations of the interest-bearing deposit system as long as they are not always able to adequately respond to the requests for the mobilization of the monetary reserves.

This is related to the capitalist social significance of the interbank organizations. One of the primary functions of interbank organizations is to enhance the acceptability of the notes issued by higher-ranked banks and the various associated deposit currencies and thus systematically amplify the credit creation function of the entire money market. The relationship between individual bank debts and the cash holdings they represent becomes more indirect, as various bank debts form multi-layered representative relationships. This is how the interbank organizations can perform the capitalist social function of saving cash as a system of interbank credit and settlement. It is self-evident that the credit business in cash is contrary to the true meaning of these interbank organizations.

This is not the only issue. As the total amount of bank credit provided to the commodity market through the interbank organizations increases, so too does the total amount of commercial transactions in the commodity market. However, the business relationships among remote commodity markets with different interbank organizations will also become more active in these instances, and the frequency of payment claims on the higher-ranked banks also increases accordingly. The expandability of the commodity market itself, which has been strengthened by the interbank organizations, ironically results in the strengthening of the partiality of the interbank organizations themselves. This is related to the quality of the commodity market expandability; strengthening the credit creation function of the interbank organizations often imparts speculative expandability not only to the commercial transactions between remote areas but also to the commercial transactions conducted within a single commodity market. For example, long-term bills that would not be discounted if the bank credit were unorganized can now be relatively easy to be discounted when it comes to the stage that the bank credit is organized, and individual banks can perform credit activities based on the premise of future re-discounts by other banks. Even if a bank can only provide short-term credit, the credit that can be provided by the interbank organization as a whole will shift to the long-term as the re-discounts between multiple banks are repeated. This prolongation of bank credit will encourage speculation in the commercial transactions, including long-term inventory formation and futures trading. When the expandability of the commodity market that is strengthened by the interbank organization is linked to its inherently speculative nature, the relationship between the commercial bill and the commodity value that the bill secures will suffer greater uncertainty. As a result, the relationship between the bank debt backed up by this commercial bill and the cash it represents becomes even more indirect. This series of events will deepen the risk of the monetary reserves of the higher-ranked banks being suddenly turned insufficient along with the cash collected from the lower-ranked banks. Strict standards must be set for the reserve rate of higher-ranked banks, since they influence the credit creation function of the interbank organizations.

However, it is not only the credit creation function that is amplified by the interbank organizations. The changes in the deposit balances of individual banks reflect the accumulation trends of various capitals in business relationships to some extent. Therefore, the concentration of re-deposits in higher-ranked banks causes a concentration of information on the accumulation trends of further capitals. This is equivalent to the situation in which the credit information concerning how much cash-forming capacity a commodity market has in the near future is aggregated in the re-deposit balance of the higher-ranked bank. As the interbank organizations get better-arranged, the deposit balances of lower-ranked banks that specialize in the deposit business also improve the accuracy of credit information. If the credit research function is amplified in this way, it is certain that the risk in the monetary reserves will be reduced.

Once again, however, the function of interbank organizations should not be overestimated. This is because re-deposit systems also create new challenges for the bank capital in terms of the value-form of its reserves. In the first place, predicting the probability and frequency of payment claims and improving the accuracy of predictions for the bank capital are not, in principle, the top priorities when trying to prevent the unexpected monetary reserve shortages. The first priority should be to maintain and strengthen the acceptability of bank debts to prevent an increase in payment claims that are caused by the weakened credibility of the bank capital. The second priority is to mobilize the monetary reserves by soliciting interest-bearing deposits and receiving the credit from other banks. However, these measures, as mentioned in Sect. 3, carry more risk of making it difficult to mobilize the monetary reserves. For example, if a bank wants to maintain or strengthen the acceptability of its own debts, it must accept payment with its own notes under the same conditions as payment of cash or notes of other banks. Accepting the payment with its own banknotes reduces the balance of banknotes and restores the reserve rate but does not increase the monetary reserves. Moreover, the debtor can choose how to pay. The bank capital is faced with uncertainty regarding what kind of payment method would be used; e.g., cash, other banknotes, or bank's own notes. A similar situation arises in soliciting interest-bearing deposits. Accepting deposits with bank's own notes to maintain and strengthen the acceptability of the bank's own debts is equivalent to accepting the uncertainty about a necessary increase in the monetary reserves in proportion to an increase in the retained deposits. Again, the depositor has the right to choose a hoarding method. The interbank organization that promotes mutual acceptance of bank debts among multiple banks and prepares the multi-layered monetary system will increase the types of payment and hoarding methods that depositors can choose. At the same time, it will reduce the probability that the bank capital will be able to obtain cash quickly. Instead of saving cash, the interbank organizations must abandon part of functionality as a system of mobilizing the monetary reserves.

Finally, regarding the limitations of interbank organizations as a system of mobilizing the asset reserves, we have already discussed this question roughly in Sect. 2. The monetary reserves are strongly required to take the form of cash as an external means of settlement. The monetary reserves should not necessarily be held as equity capital and can be replaced by borrowed capital to some extent, as long as the liquidity is not reduced. In contrast, the asset reserves that are prepared to cover bad debts are, above all, strongly required to be held as equity capital. The asset reserves could be replaced by something other than cash or other bank debts, as long as the certainty as equity capital is not diminished. However, it is clear that the interbank organizations, operating both as the interbank credit system and the settlement system, will remain a system of mobilizing the borrowed capital. For example, if the bank capital receives credit in the form of higher-ranked bank debt, this bank debt can be added to the monetary reserves of the bank until the payment date to the higher-ranked bank as a monetary claim that can be converted into cash when needed. However, it cannot be added to the asset reserves. Conversely, if the bank capital receives investment in the form of discounted bills, bank buildings, or other bank assets, it can be added to its asset reserves, even if it cannot be added to the monetary reserves of the bank. The distinction that the loaned value becomes borrowed capital and the invested value becomes equity capital is unchangeable, regardless of the value-form that it takes.

If the above limitations cannot be overcome by the sophistication of the credit system, the bank capital must demand the market system that differs from the money market, a system of mobilizing equity capital. The bank capital seeks investment from other capitals in search of equity capital that can be used as asset reserves. In this situation, the credibility of bank capital that makes up the money market means that the equity issued by the bank capital can be expected to generate more dividends and promoter's profits than that issued by the industrial capital. In addition, it contributes to the popularity of the share as a commodity in the capital market. However, if the bank capital wants to avoid nothing but the depreciation of asset reserves, she/he should show exceptionally strong resistance to investing in other capitals. The stance of bank capital on the capital combination is expected to be asymmetrical, between banks' positions as investors and investees. From this perspective, we raise serious doubt concerning the previous capital market theory. This theory ignored the bank capital's urgent need for equity capital mobilization and considered the capital combination exclusively as a bond relationship between industrial capital and commercial capital. As a result, the involvement of bank capital was limited to that of external positions, such as external credit giving and issuance underwriting. In other words, the position of bank capital was ignored when considering the position of functioning capital, which must bear the risks of defunctionalization and other risks associated with the capital combination. This question is also directly linked to questions regarding past money market theories, which explained the money market limitations from the perspective of the impossibility of long-term and fixed capital credit.[16]

[16] M. Shimizu, "Generation of Securities Market and Commercial Capital," *The Bulletin of Japan Society of Political Economy,* No. 37, 2000; M. Shimizu, "Development of Commercial Capital Theory and Capital Combination Theory," *The Kagawa University Economic Review,* Vol. 73, No. 4, 2001.

Theorizing Bank Capital: Neo-Unoist Approach

Kei Ehara

The financial industry has become increasingly global since the 1980s, and especially after the 2008 world financial crisis, economists have been paying more attention to the financial activity. Recent studies have clarified that the extent to which the financial industry has become independent from the real economy, and that US investment banks, especially those involved in the trading of various securities, have been the driving force behind the development of the modern financial industry. They have also analyzed in detail the system and the structure that are not seen in conventional financial industries like shadow banking and multi-securitization.

However, the modern financial industry is by no means unrelated to the traditional financial industry. Immediately after the burst of the stock market bubble, global capital flows rapidly shrank and central banks in most advanced countries have played a major role in stabilizing the global

K. Ehara (✉)
Faculty of Economics, Oita University, Oita City, Japan

K. Ehara (ed.), *Japanese Discourses on the Marxian Theory of Finance*, Marx, Engels, and Marxisms,
https://doi.org/10.1007/978-3-030-83324-4_7

financial system on behalf of private global actors. This large-scale intervention by the central banks has vividly demonstrated that the banking system is still at the core of today's financial system.

The modern financial system has grown into a heavily complicated structure, yet the relation between the core of the credit system within banking and the diversified securities system retains its focus as the main priority for study.

Previous studies have not sufficiently dealt with this recent issue. In Japan, studies of the financial industry are mainly conducted by Marxian economists, whose main ideas are derived from Karl Marx's *Capital* Vol. 3, Part 5 "The Division of Profit into Interest and Profit of Enterprise." As we have seen in Chapter 1 of this volume, Shigekatsu Yamaguchi developed the method called "differentiation and development method (DDM)" to reveal a three-layered market structure, viz. the commodity market with commercial capital, the money market with bank capital, and the capital market with securities capital. According to Yamaguchi, these markets and actors are created from the activities of industrial capital: industrial capital "differentiates" itself to produce the different kinds of capital, and each new type of capital creates the market and assumes the partial role originally played by industrial capital. This is, as it were, the process of developing a division of labor within the capitalist market.

Meanwhile, DDM does not examine how those three or four kinds of actors are related with each other. In Japanese Marxian credit theory, it is asserted that the emergence of banking overcame the limitations of a system based purely on commercial credit because banks can discount the bills and make them circulate widely. It is true that this intermediary function is the core of banking, though in reality, the activities of banks are not limited solely to this activity. We, therefore, need to analyze how and why banks expand their scope of operation, especially into the capital market.

It is necessary, thus, to reconsider the methodology by which the theory of finance is studied in Marxian economics. DDM falls short in capturing today's financial phenomena, where banking is deeply interconnected with other financial spheres. We need a radical methodological revolution in order to analyze them.

In this chapter, we begin by revisiting Marx's text to find the hints to enable us to overcome these problems. In Sect. 1, we will examine the terminology Marx used to depict the financial industry. Section 2 will study how the bank capital valorizes itself, providing a clear definition of the profit rate of the banking industry. In the last section, we shall propose what we are calling the "polymorphic approach," as a renewed "neo-Unoist" method for the theory of finance, which could replace DDM.

1 "Banking Capital" and "Fictitious Capital"

1.1 "Bank Capital" and "Banking Capital"

In Chapter 1 of this volume, we took a look at the term "loan capital," shown as M ... M′, and concluded that this could not be counted as one of the types of capital any longer because this M is not an equity capital invested in the banking industry. However, even among Japanese Marxian economists, there is no agreement on what word should be used to indicate the capital invested in banking. We have at least two similar terms: "bank capital" and "banking capital."

This confusing terminology has its root in Marx's *Capital* Vol. 3. In the chapter titled "Components Part of Bank Capital," Marx maintains:

> [1] Bank capital consists of 1) cash money, gold or notes; 2) securities. The latter can be subdivided into two parts: commercial paper or bills of exchange, which run for a period, become due from time to time, and whose discounting constitutes the essential business of the banker; and public securities, such as government bonds, treasury notes, stocks of all kinds, in short, interest-bearing paper which is however significantly different from bills of exchange. Mortgages may also be included here. [2] The capital composed of these tangible component parts can again be divided into the banker's invested capital and into deposits, which constitute his BANKING CAPITAL, or borrowed capital. In the case of banks which issue notes, these must also be included. [3] We shall leave the deposits and notes out of consideration for the present. It is evident at any rate that the actual component parts of the banker's capital (money, bills of exchange, deposit currency) remain unaffected whether the various elements represent the banker's own capital or deposits, i.e., the capital of other people. The same division would remain, whether he were to carry on his business with only his own capital or only with deposited capital.[1]

[1] *Marx Engels Collected Works* (hereafter MECW), Vol. 37, London: Lawrence & Wishart, 2010, pp. 461,2. All additions in the square brackets ([ ]) in this volume are made by the editor (Kei Ehara) unless otherwise noted.

This passage has not been seriously studied until recently. For example, Tsutomu Ouchi, who is a leading Marxian economist in the Uno school, asserts that Marx is completely confused here and gives us no useful guide for understanding the operation of banks.[2] However, we think that this conclusion is too hasty. A careful reading of this passage surely offers an insightful analysis of banking.

In the first part [1] of the above quotation, "bank capital" is first divided into two: "cash" and "securities." The latter, "securities," is further classified into several types, such as "commercial paper," "public securities," etc. Marx insists they are all "tangible": it is true that "stocks" are intangible assets in today's sense, but they are "tangible" in the sense that those assets are clearly perceptible and have some forms registered as the properties of the banks.[3]

In the second part [2] quoted above, "bank capital" is reclassified into the "banker's invested capital" and "BANKING CAPITAL, or borrowed capital." This shows who owns the part of the assets, not what types of these assets are. Here, we realize "bank capital" in Marx's term includes the properties that banks themselves do not own. Insofar as Marx's terminology is concerned here, "bank capital" refers to all the assets under banks' operation, regardless who owns them.

In part [3], Marx declares "the deposits and notes" are left "out of consideration for the present." If the "bank capital" includes all the assets of banks, this should not mean "the deposits and notes" are not included in the concept of "bank capital." They are certainly included in the concept, yet it is not important here whether the "bank capital" is banker's own capital or not. Admittedly, Marx insists "the actual component parts of the banker's capital ... remain unaffected whether the various elements represent the banker's own capital or deposits, i.e., the capital of other people." What is crucial here are the types of assets, which are indicated in part [1], not the owners illustrated in part [2].

Marx seemingly made up this concept of "bank capital" on the basis of the usage of the word "capital" by bankers at the time. In Chapter 28,

[2] T. Ouchi, *Credit and Bank Capital*, Tokyo: The University of Tokyo Press, 1978, pp. 166,7. Tsutomu Ouchi is famous in Japan for his original understanding of state monopoly capitalism. See K. Ehara, "The Crisis Theory and the Stages Theory in the Uno School," *Marx Engels Jahrbuch 2017/18*, Berlin: De Gruyter, 2018, pp. 108,9.

[3] In his original manuscript, Marx here uses the adjective "real" instead of "tangible." *Marx Engels Gesamtausgabe* (hereafter MEGA), II-4.2, S. 519.

"Medium of Circulation and Capital; Views of Tooke and Fullarton," Marx examines the terminology used by the bankers and considers how they capture the concept of "capital." In the following quotation from J. Fullarton, Marx says "what Fullarton means by capital" is revealed:

> the securities in the hands of the Bank of England fluctuate more frequently in an opposite direction to its circulation than in concert with it, and that the example, therefore, of that great establishment furnishes no exception to the doctrine so strongly pressed by the country bankers, to the effect that no bank can enlarge its circulation, if that circulation be already adequate to the purposes to which a bank-note currency is commonly applied; but that every addition to its advances, after that limit is passed, must be made from its capital, and supplied by the sale of some of its securities in reserve, or by abstinence from further investment in such securities.[4]

Here, the Bank of England makes "advances" by selling the securities. Marx asserts that the Bank gets "gold or banknotes" by the sale of the securities and this portion of the assets "now constitutes a part of its capital."[5] Marx sums up as follows: "In all these cases the term capital is employed only from the banker's point of view."[6]When Marx uses the term "bank capital" to illustrate the assets of banks, he seems to follow the terminology of "banker's point of view."

Meanwhile, Marx repeatedly criticizes the banking school for committing a category error by confusing the "medium of circulation" and "capital" in banking. Marx insists Tooke mistakes the difference between "*the money form of revenue* and *the money form of capital*" for that between "currency and capital."[7] Fullarton also "transforms the distinction between money as a means of purchase and money as a means of payment into a false distinction between CURRENCY and capital. This is again due to the narrow-minded banker's conception of circulation."[8]

[4] J. Fullarton, *On the Regulation of Currencies*, London: John Murray, 1844, pp. 96,7. Quoted in MECW, Vol. 37, p. 448 with slight amendments.

[5] MECW, Vol. 37, p. 448.

[6] Ibid., p. 449.

[7] Ibid., pp. 440,1.

[8] Ibid., p. 457. In this chapter, we also find the concept of capital compared with that of "means of payment": "To what extent, now, shall the bank's advance to A be regarded

It would be strange if Marx simply accepted the "banker's point of view" to develop his own concept of "capital."

In addition, it was Engels who titled this chapter "Components Part of Bank Capital." In the original manuscript that is now available in *Marx Engels Gesamtausgabe* (MEGA), the texts corresponding to Chapters 28–32 in *Capital* Vol. 3 have no titles and are divided simply by three Roman numerals. Chapter 29 is roughly part of the bundle of texts Marx numbered as "II)."[9] Hence, when interpreting the text here, we should not excessively cling to the title "Components Part of Bank Capital."

Perhaps, it might be better to seek for another interpretation of the above-quoted texts concerning "bank capital" in Chapter 29. When following the "banker's point of view," we call the assets of banks "bank capital." However, once we do not adopt this "narrow-minded banker's conception" and "leave the deposits and notes out of consideration for the present," we must focus exclusively on the "banker's invested capital." In this interpretation, part [3] has more significance than parts [1] and [2]. Parts [1] and [2] just describe a common structure of a bank's balance sheet. Thus, we can otherwise interpret the sentence "the actual component parts of the banker's capital … remain unaffected whether the various elements represent the banker's own capital or deposits, i.e., the capital of other people": the items on the right side of the balance sheet, the liabilities and the equities, have no one-to-one relations with those on the left side, the assets.

On the basis of this reinterpretation, we could assume Marx regarded the "banker's own capital" or "banker's invested capital" as the core of the concept of bank capital, excluding the "banking capital" or "borrowed capital," although he had deemed it as indicating the entire assets

as an advance of capital, or as a mere advance of means of payment?" (ibid., p. 452) Engels added a footnote to this sentence, saying "The passage that follows in the original is unintelligible in this context." (ibid.) In fact, however, the above interrogative sentence itself is inserted by Engels. In the original manuscript, Marx distinguishes the means of payment issued by the bank from the capital invested by A (MEGA, II-4.2, S. 515,6; *Marx's Economic Manuscript of 1864–1865*, Chicago: Haymarket Books, 2017, p. 551). For Marx, there is no such distinction between the "means of payment" and "capital" concerning what banks "advance." This confusing editing by Engels is pointed out in T. Otani, *Marx's Theory of Interest-bearing Capital*, Vol. 3, Tokyo: Sakurai Shoten, 2016, pp. 58–64.

[9] MEGA, II-4.2, S. 519.

of banks by following the "banker's point of view" in the first part of the quotation. Nevertheless, this elaborated conceptualization seems to be neglected when people use the term "fictitious capital."[10]

1.2 Banking and "Fictitious Capital"

The word "fictitious capital" is found in the title of Chapter 25, "Credit and Fictitious Capital." A similar phrase is also found in the manuscript as the fifth section of this part.[11] However, this fifth section in the manuscript corresponds to the texts in Chapters 25–35, not just to the texts in Chapter 25. And recent philological studies have shown that most of the texts on "fictitious capital" were originally placed in the texts of Chapter 29, not in Chapter 25.[12] Hence, we should explore the meaning of "fictitious capital" in relation to the concept of "bank capital."

Marx explains how the "fictitious capital" is formed immediately after the above-quoted passage on the "bank capital":

> The form of interest-bearing capital is responsible for the fact that every definite and regular money REVENUE appears as interest on some capital, whether it arises from some capital or not. The money income is first converted into interest, and from the interest one can determine the capital from which it arises. In like manner, in the case of interest-bearing capital, every sum of value appears as capital as long as it is not expended as REVENUE; that is, it appears as PRINCIPAL in contrast to possible or actual interest which it may yield.
>
> The matter is simple. Let the average rate of interest be 5% annually. A sum of £500 would then yield £25 annually if converted into interest-bearing capital. Every fixed annual income of £25 may then be considered

[10] David Harvey builds a consistent interpretation of Chapter 29 on the basis of this concept. See Harvey, *A Companion to Marx's Capital*, Vol. 2, London: Verso, 2013, p. 240 ff. See also D. P. Sotiropoulos, J. Milios and S. Lapatsioras, *A Political Economy of Contemporary Capitalism and its Crisis: Demystifying Finance*, London: Routledge, 2013. However, we could find another way of critical interpretation here and develop it into a more logically compelling description of financial system.

[11] MEGA, II-4.2, S. 469.

[12] Otani, *Interest-bearing Capital*, Vol. 2, Chapter 5. See also my review on Otani's books in *Marx Engels Jahrbuch 2017/18*, Berlin: De Gruyter, 2018, p. 248. This can explain the bewilderment of interpreters of this part in *Capital* Vol. 3, like shown in Harvey, *Companion*, Vol. 2, p. 203.

> as interest on a capital of £500. This, however, is and remains a purely illusory conception, except in the case where the source of the £25, whether it be a mere title of ownership or claim, or an actual element of production such as real estate, is directly transferable or assumes a form in which it becomes transferable.[13]

Marx takes the government bond as an example, saying "the capital, as whose offshoot (interest) state payments are considered, is illusory, fictitious capital."[14] Thus, when "Every fixed annual income of £25" is "considered as interest on a capital of £500," the right to gain the regular income forms "fictitious capital." Although this is an illusory concept, it is regarded as perfectly performing the function of capital: "All connection with the actual expansion process of capital is thus completely lost, and the conception of capital as something with automatic self-expansion properties is thereby strengthened."[15]

On the other hand, it is only through capitalization that the "fictitious capital" is formed. The capitalization is a process which turns what is not in essence a capital into a capital. We must admit the "fictitious capital" is different from a capital which does not need the capitalization procedure. "Fictitious capital" is a capital even though it is "fictitious." At the same time, however, we could also insist that it is not because it is "fictitious."

In the above quotation on "fictitious capital," Marx seems to consider the matter carefully and asserts that "fictitious capital" "is and remains a purely illusory conception, except in the case where the source of the £25 … is directly transferable or assumes a form in which it becomes transferable." Here, it is maintained that "fictitious capital" loses its illusoriness, i.e., stops being "fictitious," when it is "transferable." The "fictitious capital" is "fictitious" only insofar as it is not "transferable."

However, "fictitious capital" cannot be counted as a capital if it is not transferable. As Marx himself maintains, "as soon as the promissory notes [of the state debt] become unsaleable, the illusion of this capital disappears."[16] It is not to say that "fictitious capital" would turn into real capital when it is unsaleable. "Fictitious capital" stops being a "capital" here. If "fictitious capital" is transferable, it is not "fictitious"; if it

[13] MECW, Vol. 37, p. 462.

[14] Ibid., p. 463.

[15] Ibid., p. 464.

[16] Ibid., p. 463.

is not transferable, it is not a capital. "Fictitious capital" seems to be a *contradictio in adjecto*.[17]

Marx's definition of "fictitious capital" is thus confusing. Meanwhile, Marx's intention of introducing this concept is rather clear: it is to analyze "its own laws of motion."[18] This motion is depicted as follows:

> The independent movement of the value of these titles of ownership, not only of government bonds but also of stocks, adds weight to the illusion that they constitute real capital alongside of the capital or claim to which they may have title. For they become commodities, whose price has its own characteristic movement and is established in its own way. Their market value is determined differently from their nominal value, without any change in the value ... of the actual capital. On the one hand, their market value fluctuates with the amount and reliability of the proceeds to which they afford legal title. If the nominal value of a share of stock, that is, the invested sum originally represented by this share, is £100, and the enterprise pays 10% instead of 5%, then its market value, everything else remaining equal, rises to £200, as long as the rate of interest is 5%, for when capitalized at 5%, it now represents a fictitious capital of £200.[19]

In that case, the holder of this share obtains ten percent of £100, viz. £10. This is capitalized to form a "fictitious capital of £200," which is calculated as 10/0.05 = £200. Here an additional £100 is gained by the capitalization and it is mentioned as "the illusion that they constitute real capital alongside of the capital or claim to which they may have title." This is the source of what R. Hilferding refers to as "promoter's profit."[20]

Meanwhile, is it necessary to conceptualize them as a "capital"? Indeed, Marx maintains "they become commodities": they are titles which enable the holders to obtain certain monetary gains and in this sense they should

[17] Otani suggests that the phrase "This, however, is and remains a purely illusory conception, except[*ausser*] in the case where the source..." should be corrected to "This, however, is and remains a purely illusory conception, also[*auch*] in the case where the source..." (Otani, *Interest-bearing Capital*, Vol. 3, p. 165). It is certain that there would be no contradiction if this correction was made: the "fictitious capital" simply does not deserve a capital when it loses its transferability. However, this contradicting definition might be a sign of Marx's hesitation about simply setting up a new category. As we shall see, there arise some questions about this concept if we discuss it in more detail.

[18] MECW, Vol. 37, p. 463.

[19] Ibid., p. 467.

[20] See R. Hilferding, *Finance Capital*, London: Routledge, 1981, pp. 107–116.

be regarded as assets traded in the market. As we have already discussed, the assets are the items on the left side of the balance sheet; they should not be mixed with the concept of capital, which is listed on the right side of the balance sheet.

Now let us move on to see how Marx captures the concept of "fictitious capital" in relation to banking.

> A part of the banker's capital is now invested in this so-called interest-bearing paper. This is itself a portion of the reserve capital, which does not perform any function in the actual business of banking. The most important portion of this paper consists of bills of exchange, that is, promises to pay mode by industrial capitalists or merchants. For the money lender these bills of exchange are interest-bearing papers, in other words, when he buys them, he deducts interest for the time which they still have to run. This is called discounting. It depends on the prevailing rate of interest, how much of a deduction is made from the sum represented by the bill of exchange.[21]

The "so-called interest-bearing paper" should be a "fictitious capital," yet it "does not perform any function in the actual business of banking." This is because discounting the bills of exchange "constitutes the essential business of the banker" as we have seen in Sect. 1.1. Also, the bills of exchange are also "interest-bearing papers," since they bring the bank a gain, the amount of which is determined by "the prevailing rate of interest."

However, even though an interest is yielded both by the securities and the bills of exchange, these two are not the same "fictitious capital." In fact, Marx had pointed out this difference in the text in the manuscript that was later erased by himself. There he maintained that bills of exchange should be distinguished from securities because the nominal value of the bills is the same as the market value.[22] Hence it is the securities rather than the bills of exchange that are "fictitious capital" in its original sense.

Nevertheless, this view contradicts the assertion in the above quotation: "The most important portion of *this paper* consists of bills of exchange." (emphasis added) The fact is that this English translation has a problem. Both the Engels edition and the original manuscript fail to

[21] MECW, Vol. 37, p. 469.

[22] MEGA, II-4.2, S. 1070.

clarify what the bills of exchange were composed of.[23] As such, Marx did not specify in what sense the bills of exchange become important. By adding "this paper," English translation adds the interpretation that is not originally intended by Marx.

We should thus reinterpret this sentence as follows: the most important portion of *the assets of bank* consists of bills of exchange. This reinterpretation is consistent with the above notion that discounting the bills of exchange "constitutes the essential business of the banker."[24]

In addition, it is reasonable to assume the bills of exchange should be the most important portion of the assets of bank, not of the "interest-bearing paper," because it would be difficult to conceive the growth of the securities market and its crucial position if the most important portion of "fictitious capital" consisted of the bills of exchange. Today's financial phenomena show that the most important portion of "fictitious capital" lies in the financial products such as securities and stocks.

Meanwhile, Marx here deems "fictitious capital" as "a portion of the reserve capital, which does not perform any function in the actual business of banking." He also insists "The reserve funds of the banks ... always express on the average the quantity of money existing in the form of a hoard, and a portion of this hoard in turn consists of paper, mere drafts upon gold, which have no value in themselves. The greater portion of banker's capital is, therefore, purely fictitious."[25] It is true that the "reserve funds" of the banks do not function themselves in discounting the bills of exchange, also that the "reserve funds" can exist in the form of papers. It does not follow, however, that they could be called the "fictitious capital," because the "reserve funds" must be included in the assets of the bank as long as they are "existing in the form of a hoard."

In summary, the two key terms, asset and capital, are not appropriately distinguished in Marx's explanation of banking. The word "fictitious

[23] *Marx Engels Werke*, Band 25, Berlin: Dietz Verlag, 1983, S. 487 and MEGA, II-4.2, S. 524. The original sentence is as follows: "Der bedeutendste Teil besteht aus Wechseln (The most important portion consists of bills of exchange)".

[24] Otani insists that the most important portion of "the banker's capital" should consist of the bills of exchange. See Otani, *Interest-bearing Capital*, Vol. 2, p. 69. However, it is evident that a bank does not use his own capital to discount bills of exchange. The bank uses the "borrowed capital" and in this sense the most important portion of "the banker's capital" could consist of the bills, yet the "borrowed capital" cannot be the accurate terminology as we have discussed in Sect. 1.1.

[25] MECW, Vol. 37, p. 469.

capital" is based on ignoring this distinction. Using this concept, Marx was able to depict the financial market working independently from the real economy, yet it made Marx assert that the "fictitious capital" "does not perform any function in the actual business of banking" and led him to underestimate the relation between the motion of bank capital and that of the financial market. It is our remaining task to redesign an instrument to analyze the financial market without relying upon the dubious concept of "fictitious capital."

2 The Valorization of the Bank Capital

2.1 The Rate of Profit of the Bank Capital

In Sect. 1.1, we reviewed the basic structure of banking by examining the texts in *Capital* Vol. 3. The concept of bank capital should be regarded neither as money capital borrowed from others, nor as assets of the bank, but as the "banker's own capital" or the "banker's invested capital." On the other hand, this is distinctly different from the motion of industrial and commercial capital, which can be assumed to be exclusively using its own capital to manage its business. The motion of commercial capital can be shown in the general formula of M-C-M′, which is shown in *Capital* Vol. 1; also, the motion of industrial capital is illustrated in a slightly changed formula, M-C … P … C′-M′, in which P denotes the production process inserted.[26] However, we cannot apply the general formula for capital to the motion of bank capital, since the motion of bank capital can never be explained without the liabilities to others.

The bank is responsible for guaranteeing the payment of the debtors and at the same time acts as an agent for checking the credit conditions of the debtors on behalf of the creditors. Bank capital plays a role of intermediary between the two as a third-party organization, creating a credit and a debt simultaneously, as we illustrated in Chapter 1 of this volume.

This credit mediation is possible on the basis of the reliable results of the payment guarantees and credit checking. This reliability is ultimately

[26] This formula is not found in *Capital* Vol. 1, but is in *Capital* Vol. 2 as "the circuit of money capital." See MECW, Vol. 36, p. 31. It was Uno who took this illustration as the formula of industrial capital. See K. Uno, *Principles of Political Economy*, Sussex: Harvester, 1980 (hereafter Uno, *Principles 1980*), p. 15.

based on the capital invested by the bank itself. Indeed, the high performance or the established organization of the bank can be the proof of the credibility of the bank, yet they are not sufficient. When the creditor sells his/her commodity on credit, what matters for the creditor is how the future payment is secured. If the bank, as an intermediary, were not at all prepared for the possible default of the debtor, the bank would not be creditworthy, however detailed its information about credit conditions may be.

Of course, the bank does not intend to pay the creditors on behalf of the debtors. The bank tries to minimize any non-performing loans and payments from the bank to the creditors are in principle financed by the repayment from the debtors to the bank. The creditors are indifferent to whether the source of the payment is the asset of the debtors or that of the bank. "*Non olet*, from whatever source it may come."[27] However, this does not mean that the creditors pay no attention to how much the bank is prepared for non-performing debtors. From the creditors' point of view, the bank must invest its own capital even if it can normally operate without spending it.

The bank, thus, must invest the reserves, as Marx correctly put. The reserves of the bank are in various forms of assets, including securities, while the amount of the reserves corresponds to the amount of bank capital. These are the reserves for non-performing loans, but the amount of bank capital does not decrease as soon as a debtor runs into difficulties in making their repayments. If the debtor is just faced with the liquidity risk, it can be overcome by extending the credit or other operations with little impact. Even if the risk turns out to be a credit risk, in which the debtor becomes insolvent, the default loss is first subtracted from the profit of the bank, since it is part of expenses spent in the period. The amount of capital does not decrease as long as the profit is enough to cover the loss.

In case that the loss is larger than the profit, the bank will have a deficit for that period. This results in a decrease in the amount of capital. In this occasion, some amounts of the reserve assets must be liquidized in order to make payment to the creditor and the total asset of the bank will shrink. However, this decrease in the amount of reserve assets is not equal to the default loss, because the loss is partly covered by the profit in the period.

[27] MECW, Vol. 35, p. 120.

In fact, the above accounting rules apply not only to bank capital but also to all types of capital. However, for the other types of capital, the equity is not the reserve: it corresponds to the assets that must be restlessly transformed into other forms, be it money or commodities. Meanwhile, it is important that the assets corresponding to the bank capital should not be transformed. It is especially important in the case of banking to grasp the accounting rules of default, since bank capital is invested exclusively in the reserves.

The rate of profit in the banking industry can be formulated through clarifying the concept of bank capital and its structure of profit and loss. If we disregard the duration of claims and debts, the profit of the bank capital could be $L \times i - L^{'} \times i^{'}$, when L represents the claims held by the bank, L' is the debts of the bank, and i and i' are the interest rate for the claims and debts, respectively. Yet, this is not a perfect formulation, since the costs on the credit-mediating must be expended. The costs include two kinds: let the sign z denote the cost of checking the credit conditions and the sign d the default loss, then the profit of the bank should be $(L \times i - L^{'} \times i^{'}) - (z + d)$.

The bank capital is invested to obtain this profit. When the sign K denotes the invested capital for banking, the rate of the profit in the banking industry, r, should be as follows:

$$r = \frac{(L \times i - L^{'} \times i^{'}) - (z + d)}{K}$$

Bank capital competes with industrial capital and commercial capital in order to maximize the rate of profit. This competition results in the tendency for the equalization of the profit rate among all industries, including banking, consequently regulating the profit rate of bank capital: if the profit rate in the banking industry becomes recognizably higher than that in the real economy, some industrial capital should be allocated to be invested in banking, and vice versa. This formulation is indispensable if we are to consider "Finance is a well-defined field of capitalist economic activity, not a nebulous realm into which capital seeks to escape when, and if, profitability is low in production."[28]

[28] C. Lapavitsas, *Profit without Producing*, London: Verso, 2013, ebook, Kindle. See also Chapter 5 of the book. It was Michiaki Obata who first formulated the profit rate of the bank capital. See M. Obata, *The Principles of Political Economy*, Tokyo: The University

It is now evident that no capitalist would compare the interest rate directly to the profit rate. This supports the abovementioned view that the concept of "fictitious capital" is not appropriate. If "fictitious capital" was a type of capital, the rate of profit for "fictitious capital" would be equal to the interest rate. However, bank capital never compares its own rate of profit with the interest rate when buying securities: even if the rate of interest is lower than the profit rate, say $r = 0.1$ and $i = 0.05$, the bank can purchase the securities. Let i', z, d be all zero for the sake of simplicity, and the value of the securities be £200. The profit would be $L \times i = 200 \times 0.05 = 10$, but the bank does not need the equal amount of reserve for his financing activities. K can be just 100. It is only in the case of $L = K$ that the comparison between the two rates, the profit rate and the interest rate, would be meaningful, yet this case would be fatally unsuitable for capturing the nature of banking, because it means that all assets are financed by the equity. This is simply not what the banks do. The concept of "fictitious capital" would be valid only insofar as we neglected the essential role of the bank capital in the finance industry.

This is not to undervalue Marx's intention of exploring the dynamics of finance. As we shall see, bank capital plays a pivotal role in the finance industry. As Costas Lapavitsas maintains, "banks are active capitalist agents that specialize in acquiring financial assets, that is, in making loans of various types."[29]

2.2 The Credit Expansion

In principle bank capital may increase the rate of profit either by increasing the numerator and or by reducing the denominator. However, the latter proves to be difficult because the invested capital must retain reserves for the banking business. Decreasing the absolute amount of the invested capital would undermine the creditworthiness of the bank. The main way to increase the rate of profit, then, is to increase the amount of profit, the numerator.

of Tokyo Press, 2009, pp. 237,8 and M. Obata, *Critical Studies on the Marxian Theory of Crisis: The Labor Market and the Business Cycle*, Tokyo: The University of Tokyo Press, 2014, pp. 149,50.

[29] Lapavitsas, *Profit without Producing*.

Expanding $L \times i$ is more important for the bank than contracting the costs in this respect. This is because the nature of banking lies in the relative reduction of the credit-related costs. If the creditor him/herself could spare the costs for building credit relations, there would be no need for the bank. The bank intermediates multiple credits and thereby relatively saves the various costs associated with these credit transactions. The costs of checking the creditworthiness of a debtor do not increase in proportion to the amount of credit transactions. Nor does the reserves. This relative reduction lies in the economies of scale that can be achieved. This is why the expansion of sales, $L \times i$, is essential in banking.

Meanwhile, it is the level of the interest rate that has been regarded as the best indicator of the business environment of banking: for the bank, the higher the rate, the more propitious the environment. This, however, is a one-sided view, since the bank also tries to increase the amount of credit transactions, L. Indeed, the banks themselves cannot directly stimulate the demand for bank credit, but that does not mean that they will do nothing to improve the situation. As the industrial and commercial capital make all their efforts to sell their commodities even if they could not force buyers to purchase them, the banks also endeavor to open a new market.

The demand for bank credit does not change in proportion to the change in the level of the interest rate. However low the rate of interest is, the bank credit will not increase if there is no need for credit. Even if the demand for bank credit increases as a result of a reduction in the rate of interest, we do not know whether $L \times i$ will increase in total. It might not be effective to try to achieve an increase in L directly by reducing the level of the interest rate, i.

There is another factor that could lead to the increase in the assets of bank capital. The higher creditworthiness the bank capital has, the more customers it can get and more credit will be created. Both the creditors and the debtors in the bank credit must pay attention to the creditworthiness of the bank, since they receive the debt instruments of the bank in-bank credit relations.

The difference in the creditworthiness is difficult to identify quantitatively and is subject to indeterminate and unexpected changes. Indeed, large reserves could suggest high creditworthiness, yet it cannot be used as an exclusive criterion, as we will see later. Each market player exercises his/her own discretion about the level of creditworthiness of the banks and wants to have dealings with the bank that has the highest creditworthiness.

Therefore, bank capital has an incentive to maintain and enhance its own creditworthiness amid the competition for maximizing the rate of profit, even if the rate of interest is constant. The increase in the reserves is a way to boost credibility, but it leads to the decrease in the profit rate. Hence, selecting safe assets is important to avert the default and to maintain the creditworthiness.

Whereas the bank capital cannot create demand for bank credit itself, it can promote its service by creating a stable asset structure in which the amount of non-performing loans is securely controlled. The reserves are increased as a result of the increase in the size of the assets. The creditworthiness of the bank is thus strengthened in a dual process.

Particularly when the overall demand for bank credit has been reduced and the loan-deposit ratio has fallen, bank capital is tempted to buy securities in order to secure profit margins. The formula of the rate of profit for bank capital, however, does not alter when the motion of bank capital expands into the securities market.

There are two options available to the banks when they make their way into the securities market. The first is to buy assets with the highest possible income and capital gains, with the aim of maximizing the rate of return on each asset. This can be called a risk-taking option. The other option is to seek for stabilizing the asset values by offsetting the price fluctuations of various securities through diversifying the assets. When some of the bank capitals focus on the risk-taking activities, the latter risk-averting option could be effective in that it would result in a relative increase in the creditworthiness of the bank and thereby raise the amount of profit.

Therefore, it must be noted that the finance system is not immediately destabilized even if bank capital extensively engages in the securities market and we begin to see something that resembles what Marx depicted as the motion of "fictitious capital." This is because bank capital has an inherent incentive to maintain and augment overall creditworthiness based on its motivation to maximize the profit rate, consequently contributing to the stability of the credit system as a whole.

However, this is true as long as the securities market is not booming. This is because credit maintenance is not an end for itself as far as bank capital is concerned. If the prices of securities cumulatively rise, it is easier for bank capital to speculate on the securities market than to steadily keep its focus solely on credibility. In such a case, every bank capital becomes a risk-taker, which results in an overall expansion of credit in the system.

The credit expansion here cannot be the same with the proportional increase in the credit as the size of social production gets larger. In this chapter, the term credit expansion is to be used exclusively for the quantitative expansion of credit at a particular stage in the business cycle, in which we observe a speculative rise in asset prices. This credit expansion occurs when the bank capital abandons the policy of risk-averting option.[30]

The speculation conducted by bank capital is different from that by the other types of capital, in that bank capital can manipulate, or at least influence the level of the interest rate, which affects the price of securities. Moreover, when bank capital itself is involved in the buying and selling of securities, the credit expansion can be self-fulfilling: more purchasing power is created as more securities are obtained by the banks. Admittedly, we cannot assert that the cumulative rise in securities prices is caused intentionally by bank capital, because other players in the securities market also affect the level of prices. Nevertheless, bank capital has a dominating influence over the asset market that cannot be exercised by other types of capital.

To sum up, financial stability in the capitalist market is inseparably linked with the risks relating to credit expansion. Bank capital stabilizes the market as a consequence of its profit-seeking activities, but it is true only insofar as the speculative rise in the securities market is effectively prevented. Once the rise in the prices of securities occurs, bank capital can accelerate the process which results in credit expansion. What Marx deems to be the motion of "fictitious capital" should be considered in relation to the motion of bank capital, which is based on credit transactions and also expands into the securities market. As we properly relate the motion of bank capital to the securities market, we can effectively avoid

[30] David Kotz maintains, in the midst of neoliberal deregulation of finance, "Some old-line financial institutions resisted a descent into highly risky activities, but the growing competitive pressure from rivals that had already moved in that direction eventually compelled them to follow suit." D. Kotz, *The Rise and Fall of Neoliberal Capitalism*, Cambridge, MA: Harvard University Press, 2017, p. 108. For more detailed description of newly invented financial instruments in this period, see ibid., pp. 130–141.

the simplistic view that assumes the securities market is incessantly subject to "financial instability." The capitalist market is not quite that simple.[31]

The valorization of bank capital is thus at the center of the theory of finance. In order to incorporate this view into Marxian theory of capital, we need a methodological change in the way we conceptualize the concept of capital.

3 From DDM to the Polymorphic Approach

As we have noted in Chapter 1, Japanese Marxian economists have successfully explained the fundamental relations of the credit system by adopting DDM. The method was largely seen to have resolved a number of misunderstandings, and especially the dogmatic view that the creditor lends idle money to the debtor in the commercial credit relationship. This is simply wrong, since the creditor does not lend his/her money but gives credit to the debtor and thereby creates additional purchasing power.[32] If the creditor lent his/her own money to the debtor, the amount of the credit would be limited by the amount of money held by the creditor. In reality, the amount of the credit is limited by the possibility of the debtor to pay back. This is what credit creation is all about, and in the history of Japanese Marxian studies, it was revealed by DDM as an analytical method.

Nevertheless, DDM was not applicable to the study of the interrelation between the different types of capital, such as the relation between banking and the securities market. DDM is a method to describe the process of "differentiating" the functions of industrial capital into other independent capitals. Here, industrial capital is regarded as fundamental

[31] Harvey's study of banking system that first published in 1982 is still intuitive in this respect, especially in that he observes the two conflicting characters in banking and explains the necessity of the central banking system therefrom. See D. Harvey, *The Limits to Capital*, London: Verso, 2006, Chapter 9.

[32] The wrong view of credit relationship lies behind the finance theory of mainstream macroeconomics, which insists that "the global saving glut" in the emerging economies flowed into the US financial market and fundamentally caused the financial instability in the developed world. See B. Bernanke, "The Global Saving Glut and the U.S. Current Account Deficit," Speech at the Sandridge Lecture, March 10, *BIS Review*, 16/2005; B. Bernanke, "Global Imbalances: Links to Economic and Financial Stability," Remarks at the Banque de France Financial Stability Review Launch Event, Feb. 18, 2011.

to the capitalist market and the rest of them are supplementaries. The interrelation between these supplementaries, e.g., bank capital and securities capital, is a very minor issue for DDM. Hence its weakness in analyzing today's "financialization."[33]

We must admit, however, that this industry-centered view is deeply rooted in Marxian understandings of the capitalist economy. Marx first introduces the conception of capital in Chapter 4 of *Capital* Vol. 1, "the Transformation of Money into Capital." Here, the general formula for capital is given as M-C-M′, and Marx defines the "increment or excess over the original value," or M′ minus M, as "surplus value" and maintains that "[it] is this movement that converts it [money] into capital."[34] Nevertheless, he immediately goes on to points out the surplus value cannot arise as long as every commodity is exchanged with its equivalent, thus there are "Contradictions in the General Formula of Capital."[35] This contradiction is solved as the concept of labor power is introduced and the mechanism of exploitation is revealed in Chapter 7, "The Labour Process and the Process of Producing Surplus Value."[36] In this vein, the concept of capital in Marxian terms is defined in terms of the systematic structure of industrial production.

In fact, Uno's "theory of circulation" was an attempt to redefine the concept of capital in terms of the motion within the market. The "theory of circulation" comprises the first part of Uno's principles of political economy and has three areas of study, viz. commodity, money and capital. There Uno suggests three formulae of capital: "M-C-M′" as the formula for "merchant capital"; "M … M′" as the formula for "money-lending capital"; "M-C … P … C′-M′" as the formula for "industrial capital."[37] Uno thus emphasized the aspect of the market that cannot be reduced to the characteristics of the capitalist mode of production in conventional

[33] When Yamaguchi discusses competition among capitalists in his most systematic textbook, he is referring to competition among industrial capitals. And this competition is supplemented by the three types of capital, i.e., commercial, bank, and securities capitals, which are "differentiated" from the industrial capital. This view is clearly shown in the table of contents of the textbook. S. Yamaguchi, *Lectures on the Principles of Political Economy*, Tokyo: The University of Tokyo Press, 1985.

[34] MECW, Vol. 35, p. 161.

[35] Ibid., p. 166.

[36] Ibid., p. 187.

[37] Uno, *Principles 1980*, pp. 14,5.

Marxian analyses. The "theory of circulation" is what distinguishes the Uno school theorists from other Marxists.[38]

However, Uno's reconceptualization was not perfect. As we have repeatedly noted, the formula M ... M′ is inappropriate for grasping the structure of banking. Moreover, we assume this "theory of circulation" is also subject to the industry-centered view: Uno himself suggests that the first two formulae, merchant and money-lending capitals, cannot "be regarded as an accomplished form of capital, possessing in itself a real source of surplus value," concluding that capital "cannot secure a firm foundation for its value-augmenting activity unless it goes a step further than mere resale business and *produces* the commodity that it sells by means of the commodities that it purchases."[39] The logic for re-introducing industrial capital is derived from Marx's deductive presentation of surplus value.[40] Indeed, in the latter part of Uno's principles, the first two formulae are reformulated as commercial capital and "loan capital," respectively, and these two types of capital are regarded as subservient to industrial capital.[41]

It is certain that the market itself lacks the social foundation for valorization. However, it does not follow that individual capitalists lack incentives for valorization. The capitalist process takes a step forward whenever there is a slight chance for profit-seeking activities in the market, in which incessant and unforeseeable fluctuations occur amid the anarchic motions of individuals. Even if it turns out to be a zero-sum game, the players do not give up maximizing their own gains. Uno has introduced the existence of commodity owners within value-form analysis and this method of analyzing the economic incentives has been inherited by the DDM model, as we have noted in Chapter 1, yet it has not sufficiently theorized the concept of capital in relation to the structure of the market.

38 As for the formation of the "theory of circulation," see M. Obata, "How has Marx's *Capital* been Re-read in the Process of Capitalistic Development?," *The Proceedings of "Marx in the 21st Century" Project in Japan*, Vol. 1, 2019, pp. 37,8.

39 Uno, *Principles 1980*, p. 15.

40 Therefore, I assume that it is not appropriate to assert that "Uno ... altogether omits Chapter 5, 'Contradictions of the General Formula' of Capital (M-C-M'), and, in direct relation, Chapter 6, 'The Sale and Purchase of Labour-Power'." (E. Lange, *Value without Fetish: Uno Kōzō's Theory of 'Pure Capitalism' in Light of Marx's Critique of Political Economy*, Leiden: Brill, 2021, p. 267) The same misinterpretation of Uno is found in E. Lange, Geldtheorie ohne Fetischcharakter: zur problematischen Rezeption des ersten Kapitalbandes bei Uno Kozo und der Uno-Schule", *Zeitschrift für kritische Sozialtheorie und Philosophie*, Jahrgang 4, Heft 1-2, 2017, S. 196.

41 Uno, *Principles 1980*, p. 109.

As a result, the whole dynamics of finance is considered as secondary to the industrial conjuncture.

It is necessary, therefore, to revise the theory of capital in Uno's "theory of circulation" so as to incorporate the redefined concept of bank capital discussed above. Uno himself considered that the first two formulae, merchant and money-lending capitals, must be distinguished from the last formula of industrial capital on the ground that these two can be found in pre-capitalist societies. The same idea can be found in Marx's *Capital*: "in analysing the standard form of capital, the form under which it determines the economic organization of modern society, we entirely left out of consideration its most popular, and, so to say, antediluvian forms, merchants' capital and money lenders' capital."[42]

However, if we are to pay attention to the concrete trading procedures entailed in the formulae, it should be noted that the formulae for merchant capital and for industrial capital have common characteristics: both are basically formed by the buying and selling of commodities, which is absent from the formula of money-lending capital. If we reject the formula for "money-lending capital," we can, therefore, group the remaining two formulae into a single category, which could be described as a metamorphosis formula.[43]

On the other hand, the motion of bank capital does not involve the process of buying and selling. The bank is mediating the creditors and debtors and thus creates additional purchasing power, as we have seen in Chapter 1. As Yamaguchi suggested, this is an act of credit creation. We could refer to it as a credit-creating formula.

In our analysis, these two formulae of capital, viz. metamorphosis and credit-creating, are both logically valid as a way to stimulate valorization. Capital chooses which of these formulae to engage in, comparing the rate of profit in each form. In the conventional Marxian theory of capital, including that of the Uno school, industrial capital occupies the dominant position. In contrast, we propose that there are two logically equivalent formulae for capital and that the capitalist market exhibits flexibility

[42] MECW, Vol. 35, p. 174.

[43] The word "metamorphosis" is used by Marx when he describes the buying and selling of commodities mediated by money when it functions as a means of circulation. See MECW, Vol. 35, p. 113 ff. Uno criticizes Marx and asserts the concept of metamorphosis should be employed only for M-C-M′ movement, not for C-M-C′ process. See Uno, *Principles 1980*, p. 17. I assume this contention of Uno is not persuasive and misled Uno's followers into thinking that commodities play no role as value in motion. In fact, commodities have values themselves, just as is the case with money, and the discrimination is of little use in describing the process of valorization.

according to its historical conditions. The motion of bank capital, along with its financial dynamics, is thus regarded not as supplementary to the industrial production, but as possessing equal significance in describing the capitalist market system.[44]

In Japan, younger generations of Marxian economists have been increasingly adopting this new method in detecting multiple cores within the concepts of capitalist society and searching the historical conditions of the transformations between them. It was Michiaki Obata who launched this new research trend and he labeled it the "polymorphic approach."[45] The concept of capital is polymorphic in that it has dual forms which can satisfy the essential requirements of the motion of capital.[46] While this method is completely different from that employed by the Uno school, viz. the assumption of a pure capitalist society through a single theoretical model, it remains in line with the Unoist tradition since the polymorphic

[44] This is in essence an extension of Uno's "theory of circulation" and his formal theory of capital. According to E. Lange, it "indicates not only his disavowal of Marx's specific cognitive interest in the problem of the fetishistic approach to surplus value … but also wittingly undermines the social dimension that the allegedly 'formal' relation between commodities entails: namely that between capital and labour." (Lange, *Value without Fetish*, p. 257) As we have noted above, this understanding of Uno is not relevant, but also underestimates what has been achieved through non-fetishistic approach in Japanese political economy. It is not only the critique of fetishism but also Unoist theory of finance that can effectively be counterposed to neoliberal economics, as noted above in relation to "the global saving glut" view. From this viewpoint, Unoist conceptualization of capitalist finance can complement the theory of fetishism.

[45] In Obata, "How has Marx's *Capital* been Re-read in the Process of Capitalistic Development?," pp. 41,2, Obata gives an example of the concept of money in the polymorphic approach. It is maintained that money has two forms in principle: metallic money and the inconvertible banknote. In the theory of money utilized in the polymorphic approach, we aim at deducing both of these two forms as logical consequences of value-form analysis. Meanwhile, fiat money is excluded as inexplicable in the realm of fundamental theory. See M. Obata, *The Principles of Political Economy*. This approach would provide a renewed theory of money as "neo-Unoist" that is different from an "old-Unoist" style seen in Lapavitsas, *Profit without Producing*, Chapter 4, for example, in which metallic money is regarded as a unique fundamental form of money and all kinds of intangible money, including fiat money, are allowed as derivative forms. This new trend of theoretical studies of money has recently gained more and more attentions in Japan and needs further introductions and elucidations in English.

[46] Obata's theory of capital is different from the view in this chapter. Obata maintains that an individual capitalist and a joint-stock capital should comprise the dual concepts of capital in theory. M. Obata, *Critical Studies on the Marxian Theory of Value*, Tokyo: Koubundo, 2013, Chapter 3.

approach appreciates Uno's formulation of the "theory of circulation," where the market structure itself is independently discussed. Hence the scholars who take the polymorphic approach should be considered as "neo-Unoists."

The polymorphic approach attracts wide interest because of the possibilities it offers for interpretation of contemporary capitalism. Though we have not yet conducted detailed studies of its application, some hints of its utility are provided by some very brief sketches here.

Many Marxists associate today's "financialization" with the concept of "finance capital," which was coined by Hilferding. However, they cannot help adding that there is a notable difference: while "finance capital" was formed through coalescence of industrial monopoly capital into a large bank, "financialization" is characterized by the disconnection between production and finance. Despite this difference, Marxists have been forced to depend upon the concept of "finance capital" because they had no other theoretical apparatuses with which to study financial phenomena.[47]

We consider this difference to be substantial enough to lead us to the view that the conventional concept of capital is outdated and that there must be a fundamental transformation in the way we conceptualize the trajectory of capitalist development.[48] By rethinking the conceptualization of capital, we could escape from the clumsy usage of "finance capital." The age of "finance capital" took place within the phase of industrial development continuing from the nineteenth century, and was dominated by the process of the metamorphosis formula of capital in our terminology. By contrast, the neoliberal deregulation of finance from the 1980s onwards allowed bank capital to flourish in the asset market, consequently letting the credit-creating formula prevail over the metamorphosis type. Both stages are inherent in the concept of capital and the potential is realized through the catalyzing effect of a myriad of historical conditions.

[47] The claims that "financialization" is related somehow to the concept of "finance capital" include G. Arrighi, *The Long Twentieth Century*, London: Verso, 1994; G. Dumenil and D. Levy, *Capital Resurgent: Roots of the Neoliberal Revolution*, Cambridge, MA: Harvard University Press, 2004; J. Bellamy-Foster and R. McChesney, *The Endless Crisis: How Monopoly-Finance Capital Produces Stagnation and Upheaval from the USA to China*, New York, NY: Monthly Review, 2012.

[48] See Kotz, *Neoliberal Capitalism*; C. Lapavitsas, "Financialised Capitalism: Crisis and Financial Expropriation," C. Lapavitsas ed., *Financialisation in Crisis*, Chicago, IL: Haymarket Books, 2013, Chapter 1; Lapavitsas, *Profit without Producing*; R. Westra, *Periodizing Capitalism and Capitalist Extinction*, London: Palgrave Macmillan, 2019.

For Japanese Marxian economists, and especially those in the old-Unoist group, the modern capitalism diverts itself from its normal developmental process, confronted with unprecedented events. They thereby assume that capitalism is in crisis, or that a post-capitalist system has begun to emerge.[49] On the contrary, we consider that the contemporary socioeconomic situation is nothing other than full-fledged capitalism and that the multiple crises today are those aroused by the motion of capital itself.[50] The way we conceptualize capital is thus linked to the way we evaluate today's society. Our dual concepts of capital suggest that today's "financialization" is unique to the neoliberal age where the movement of bank capital has been fully unleashed. We conclude that Marxian capital theory continues to provide the most effective framework for studying contemporary capitalism, albeit with a few amendments.

[49] Makoto Itoh maintains that neoliberal capitalism is a process of going back into the stage of liberalism with a symptom of its decline, labeling the tendency a "spiral reversal." See M. Itoh, "Spiral Reversal of Capitalist Development: What Does It Imply for the Twenty-First Century?" in M. Itoh, *Value and Crisis*, 2nd ed., New York, NY: Monthly Review, 2021. John Bell and Thomas T. Sekine assert that we are now experiencing "ex-capitalist transition." See J. Bell and T. T. Sekine, "The Disintegration of Capitalism: A Phase of Ex-Capitalist Transition," in R. Albritton, M. Itoh, R. Westra and A. Zuege eds., *Phases of Capitalist Development: Booms, Crises and Globalizations*, Basingstoke: Palgrave Macmillan, 2001.

[50] In this sense, we assume that our recognition of contemporary capitalism would be in essence similar to the one in which "financialization" is considered as the ways in which capitalism transforms itself, though the advocates do not stress the roles of bank capital so much as we do. See D. Bryan, R. Martin and M. Rafferty, "Financialization and Marx: Giving Labor and Capital a Financial Makeover," *Review of Radical Political Economics*, Vol. 41, No. 4, 2009; Sotiropoulos et al., *Contemporary Capitalism*.

Index

K. Ehara (ed.), *Japanese Discourses on the Marxian Theory of Finance*, Marx, Engels, and Marxisms,
https://doi.org/10.1007/978-3-030-83324-4

The manufacturer's authorised representative in the EU is Springer Nature Customer Service Centre GmbH, Europaplatz 3, 69115 Heidelberg, Germany. If you have any concerns regarding our products, please contact ProductSafety@springernature.com

Printed and bound by CPI Group (UK) Ltd, Croydon, CR0 4YY
30/09/2026
02225459-0002